WINNING SALES AND
MARKETING TACTICS

WINNING SALES
AND
MARKETING
TACTICS

John Winkler

BUTTERWORTH
HEINEMANN

Butterworth-Heinemann Ltd
Halley Court, Jordan Hill, Oxford OX2 8EJ

PART OF REED INTERNATIONAL BOOKS

OXFORD   LONDON   GUILDFORD   BOSTON
MUNICH   NEW DELHI   SINGAPORE   SYDNEY
TOKYO   TORONTO   WELLINGTON

First published 1989
Reprinted 1989
First published as a paperback edition 1991

British Library Cataloguing in Publication Data
Winkler, John
Winning sales and marketing tactics
1. Marketing—manuals
I. Title
658.8

ISBN 0 7506 0054 3

Printed and bound in Great Britain by
Redwood Press Ltd, Melksham, Wiltshire

Contents

●

v

Acknowledgements

•

I churn out about two hundred thousand words a year in business. So in seventeen years, Pat Clark has typed over three million words for me, including six books now. Thanks, Pat. Don't know how you do it. Fingers do grow again.

When we started our business, Katrina Barnes-Hughes was three. I had to wait another twenty years before she could join us to keep our clients happy on the telephone. She bubbles at them, bubbles at me, and she read this book in draft between bubbles. Thanks KB-H. I'll do the coffee.

DEDICATION

We started out with five hundred £1 notes in the business. At one stage, Ben Thomson and I went through the *Yellow Pages* to see what sort of business we would go in for. Fate provided the one we have. And fate provided me with the best chairman that one could wish for. Never a single cross word in just under twenty years. Never a disagreement over policy. Just ruddy good fun, from beginning to end. Well, more or less. Thanks Ben for teaching me half the tricks in this book. The book is for you.

Introduction

●

If someone says 'communications' to me, horrible word, then I immediately think of how to get the other person involved. Lecturing is pretty inefficient. One-way communications. So is writing. No feedback, you see.

But conversation, questions, dialogues, games, they get both parties involved. That's my kind of communications.

I've been trying in the past few books to get more reader involvement. I cannot have conversations with readers. But we can have a contorted sort of dialogue if I set up some forced choice questions, and play some games with self-assessment tests.

HOW MANAGERS READ

Our market research with readers of the previous books told us that managers buy books and then stick them on shelves for months. Occasionally they dip into a book either to solve a particular problem, or to seek fresh ideas on an old subject. This skimpy reading is guided from the contents page. Seldom does the reader go from beginning to end. (They do sometimes.) They read about thirty minutes a time. It is done in bed, on trains, in hotels, on aeroplanes.

So, fine. That gives us the outline for the book structure.

WHAT WE ARE TRYING TO DO

The basic aim is to point out strategies and tactics which will make the reader more money in his business. In one way or another we want readers to sell more, or reduce cost, or get better prices. They are the only ways I know of making more money.

We can only give you the main tactic – there are thirty-eight of them here – and you have to fit them to your business yourself. So to help broaden each tactic in the reader's mind we start with some forced-choice questions leading into the tactical issue. There are ninety-nine questions and I don't expect you to agree with all my answers, particularly if you get poor scores. The main tactic is summarized fairly freely, with some examples, in about five minutes of reading time.

1

Then there are another thirty-three self-assessment tests, to position each tactic in a way you might find useful for yourself. Then we show a wider set of applications for the tactics we call Action Point ideas. There are over 150 of these.

Finally, we would like to think that you would make a summary note and a small plan to apply specifically in your company. No point in buying a book like this unless something happens afterwards. Each of the tactical chapters takes about twenty minutes to read, summarize and think through. Just about the time it takes for your cocoa to cool in the hotel room.

WOMEN

Surrounded as I am by majorities of women at work and further majorities of women at home, it would be surprising if the idea of women's lib had not forced its way through the quarter inch of human skull of even such a potential blind chauvinist as myself. So I do not excuse what I've done in this book but seek only to explain why.

If you write a book like this using direct language, English as she is spoke, and addressing the reader as 'you', then you are going to come up against the he/she problems practically every time you use a personal pronoun. I tried it. It is horrible, absolutely awful. I tried then to escape by using the neutral 'they' in the third person plural, and that was worse.

So I am truly sorry, but I made a decision, right or wrong, to assume that all business personnel are male. The fact that most of them are, in real life, is to be regretted. I am not patronizing anyone. I've said I'm sorry. It's a decision.

(P.S. What my clients do not know, because to my shame I never tell them, that the first thing I do when running an in-house seminar is to count the number of women in the audience. Last year I had a total of 485 personnel at in-company audiences, apart from public seminars. A total of 452 were male. It helps to form a picture for me of the company's flexibility, free-ranging attitude and enterprise. Or not, as the case may be.)

FAST READING

It is easy to fast read this text. The purpose is for you to see roughly where your chosen section is taking you so you follow a map. It also helps to set up your memory – there is a strong element of reinforcement.

Here is a simple description of how to use fast reading as a technique. I have to read a great deal of material, much of which is boring or technical in the form of reports and books. I can absorb 120,000 words of technical material in a total of six hours (not done all at the same time though). That's two novels, which would normally take sixteen hours of study. With fast reading and mind mapping your recall of comprehension will be up to 80 per cent. But with normal studying your recall will be less than 50 per cent and it will take you twice as long.

Fast reading works because:

1 You can get the meaning of most sentences without needing all the words. ('Meaning, sentences, few words' gives you the same meaning.) So many words that we use in language are redundant.
2 Reader's attention drifts off. Have you ever read a paragraph and then gone back to it again because you did not take it in? It happens in reading sentences, too. The eyes drift back again to make sure we get all the words.
3 For the purpose of storing things in the mind, most people read for too long a period at one time. The attention wanders.
4 There are only a few crucial elements in most messages which we need to read for our purposes. Have you read through a long laborious book only to find that three chapters were the only ones worth reading?
5 Fast reading works well when it is combined with short sessions, highlighting key factors, mind mapping key elements and a later review.

When fast reading does not work

When you want to read for enjoyment. Or when you cannot discipline yourself for the task.

Basic approach

STEP ONE
Survey the material to be studied. (Read the contents page; look for summaries/conclusions. Decide what you want to read in depth. Dump the useless stuff.) Survey each chapter you want to fast read

in the same way. (That way you'll know where the important stuff is and you can slow down a bit.)

STEP TWO

Train the eye to move quickly for a two-minute test. The eye moves from left to right when reading at a speed which is comfortable to you. We want it to move fast, much, much faster. It does not matter if it does not pick up all the words. The words the eye will leave out are the redundant words – it will pick up most of the hard words which contain the meaning. The eye will automatically dump complete sentences. Don't regress, don't go back. Move the eye quickly left to right and in this training session go through whole pages gathering speed until you are doing a complete page in a few seconds.

After a couple of minutes your eyes will be moving a lot faster – you've trained them. (Just as when you come off a motorway at 70 miles an hour into a built-up area you find it difficult to bring your speed right down.) After two minutes of testing, you are ready for fast reading.

You also need to use an aid to rapid eye movement. A pencil swung quickly from left to right just below the lines you are reading will do this. Or, if you just lower a sheet of paper down the page as you read and you concentrate upon the words in the middle of the line this will do as well. See which system suits you.

STEP THREE

Fast read for only twenty minutes at a time, add on ten minutes for review and mind mapping. This way you pick up the benefit of retaining the material at the beginning of the session and at the end. As you read, use a highlighter marking pen to select key phrases, words. After twenty minutes complete a mind map of the material you have read. In this twenty minutes you should have completed about 20,000 words (a third of a standard novel).

STEP FOUR

At the end of the day i.e. much later than when you fast read the material, look up your mind map and review the material.

STEP FIVE

At the end of the week do the same thing again. Only a few minutes is needed for this. Complete a simple mind map summary of the key facts you can remember without help. This is to help the material go into the long-term memory.

Summary

- Survey the material first
- Train the eye in a practice session
- Fast read and highlight
- Mind map the material
- Review later

MIND MAPS

The basis of the mind-mapping technique is that the brain does not work in a completely logical way, for instance in a vertical format starting at the top of the page and working down to the bottom, reading from left to right. The mind is much more chaotic, but within the apparent chaos a pattern can be identified.

The mind map produces a record in a pattern that replicates the working of the mind. Because the note is directly related to the individual producing it, the patterns can take a variety of forms and to another person can be unintelligible and almost indecipherable. This is perfectly acceptable.

A variety of formats can be used, the criterion being that they are meaningful to the map maker. Colours can be effective, as can symbols enclosing parts of the map. Arrows from one part of the map to another can link similar or related subjects. Symbols such as asterisks, exclamation marks, question marks and so on will highlight important parts of the note.

The most important aspect in the construction of the map is the summary of the key elements of the subject, using words that are meaningful to the map and recall the more detailed aspects of the particular point.

Mind maps of this nature can be used in a variety of ways, including:

- To record a training session
- To summarize a meeting
- Preparing for the compilation of a report
- Preparing a talk or training brief
- Reminder notes for the stages of an exercise or activity

Mind maps are very personal to the individual who makes them. They can be used for all kinds of note taking and help the memory to store dates. Use them with added pictures and with memory joggers. First prepare the mind map; then review it after half an hour then again after a week. It's a marvellous technique for reducing long-winded books and reports to simple terms. You can prepare plans with them; sort out priorities. I use them for preparing new seminars and speeches. Here is my own mind map of the subject.

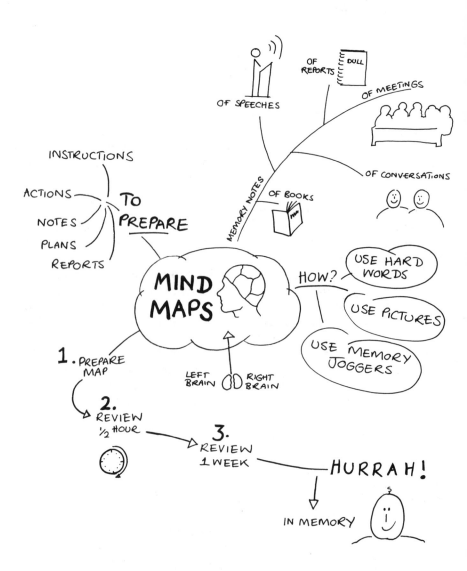

Part One

Five Tactics to Manage Yourself and Others

LET US START WITH YOURSELF

Nothing like getting to the meaty bit at the outset. Let us find out about you, the reader. Who you are, what you are good at, what you are not so good at. Start by filling in the Winkler Profile form printed on the inside of the book jacket or obtainable from Winkler Marketing at 6 St Georges Place, Brighton BN1 4GA, UK. Now. Have fun. Make money. Find out what you want from business life.

1

So how do you achieve your results?

•

> If you ask someone to tell you what they are
> like, then they will probably be fairly
> accurate. Psychometric instruments are a
> means of showing how people cope with
> their environment. *If you are going to fill in
> the form printed on the inside of the book
> jacket, and assess yourself, you should
> complete it first, before reading this.
> Otherwise your answers may be biased.*

For a long time, since the 1920s in fact, psychologists have used testing systems which show how two different styles of behaviour, passive and active, operate under two sets of conditions, favourable and challenging. Each one of us is sometimes passive and sometimes active; each one of us has to operate both in favourable and in challenging circumstances.

So each of us finds a way of coping with our environment which obtains for us results which are personally satisfying. And although our behaviour may be very rich and varied, it is likely that we obtain more satisfaction from one style than from another.

So they developed tests which discriminate very crudely between those who enjoy using positive actions in challenging situations, those who enjoy using positive actions in favourable situations, those who prefer a passive role in favourable situations, and those who enjoy reducing the degree of challenge by cautious and passive responses.

It you try and discover these styles of coping from an interview, you will find the task extraordinarily difficult. So the psychometrics test was developed as an aid in recruiting, to be added to personal judgement and not to replace it. There are many systems and many of these, but not all, are based around the four dimensions described above.

Basically the tests ask people to report on whether they search for and react best to situations which are fairly challenging or which are basically favourable; and whether they respond to these actively or passively. The system used here describes a fifth factor as well. This is very important in a working environment – it is the ability to generate new ideas. It shows an attitude towards the environment, a way of thinking and is a very important part of the self-image.

In this system those who get most satisfaction from favourable situations in which they can operate well with passive agreement, will score strongly on the S factor. Those who enjoy being active and positive in challenging situations will score strongly on the D factor. Those whose pattern of interaction with others works best by being positive in a favourable environment will score strongly on the E factor. Those who are imaginative and enjoy developing creative solutions to life's situations will score strongly on the T factor. Those who seek to reduce tension or antagonism by taking a cautious or orderly approach will score high on the C factor.

ADVICE TO THE STRONG S: THE STABLE PERSON

If the rest of the world's people were like you, it would be a much nicer, healthier, more peaceful place. We would have little nastiness, and no wars. People would get on well together.

Get into a job which does not involve too much exposure to risk. Don't work for new organizations, or small companies, or fast growth organizations – they'll push you around, make changes all the time and they lack security. You don't like any of that.

A job where you can look after things, mind the shop, provide service, and advise others is just what you need. You are very good at looking after today, you are concerned with the present time. You work best in an environment which is non-competitive and where the work is measured by intangible results.

You are a good listener, and this is a very important attribute in a world which is led by the noisy, all-action heroes. People come to you for help, and you will always provide assistance, without taking over.

Your great strength is that you can see the traps and the dangers involved in a project which others miss. You are excellent at stopping others from making mistakes or making decisions too quickly. This asset is not always appreciated by others, yet they need you badly.

If you also have a strong C, (and a weak D) then work with others who can bring you out and listen to you. You will not impose yourself on others and you may not value your own very high skills properly. You may generally undervalue yourself, because you do not make waves and you are often disinclined to shout above all the din. Too many all-action people around you will wear you out.

Your difficulty is that you enjoy doing one thing at a time, and you will often take a long time over things. Others can push you into a panic. Use your close friends. Try and schedule your own work better by doing it in small bites at a time. You tend to leave tomorrow to look after itself, but a little effort today can ease a lot of tomorrow's problems. Use your boss for advice.

Your loyalty is amazing. You will work steadfastly through thick and thin. You will continue to work in situations which others would not tolerate for a moment longer. You are a joy to behold in situations which frustrate and annoy others. Don't write yourself down.

Don't let the strong D roll over you. They learn to appreciate in you something which they have not got in themselves. With you, they can enjoy today. They often end up marrying you. The trappings of success do not turn you on particularly, nor does a lot of money beyond what you need to be comfortable. But you do want sound insurance policies with good companies and a well-funded pension.

ADVICE TO THE STRONG C: THE CONSCIENTIOUS PERSON

Life for you is about proper organization and taking care. How sensible, orderly and thorough you are! If only others would take as many pains as you do, there would be fewer mistakes made and the world would be a more orderly place.

Get into a job where your skills of method and procedure are going to be needed. You need a well-defined job structure, a clear policy to work within and then you will set about the task of getting everything right. You need notice of new ideas. You need time to get used to things. You do not mind a challenge (though you will not like personal challenges) and you will try to reduce any conflict or risk by being accurate, tidy and careful with what you do. Technical problems you will enjoy for their own sake.

Money is not the be-all and end-all for you, neither is achieving power, glory or fame. But you do enjoy tangible, measurable results. Remember, though, that perfectionists are sometimes difficult for others to live with. Just as other people irritate you with their irrational and emotional approach to life, so you can be trying for others who want you to speed up, accept change, and get things done more quickly. Others often want to pile too much on top of you, and that gives you problems.

You are not likely to be a fighter (unless you are a strong D as well) so you may tend to duck and weave around situations you do not like.

You are a good listener. Others do not feel threatened by you. You make a good specialist.

One thing that others often do not appreciate is that you are also a good team player. You enjoy being a specialist or expert in a team, you will have your say and then not be too upset if the group decides to go another way. You like having other people's views and opinions before you make decisions. You want all the facts, all the figures, all the data before you when you make decisions. You work on the problem logically, by calculation. You can be creative and imaginative, and if you are, this may show up as a strong T factor.

Organizations are built upon folks such as you. The world crumples into a mistake-ridden chaos without you. You are a massively good investment for an organization which wants to provide sound accurate service which involves problem solving and routine.

ADVICE TO THE STRONG D: THE DRIVER

So life for you is an opportunity and a challenge. What great constructions, what great triumphs, but how you can wear others out!

Get into a job where you can negotiate objectives with your superior and then ensure you are then left free to achieve these aims with little interference. You need room to move, you need variety, you need many things to be happening at the same time.

You are an exploiter of opportunities, and you often make such decisions quickly. If you are a strong E as well then you will get into control of other people and you will get your results through them. You are a tough persuader. And you want to be respected for it.

If you are also a strong C, then life is a little more complicated, (particularly if you are also a weak E). In this case you don't worry too much about what people think of you, and you can be seen to be a bully. There are also inner tensions within your make-up. You want to get results, but you also want perfection. Not an easy combination for others to live with.

You like money, because money is a means to an end for you. You do not tolerate fools gladly. You respect strong, active motivations in others, but you respect power most of all. You could possibly be a dedicated workaholic, successful, and ambitious to your old age. Others may wonder why you do it – particularly when apparently you have most of the things you want. The answer is that you do it because you have to, because you enjoy it.

Just stop sometimes and ask yourself what it is all for. Introduce some slowness here and there – you do not want to become ill later, do you? Get some variety of pace. You can relax by applying your energy in a completely different field. It may stop you becoming too narrow.

And listen to other people from time to time. Particularly listen to the quiet, slower ones. They have a great deal to contribute to your aims, but you will have to draw it out of them. Be careful with other strong Ds. If you clash it can be painful for you both. Watch your priorities. Just be content to win the big battles. Trying to win them all is a mug's game.

You are always building for tomorrow – you will sacrifice a lot of today's comfort for tomorrow's result. Just remember that when tomorrow comes you will be looking for the result on the day after that. So what is it all for, you may ask?

You like numbers. You measure yourself by numbers, and control, inspire, motivate and measure others by numbers too. Remember, not everyone enjoys the numbers as much as you do.

ADVICE TO THE STRONG E: THE EXPRESSIVE PERSON

Life for you is about friends, other people, and having fun. People revolve around you, they pay attention to you, and you know them well. Not many people enjoy making new friends, meeting people for the first time – but you do. You turn on the charm, you shine, and there you go again being popular.

Get into a job where you can circulate. If you can be a star as well, then so much the better. You need to use your talents to mould teams, create high motivation, develop team spirits, and get your results through people getting on well together. Who needs antagonistic situations, when you can be out enjoying yourself?

If you are also a strong D, then behind all this bonhomie and goodwill there will be some personal aim in mind, some ambition of yours disguised amongst the friendship. You might possibly be a little quick to discard people if they are not much use to you. You like an active life. You like working with others. You enjoy leading, and you will go along with what others want to do.

You do not care much for nasty, antagonistic situations (particularly if you are strong C, or strong S), but you will take them in your stride if you are a strong D. If you are also a strong T, you are full of ideas and people always ask you to suggest what should be done next.

You take life as it comes, tomorrow is another day. You have a lot of self-confidence to carry through most situations, so detailed and systematic planning or reporting is not your strong point. You may sometimes be a bit superficial with others, a bit too much on the surface. Don't work with people who might be critical of you, because you will definitely not be happy.

Do not work in organizations which are losing, because the morale will be low and you will start seeking your satisfactions outside work. You enjoy variety, you like a fast pace (usually). You are just a friendly fun person. Is that not what people are supposed to be like? You like fast cars, big houses, the trapping of success and the money that can buy you these things.

ADVICE TO THE STRONG T: THE THINKING PERSON

Bright, inventive, open-minded, that's you. But the style you use to cope with your environment will be shown up by the other factors. So, as well as being strong on the T factor, where else are you strong?

The rest of your profile can be read normally, but it may also determine the way in which your schemes and ideas are generated. If you also have a strong S factor, your ideas may often be romantic or artistic. Your ideas will tend to be about immediate issues, and will often concern friends and family. You are unlikely to force your ideas on others, and you need other people to appreciate you.

If you also have a strong D factor, then you will be a mass of realistic schemes for tomorrow. They will involve breaking down barriers, doing things a different way. Your ideas will tend to be instant, forceful and opportunistic. You are likely to be a fast copier from other fields. If you have a strong E factor, then your ideas will concern other people, things you can do together, for example. They will be intuitive, free-flowing and be expressed with confidence and optimism. You are likely to be fun to be with.

If you are a strong C, then you will be happy working out your schemes alone, worrying away at your inventions. Sensitive and quick to spot connections, your ideas will involve abstractions, systems, things, rather than people. Others will appreciate your original mind, so long as they listen to you. You may have to struggle to make them hear, though. You like getting the details right and others can get impatient.

Get into the kind of job which suits your other profiles. The strong Ss and strong Cs need can sometimes be helped by a group which listens seriously to them and appreciates their ideas.

SO HOW SHOULD YOU BUILD YOUR SALES TEAM?

There are no simple answers to this question. The ideal sales team involves matching up the right kind of style to each individual account.

And that makes life complicated. A theoretical solution would be to identify the best producers in your existing sales team, score their profiles and then search for recruits to fit this profile.

But this suffers from several problems. First you are going to get a mixture of profiles when you do this. Second, you need a large sample of high producers to produce statistical stability. And who has a hundred top selling producers in their sales organization? Third, people develop their results over long periods. Fourth, what is right in one situation with a customer will be wrong in another situation later with the same customer. Fifth, you will find many people in your organization with the right profile for success yet they may be useless.

So one thing cannot be stated strongly enough. Truly, you cannot really compare different people together on the basis of their profiles. Whatever they are like, whatever their level of skills and ability, each person will still produce a profile. What the profile tells you is that the person you are examining has a preferred style and the chances are that whatever results he gets, he gets them through the use of that style.

WHERE TO LOOK TO MATCH THE RIGHT STYLE WITH THE SALES JOB

The classical sales profile is one with a strong E (particularly if there is strongish D, above the line, to go with it). To make contacts, to establish a network of relationships, to represent the organization as being easy, nice, pleasant to do business with, then put in a strong E. The strong E will do well where you need rapport. But they are not dedicated killers.

To establish rapport

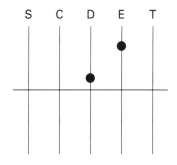

The classical manager, tough guy, hard nose is the strong D. Provided
there is a strongish E to go with it, then this one will handle difficult
accounts, awkward buyers, big deals, challenges and conflicts. He may
even cause a few of his own. This one *is* the killer.

To close deals

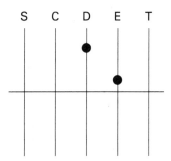

Some of the most successful long-term relationships with customers
have been built up by the strong Ss. They often appear quiet and
perhaps too tentative for successful salespeople but customers requir-
ing a high level of service and back-up love them. They make customers dependent upon them.

To service customers

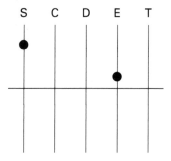

When even deeper service is required, when technical problems must
be solved, when technical support people must deal with their opposite numbers to ensure that things are accurate, efficient and working
well then put in your strong C. You will have some difficulty in getting

one with a strong E, but let them free to deal with their opposite numbers in the customer organization. They will not shine at the big deals, the big shoot-outs. They just keep the account for you. That can't be bad.

Technical support

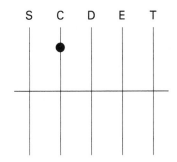

DEVELOPING TEAMS FOR REALLY MAJOR DEALS

At the early stages put in the expressive person the strong E. Keep them there throughout to maintain warm relationships with everyone, while the deal is going on. Get the driver, the strong D in next to meet his opposite number high up in the organization. Let them set up the heads of agreement, or outlines of the deal to be negotiated.

Now put in your patient Ss and Cs in particular to sort out the technical problems. Let the strong E head this team, but strap your team down tight on the limits to the deal they can negotiate. In a crisis, Ss can panic, Es can give it away on an impulse, and Cs avoid trouble when they are under pressure from the other side. So you have to give your team no room to move without referring to head office. When the timing is right, put the strong D back in to close the deal. Subsequently, let the strong S service it, the strong C supply technical support and the strong E keep everyone happy. Keep the strong D in reserve to get the prices up, to renew the contract on new terms and to resolve bad disputes.

2

Selling to the hard driving personality

●

> How to recognize the high achiever, and how
> to sell them on your deal.
> Sales executives often say these are the most
> difficult people to sell to. They are not.

Q.1 *The buyer sits behind a big desk, facing the door. There are trophies in a glass cupboard. He sits in a big chair, his visitor's chair is small, quite low and situated opposite him. As you come in he continues to write, without looking up. You are in the room of somebody powerful.*
How are you going to handle the sales interview?

(a) By getting out quickly, letting someone else take over.
(b) By taking extreme care for the first five minutes.
(c) By being prepared for a fight if necessary.
(d) By giving him what he wants.

Q.2 *He says he can spare you five minutes. He tells you what he is trying to achieve and asks how you can help him. How do you think it is going?*

(a) Brilliantly.
(b) It is going to go bad later.
(c) You cannot tell at this stage.
(d) You feel you'll have to make him like you first.

Q.3 *What makes these hard driving people afraid?*

(a) A big challenge.
(b) The prospect of not succeeding.
(c) New activities.
(d) Other people.

18

ANSWERS

Q.1 (a) 0 points Wimp.

(b) 5 points Don't be too relaxed for the next fifty-five either.

(c) 3 points But you will have to be very courteous if you fight him. He is a brawler if he is in a powerful position. You'll have to be Mr Tough but a nice guy with it.

(d) 3 points Be careful he does not kick you all over the place if you keep giving him what he demands.

Q.2 (a) 5 points It is. He is in a hurry, he wants results, he is asking you for help. What else do you want? Go get the business.

(b) 3 points Mildly wimpish. Everything is going to go bad sooner or later. In the long run we all end up dead.

(c) 4 points You can get a clue, you know. This person often makes up his mind quite quickly about you.

(d) 2 points He does not even notice you, let alone like you. He only likes getting results. Don't sweet-talk him too much

Q.3 (a) 0 points No, they love a challenge. If they do not face one, then they'll create one.

(b) 5 points Yes, this is their Achilles Heel.

(c) 2 points Most of them love change, new things, disrupting the old order.

(d) 2 points No, they are fighters. Only other even more dominant personalities can make them nervous

SCORES

12–15 points   Pretty good.

8–11 points   Read the text carefully, then read the questions again. It all checks out.

Up to 7 points   Work at it

●   ●   ●

SELLING TO THE HARD DRIVING PERSONALITY

Many people in this world seek to be master of their own affairs. Many seek control over others. Many people are competitive and forceful. They drive their own lives, and they drive others' lives, too. All of this adds up to a very effective manager, a very effective buyer. He is going to run things his way, and woe betide the person who stands between him and his goals.

We are going to describe three basic personality types we have to negotiate with, starting with the hard driver. These three are easy to recognize from the signs and signals they give off. Once we spot them, then we will know how to construct propositions which will suit them. Every one is different. The propositions and arguments which will suit one, will not suit the other two.

So, start by thinking of someone who is fairly dominant, someone who is not afraid of pushing you, not afraid of arguing and not afraid of telling you straight, when he does not like something. You have now got the hard driving dominant personality in your sights.

Remember that to make a proper judgement you need to look at the whole of the person and not rely on single clues. Also, everyone has a different mixture of personality styles, so you can have driving brutes and driving nice guys.

How to spot the driver

The desk. We all know about this, because we have learned it at the University of Life course we have been attending all these years. Think of a driving personality you have known. What size of desk does he have? It's a large one, isn't it (assuming that he is free to choose his own room and desk)?

Desk position. Where is it positioned? More often than not, the driving personality will position his back to the window, so that he is facing the door. So will many other types of people, of course, but this is particularly true of the driver.

The greeting, the eyes, the handshake. The greeting will be fairly formal, and only warm if the person is also high on the people scale. If he is low on the people scale, the greeting may be positively rude. Such a person may even remain seated when greeting you. He may not care what you think of him. Such a person is the type to keep you waiting for a very, very long time. Keeping you waiting regularly for half an hour or an hour is nothing for a high-driving, low-people type.

His eyes will be direct, and the gaze usually firm. His handshake will also be firm, often quite strong. If he is very dominant – as Alan Pease, the Australian specialist in non-verbal behaviour, points out – he might even twist his hand so that it is on top of yours when shaking hands.

His room. This man is a high achiever. He will have signs of success in his room. This is the person who has sales charts, graphs and performance awards around his office. They will show up his achievements and successes in some way.

The fundamental drive of the high achiever personality is a fear of failure. He is opinionated. He does not alter his views easily. He is a tough opponent. He does not tolerate either fools or incompetence. If he is low on the people scale as well, he may be inclined to be derogatory or insulting. If he is high on the people scale as well as being a high driver, he has the profile of a successful chief executive. He is a leader. But he does not brook opposition to his views.

How should you sell to him?

This is the type of personality which, when allied to a strong orderly type, makes for the ideal professional buyer's profile. This kind of personality is being hired today by all the leading retail groups.

He is a difficult type to sell to. You must not oppose him with an argument, yet you must stand your ground. You must let him appear to win, but you must not let him roll over you. You must be prepared to distance yourself, yet do so with politeness and finesse. In short, you must achieve a position of equality and balance with him. Then he will respect you and behave himself.

The first five minutes are crucial when dealing with this man. In this time he decides whether you are worth his while. If he decides you are too weak, too junior or do not know your stuff, he will wrap up the meeting quickly and pass you on to his subordinates.

He smells your anxiety at a distance of five miles. He is used to it. Many people fear him, and have done so all his life. He senses it and has no time for them. What he needs is very professional and confident handling. He may come to realize that he is being handled, but he admires that. He knows he presents difficulties to people. He often tends to marry someone who has an opposite profile to his, say a high stability type who can put up with his drive and determination and carefully turn it around. His wife can handle him easily, and he knows it.

He has a strong ego, knows it and this ego needs to be massaged a bit. But don't overdo the flattery or creeping to him. He'll dominate you if you do. He does need the utmost patience. On no account get rattled. And don't make concessions easily to his personality; if you have to give something away, you must make sure you get something back for it. He will appreciate that and respect you for it. He admires confidence, technique and style. In short, be professional.

The high-driving, low-people character is a bully. He knows it and does not care. The high-driving type, combined with high people, is a person who gets his own way with others through reading them well. There is a high proportion of good sales managers with these two characteristics. Are you one of them? If so, remember that people find you difficult too. You silver-tongued bully, you.

ACTION POINT IDEAS

1 With this person, always be a little wary. You can cross him easily, one wrong word can draw him into a fight. He can be irritated if you waste too much time. Just be practical and businesslike.
2 Ask him, fairly directly, what he wants to achieve. You can even ask him what he wants to achieve personally, and it will be acceptable to him. He knows that he makes people nervous and he is quite pleased when he finds someone who is confident. Always support his goals.
3 If he is rude or insulting to you, then go very cold. Withdraw all the warmth. Don't be rude back, but if you can gently wave the red flag and indicate that this kind of behaviour is not going to get him what he wants then this will stop him. If he threatens you, then just tell him quietly that your company policy does not allow you to negotiate under threat.
4 His staff often don't like him, and neither do his colleagues. Don't join in their conspiracies. If he is in middle management, then don't go over his head. Remember he is going to be there every day, and every day he will chip away at you until in the end he will get revenge. He makes a bad enemy.
5 Remember he is going to be the best long-term customer you'll ever have. Do the first deal with him, don't foul it up, and you could be dealing with his organization for the next ten years. You might not even see him again in the future, but you will still get the business. He is on to bigger and better things by then.

YOUR MIND MAP

YOUR ACTION PLAN

Think of a couple of tough driving people you deal with. How are you going to handle them now?

CAN YOU SPOT THE DRIVER?

Think of a driving personality. Answer this set of questions about him.

		Yes, very like him	A little like him	Not at all like him
(a)	He displays a very firm, very self-confident manner. He seems sure of himself.	———	———	———
(b)	He has got the trappings of power. Signs of his ego are all around. He talks a lot about himself and his ideas. Big desk. He likes to control the situation.	———	———	———
(c)	He is not afraid to challenge you or others. He will argue, interrupt. People find him difficult. He takes a lot of persuading to different point of views.	———	———	———
(d)	His voice can have a hard edge to it. He gets others to do things for him. He may be polite but behind the pleasantries, he is still directing others.	———	———	———
(e)	He likes a challenge. He likes doing things other people cannot do. He is competitive. He likes measurable success, numbers, results, growth, ownership of things.	———	———	———
(f)	Money is important to him.	———	———	———

SCORE

4 in the 'Yes, very like him' column and Yes, you've got one. Good luck.

3

So you think that salesmen make lousy buyers? This is why

●

> Selling to the expressive person – If your buyer is warm, easy and friendly, then thank your lucky stars.

Q.1 *You have three candidates for the job of purchasing officer for your company. Which do you pick?*

    (a)   The warm friendly person, who will obviously mix well and is socially at ease.

    (b)   The cool, blunt, awkward one who asks about your company performance.

    (c)   The quiet, rather gentle candidate who listens carefully to what you say while making notes.

Q.2 *Your buyer gets up from his desk, smiles genuinely to meet you, shakes hands, and with his other hand on your elbow he ushers you to sit in an easy chair, alongside him. He puts you at your ease. How do you handle the sales interview?*

    (a)   Let him do the talking, make the running.

    (b)   By your taking control quickly and running things.

    (c)   By concentrating upon results and performance.

    (d)   By making him like you.

Q.3 *What makes this type of buyer afraid?*

    (a)   Criticism.

    (b)   Strong people.

    (c)   Failure.

    (d)   Rejection.

ANSWERS

Q.1 (a) 0 points   He will get on too jolly well with
                           salesmen. The clever ones will rip him
                           off.
     (b) 5 points.   He'll make them work hard for his
                       business. He can be too blunt and
                       awkward for his own good though.
     (c) 3 points   May find it difficult to make decisions,
                       but will be quite thorough, though. No
                       good in a real crisis.

Q.2 (a) 5 points   Key customers you can service easily.
     (b) 1 point.   (I don't want to give you nothing,
                       because that might de-motivate you.)
     (c) 1 point   (Also if I gave you nothing, you might
                       reject me, and that would de-motivate
                       me.)
     (d) 5 points   Nothing like getting 5 points for a bit of
                       motivation.

Q.3 (a) 5 points   He does not like criticism. Few people
                       do. But this one in particular does not.
     (b) 2 points   No, he likes strong personalities so long
                       as he can handle them socially.
     (c) 2 points   Not a big problem for him.
     (d) 5 points   A big problem for him.

SCORES

12–15 points	You are lucky here. You had five chances of getting 5 points.
8–11 points.	Just missed it.
Up to 7 points.	You might seriously think about taking up nuclear physics as a career.

●   ●   ●

As you read this, I'd like you to look around your office. I can tell you what it looks like. I'll even give you odds.

Let us assume that most readers are fairly good salespeople. Some are sales directors and sales managers, and many have come up through personal selling skills. And to be promoted you usually have to be good at selling. The people who are good at selling, 80 per cent of them anyway, fall into certain personality profiles. Not only that, but you can tell what sort of profile they have from looking at their office. So look around you.

Look at your walls. Do they show pictures, graphs, awards, club memberships? Do these generally reflect your status as a pretty expert person? If they show signs of success, such as rising sales graphs, this means that you may be combining a driving personality with a great deal of people awareness. Most really successful managers are like this. They are skilful socially, but they also desire success. A typical 'A' – high achiever with social flair. Is that you? It can be a lethal combination – for your staff.

Look at the way you are dressed. Would other people say you dress well? I don't mean outrageously well, but enough to be recognized as a person of importance in the group to which you belong? Have you got management toys, executive games, plus executive diaries on your desk? When someone comes in to your room, a visitor, do you stand up to greet him? Do you smile at him? (Not everybody does. Hard-nosed buyers don't smile when you come in, and they are sometimes quite reluctant to get up out of their chairs to greet you.) Do you go around to your visitor's side of the desk? Or take him over to a side table and low chairs to sit alongside him?

It's all a dead giveaway if you do. You are a people person. You like people and want people to like you. You'll accommodate them, be nice to them so long as they are nice to you. You'll go out of your way to be courteous. You are nice to junior staff. (You might get stroppy sometimes too, but that's only your high drive coming out.)

THE ACHILLES' HEEL OF THE PEOPLE PERSON

If you are saying yes at this point, then you are admitting that you have the qualities that make a good salesman. You can get people to do what you want them to do. It's the thrill of the job for you, working with other people. But I must tell you something else, something you won't like. I know what your Achilles' heel is. I know what you fear. Rejection. That's the problem which faces you. You are probably very sensitive to criticism, particularly in public.

And I haven't told you all the bad bits yet, because there is something else which you might or might not like. You'll probably make a poor buyer. You'll be an easy touch for a salesman you like. You are probably too quick, you do not consider things long enough. You can tell such buyers by their warm handshake, their friendly approach, their snappy dressing, their smile. Oh, and they do one other thing. They talk a lot.

They like to impress you. So when you meet one of these buyers, lie back and enjoy it. Let him impress you. Be talkative with him. Make him like you. Admire his room, his decor, his company, his product. Ask him about the certificates and awards on his walls. Give him half a chance and he will talk himself into the deal.

But this sort of person likes to make many contacts, he likes to be in a crowd. He can be influenced just as easily by the salesman who comes in after you. So if you do not tie up the deal properly when you are with him, then you might lose it later. He is not the world's best planner. He does his calculations quickly and his preparation is on the spur of the moment. So it can pay you to work things out for him and make his life easy.

He loves praise, he basks in the warmth of others. So construct your propositions to feed this motivating factor. Show him how this might help him with other people, show him some glamour, show him your proposition is up to date, in fashion, the latest thing.

He does not give you a great deal of time – he has got other people to meet, remember. But he is an enthusiast, an optimist. He likes other enthusiasts, optimists. He is strong on ego, so do not criticize him. That is a real turn-off for him. Have fun with this kind of buyer. There are not enough of them about.

ACTION POINT IDEAS

1   With this person, just relax and be yourself. Like him, be warm and friendly. A little introductory socializing will be fine. Keep the conversation loose and open. Treat him in the way you would treat a friend. This one enjoys people, he enjoys fun. Give him some fun.

2   He operates best in a non-threatening situation so don't needle him. He has a strong ego – there may be a touch of the actor in him. So he can be wounded easily. Avoid anything he can take to be criticism – in fact if you can shore up his ego by showing that you respect and admire him, that is a good posture.

3   He tends to operate on the surface. So do not expect him to do too much deep thinking, research, preparation or too many calculations. He is not afraid of taking chances, so you do not need a great deal of safety and reassurance in your proposals. He is an all-action person and will respond positively to suggestions that he should meet other people, join in socializing events and so on. He will join in sports, games and events if they give him a chance to meet new people.

4   Construct propositions for him around his need to be a star and to be the centre of attention. Show him how we will do well with other people from the proposal.

5   But close him then and there while you are with him. Pre-sell him
    beforehand on the need for him to take a decision when you meet.
    Otherwise he may defer it and when you leave him you'll think you
    have got the deal. But then he may meet someone else afterwards,
    whom he also grows to like. And *he* may get the deal instead of
    you. The people person can be like that.

YOUR MIND MAP

YOUR ACTION PLAN

Think of a couple of warm friendly buyers who do *not* give you business. How are you going to land them, now?

CAN YOU SPOT THE PEOPLE PERSON?

Think of a warm, friendly, open personality. Answer this set of questions about him.

		Yes, very like him	A little like him	Not at all like him
(a)	When he greets you, his smile is warm, he stands up, comes forward towards you.	_____	_____	_____
(b)	He has the trappings of influence and ego all around him. Smartly dressed. Expensive tastes. A little star quality, perhaps, about him?	_____	_____	_____
(c)	He is self-expressive. Seldom embarrassed. Can handle any social situation. Talks a fair amount.	_____	_____	_____
(d)	When there is trouble he goes quiet. He withdraws a bit. Doesn't shine any more. Trouble is not his style.	_____	_____	_____
(e)	Money is for spending – on himself, on others, on fun. Praise is even more fun, for him.	_____	_____	_____
(f)	Everyone seems to know him. Even in a short space of time, people high and low know his name and are familiar with him.	_____	_____	_____

SCORE

Four in the 'Yes, very like him' column and you've got one. Enjoy yourself.

4

Watch the 'Leave it with me to think over' brigade

●

> Selling to quiet, not very expressive people can be very difficult indeed – Take care, the stable or conscientious buyer can be the trickiest to handle.

Q.1 *The buyer is sitting in a normal-sized office. Ordinary desk, perhaps side on to the door or the window. The furniture is not very impressive, there are photographs of the buyer's wife and children on the desk. How are you going to handle the sales interview?*

(a) Try to get a decision today.
(b) By getting to know them well, making friends first.
(c) By showing what results can be achieved.
(d) By taking things very slowly, very carefully.

Q.2 *He tells you he is 'just looking', not really intending to buy anything.*

(a) Is he telling the truth.
(b) Is it a gambit to put you off.
(c) Is he not the decision-maker.
(d) Is it normal behaviour for him.

Q.3 *What will make this person afraid?*

(a) Criticism.
(b) Antagonism.
(c) Risk.
(d) New ideas.

ANSWERS

Q1 (a) 0 points. Just the worst you can do.
     (b) 2 points. Getting to know them OK. Making friends quickly is a bad idea. They'll draw back a bit.
     (c) 3 points. It's not really on his wavelength.
     (d) 5 points. Yes, whether they are very orderly, or very stable personalities, they will want to take things slowly and carefully.

Q2 (a) 4 points Yes. He does not make up his mind quickly, if at all.
     (b) 1 point   No.
     (c) 3 points Maybe he is not. Does he look like, sound like a decision-maker?
     (d) 5 points Yes. Does it all the time.

Q3 (a) 1 point   Very unlikely. Also very unwise.
     (b) 3 points These folks do not like it.
     (c) 5 points Don't like this even more.
     (d) 3 points Nor these much.

SCORES

13–15 points   You are really getting the hang of these questions now.
9–12 points   You'll soon get the hang of these questions.
Up to 8 points After you've read this book you'll get the hang of these questions.

● ● ●

A lot of standard sales training is wrong. Just plain wrong. Much of the theory of selling was developed in the days of the 1930s for people selling typewriters, office equipment, carbon paper and insurance. A characteristic of these products is that they have a tendency to be one-shot deals – that's not totally true, but like people who sell cars, if the salesman does not close on a deal when the customer is in front of him, then he will lose the deal entirely. The customer will go away, use the price to squeeze someone else and place the business elsewhere.

So most sales training puts *closing* high on the list of skills. And there is another reason for this. Many new sales recruits will lack confidence when facing the buyer. They will be afraid to ask for the business even when they can get it. No sales manager likes his salesmen to walk away from a customer if there is a chance of closing the business there and then, so they push their people into hurried closing routines even though it might be counter productive to do so.

So when I say that there are some customer types who should not be closed too quickly, I do not mean that if a deal is there to be done then I would allow the salesman to walk away from it. Furthermore, for the one-shot dealers of this world, everything they do must lead to good timing on the close, because they'll only have one chance.

But there are some personality types who should be given time and taken more carefully if they are buyers. And most people who sell things successfully for a living do not need verbal closing tricks to land business. Ask yourself, are you successful at selling or not? So when was the last time you yourself said 'Would you like delivery Thursday or will next Monday be early enough' or whatever little verbal game-play is popular in your market? How often do you find that you need the so-called LAAPAC technique, and when you used it last would you have got the deal in any case? Yet thousands of people get trained in the use of this technique each year and not one of them is told which types of people *not to close too quickly.*

Well, I'll tell you. Have you ever met a buyer who appeared a bit wary? One who calls you 'Mr —' perhaps, one who might even appear to withdraw slightly if you get too familiar with him. A solicitor type, perhaps or maybe an accountant? Well, give them space, give them room, back off a bit and you'll stand more chance of doing business with them. For these people have a strong stability factor in their personality, or they are very orderly people.

Ever met a buyer who is very slow? Not very energetic perhaps, keeps on procrastinating, cannot make decisions? There you are again, that's a high stability factor. I'll tell you more about this type. He, or she, will keep you at arms length, they'll keep things formal. They'll probably have a fairly untidy desk or room, but they'll know where things are kept. They'll have photographs of their family on their shelves or desk. They will put a desk between you and them and will back away if you get too close.

If you push him too hard, then he may give you the impression that you will get the business, but for one reason or another he must think it over. He will say he has other people to talk to. He needs more information. He will delay things. And you must give him this time, this breathing space. He is wary and does not trust people easily. He can be a nice pleasant person, or he can be impressive, but either way he is one of the most difficult types to sell to.

Don't push him. Feed him general information, facts and figures and re-assure him. Give him written or visual 'proof' of the claims you make. Give him third-party references and supporting data. Leave yourself always with some important information that you will have to get back to him about. Don't tell him everything at once. This type of person 'feels' his way gradually towards a decision.

Don't rush him. Don't crowd him. And when you sell him once, you will sell him all the time. But he has got to trust you first, so never over-promise, always deliver more than he expects. He can be worth a fortune to you over the years, because he sticks to tried and trusted suppliers. He hates taking risks.

So does the orderly type. This person is a conformist, he keeps to the rules. He likes playing within a team but the procedures are more important to him than the results.

His desk is clear of mess, the only piece of paper on it will refer to the meeting with you. (Not like you. If you have a clear desk for a meeting, it is probably because you are concerned about the impression you are making and you have just opened the drawers and cleared all the clutter away while your visitor sits in Reception. Not for nothing are you a people person. Well, you are successful in selling are you not?)

Selling to the orderly type is easier, provided you know what turns him on. He likes data, lots of it. In very fine detail, he likes it, so he can use it to comfort himself. Give him analyses, reports, facts and figures.

Sell him on precedent. Sell him the same deal he had before. He does not go for new ideas until they have been around for a long time and everyone else thinks they are old hat. Give him third-party references from solid companies. Don't be unusual, don't be too creative with him. He is the one type of person who might start discussing your terms of business with you. God, how boring can some people be?

Confirm things in writing. Make him feel safe. But when you have got him totally assured, and you can feel his agreement is in sight, then close him. Don't let him get away then. But you have to get him into a situation where he will put himself in your hands. Having made the decision he will not reverse it. Just make sure you do not pressure him too much. And don't play games. If he catches you out in breaking his rules of conduct, then he will never deal with you again.

ACTION POINT IDEAS

1   You have two different kinds of personality here, the stable and the orderly. They both behave in a similar fashion and each needs a similar approach. Remember that the stable personality wants to reduce risk, he is concerned with security and safety, and does not want things to go wrong. He takes a long time to make up his mind. His room will be slightly untidy, or perhaps spartan of furnishings and he will cover himself with family photographs. He

is unhappy away from home. He is unhappy with unfamiliar circumstances. He needs space and time. Give him both.

2   The orderly personality reduces the prospects of antagonism or conflict by working things out in meticulous detail. He prepares well and thoroughly. He also takes a long time. Give him detail and lots of it. His room will be tidy, meticulous, neat. The files will be well organized – his life will be also. Do not upset the order of his existence.

3   Look for strong decision-influencers behind these two. They often turn to others to help them reduce risk. So people behind the scenes whom you might never meet can swing the decisions against you. Prepare the ground well, and help them sell to their boss, if that is necessary.

4   The safest decision for these two to take is the one they took last time. This works to your disadvantage in one way. It makes it difficult to get them to adopt a new idea or a new supplier unless you can show there is no danger of things going wrong and that they will be safer with you than with their present supplier. You must at least match the present supplier with your service. Yet, in another way, there is an advantage for you in dealing with them. Once you have them as customers, you will keep them. Other people will find the same difficulty in unseating you. Unless you muck up their service, of course.

YOUR MIND MAP

YOUR ACTION PLAN

Think of some quiet stable buyers you have been trying to sell to. Can you change your approach to them now? Where were you going wrong?

CAN YOU SPOT THE RISK AVOIDERS?

Think of a quiet, soft spoken personality who is in buying. Answer
this set of questions about him.

		Yes, very like him	A little like him	Not at all like him
(a)	He has a quiet, peaceful, soft-spoken non-aggressive manner.	_____	_____	_____
(b)	His office is unassuming, no signs of power, no signs of ego, just a place to work.	_____	_____	_____
(c)	He listens carefully, does not probe hard or use awkward questions or try to trap you. He does not demand improved terms or use any kind of threat to you.	_____	_____	_____
(d)	He wants all the details of everything. He wants facts, figures, literature, proof. He has little sense of priority over this. He just feels more comfortable with all the data.	_____	_____	_____
(e)	He joins in with other people without being a show-off, without wanting to lead all the time. People come to him sometimes for advice.	_____	_____	_____
(f)	He is the sort of person who is unlikely to become a millionaire, but you can imagine him joining a company because of its good pension policy.	_____	_____	_____

SCORES

Four in the 'Yes, very like him' column and you've got one. Either
stable, or orderly. Hope you have enough time to spare.

5

Become a millionaire the easy, safe way

●

> Personal career development – This is just addressed to you, the individual. It shows how to become rich.

Q.1 *You want to build £1 million after-tax worth of personal assets. How will you do this?*

(a) By marrying the chairman's daughter.

(b) Through putting £10,000 a year away into a pension fund, for sixteen years.

(c) Through running your own business.

(d) Through continuously buying and selling the house you live in, buying cheap and selling dear.

Q.2 *You have two friends who want to join in with you on your new business venture. The idea is all yours but you need them to get it going. How will you divide the shares? You will all be expected to put up finance for your share of the equity.*

(a) One-third each, equal amounts of finance to come from all three.

(b) 60 per cent to you, the others 20 per cent each, with you putting up 60 per cent of the finance.

(c) 100 per cent to you, all the finance to you, pay them big salaries to join you.

(d) Run it as a partnership, sorting it out later when everyone has proven their worth.

Q.3 *You are invited to join a private company by the owner who suggests a shareholding to you. The venture is new, the*

*owner has the resources but you are the one with the talent
and experience. Which option do you argue for?*

(a)   No shares now, but an option on 40 per cent of the
      shares in five years time, at today's price.
(b)   Equal fifty-fifty.
(c)   Accept his suggestion of 40 per cent now.
(d)   10 per cent now, but an option on another 30 per cent
      in five years at the price ruling then.

ANSWERS

Q1   (a)   2 points   You've got your head screwed on the
                          right way. But she'll be the millionaire,
                          not you.

         (b)   4 points   Yes, it will; but the fund will be locked
                          away, so you will never actually be able
                          to lay your hands on the million
                          smackers or hand it on.

         (c)   5 points   You should be able to do this with
                          reasonable success. But it has got to be
                          more than a newspaper shop business
                          and you have got to be at it for a long
                          time.

         (d)   4 points   Yes, it can be done. Buy worn out
                          properties on the edge of areas
                          becoming fashionable. Do them up, sell
                          them and move on every four years. But
                          it is very disruptive to your family life.

Q2   (a)   1 point   A lot of people actually do this and they
                          never gain control. This business will
                          probably break up because three is the
                          most difficult number to run an
                          operation. Even four is better than three.
                          For a new business two or one owning
                          it is best.

         (b)   5 points. This is pretty good. You have control
                          and there is enough in it to interest the
                          others, particularly if they have their
                          money in it, too.

(c) 1 point   They are no more than expensive staff. And the last thing you want is expensive people who have no real commitment.

(d) 3 points   Quite like this. Sorts out men from boys, but you have to have great confidence in your own ability to come through as top performer. Three are going to break up sooner or later.

Q3 (a) 3 points   But you must tie up the deal contractually so he cannot escape from his commitment. This is the easiest way for an owner to skin you. He may fire you in a year.

(b) 5 points   Yes, if you can get it. But ask yourself, why does he need you so badly he will give you half of what he has got?

(c) 4 points   Minority shares are always difficult when you want to get out. Who is there to buy them? And at what price? You want to arrange a get-out clause in the contract confirming your right to sell when you want, and to whom you want, and the basis of the valuation when you do want to sell. All difficult, eh?

(d) 0 points   At 10 per cent he can claw back your shares at any time he wants and you can do nothing about it. And when you do buy the extra shares in five years the price then will have been built up by your own successful efforts. Don't be a chump.

SCORES

11–15 points   A wide band here for the top score. They are not questions which come up every day in the normal person's experience. Of course, if you get high scores, this could be an indication of your abnormality.

8–10 points   Think twice about these issues before going into your own venture.

Up to 7 points   Think three times before you go into your new venture.

●   ●   ●

THE WAY TO BECOME A MILLIONAIRE

Becoming a millionaire should be easy enough these days. There are thousands of them. But there should be many, many more. I see them all the time in all kinds of companies. People with energy, drive, common sense and an eye for the main chance. But they will never become millionaires because they trap themselves. They hide behind their monthly pay cheque.

You are very unlikely to become a millionaire if you work for someone else. It can be done – just – but look at what a struggle it is. Lord Hanson has made a few of his boardroom colleagues into millionaires. Sir Owen Green has made a few more. But these are just a handful of people running really big organizations. It is very difficult to become a millionaire if you also want the guaranteed security of a monthly pay cheque. And if, by the way, you think that working for a big organization will guarantee a monthly pay cheque forever, think again.

It's not too late

Here is a good way to become a millionaire. Even if you are in mid-career, it's not too late. Run a small business, where you own 51 per cent of the equity. Make sure that it makes £10,000 profit a year. Don't leave the profit in, or the government will take it away. Put it into your pension fund. Do your homework, invest it properly and it will grow at 20 per cent or so a year. Don't rely on advisers or any other berks who make commissions out of investing your money. Otherwise, you'll only make 15 per cent a year or less. Pay in your £10,000 profits every year for sixteen years, and you will build £1 million. That will give you a reasonable amount to spend, and a good income for the rest of your life.

Now, you can't call £10,000 net profit a year much, can you? After all, some people can make that on a sales turnover of £100,000 or less. No, the real problem is that you must have that extra one share above the fifty mark. It's the central cog in the whole wheel. Once you've got it, never give it up. (Well, never is too long. You must get out sometime.)

The one share gives you control

That one extra share above the 50 gives you control. With control, you can vote for yourself becoming a millionaire. Just try and vote for yourself becoming a millionaire through the democratic process, without having control. You'll have no chance. Dictators become millionaires. Love-thy-neighbour merchants do not. In this world, you can make big money from nothing in only three ways: taking risks, raking in profits, and making big sales.

Take a little risk

First, you must be prepared to take a little risk. Most people are too nervous to take out a second mortgage on their home. It's not a question of not having the right idea, either. Every businessman worth his salt has plenty of unused ideas just waiting for someone to work them up. Often, they'll join in a joint venture themselves, and provide some backing.

The trick is to limit your personal risk. Keep your job for a start. Begin with two years' advance planning for your new business. Work at it at night and at weekends. Earn yourself pin money so that on day one, you have got something coming in.

Four years ago a pal of mine bought the freeholds on a parade of shops costing £200,000. There were ten shops with an average rental of £2,000 a year each. The bank put up 80 per cent and he put up 20 per cent. For the first three years he was paying out more in interest than he was earning from rents. But after three years he put up the rents to about £3,000 a year so his interest payments were covered, and the property is now worth £300,000. He sends out quarterly demands for the rents. That's all he does and he stayed in his job. See what I mean about reducing the risk? Millionaires-to-be appear to take big risks, but if you ask them, they'll tell you that they were hedged the whole time.

Force the profits

The second way to become rich is to make big profits for people. If you get into a position of profit responsibility in a company, make the figures sing. Hammer the costs down first. Push the sales up second. Force the sales of profitable things and ruthlessly cut out the things which do not make much money. Run a tight ship. Keep the fixed costs low.

Seek the profit edge the whole time. You do not need great strategic flights of fancy, advanced management skills or superior brain power. You need commonsense and an eye for the main chance. You need very good financial controls, very good figures. You need to be fast on your feet and, when things go wrong, you should cut, and cut fast. Don't stay with losers, whatever you do. You'll make a lot of money. People will promote you to bigger jobs. You'll learn to do these things on a big scale. Then you can name the money you want, and people will have to pay it.

So the second way to become rich is to make profits, big profits. But that means taking on profit-responsible jobs.

Build big sales

Building sales can also make you into a millionaire, but it's not as good as the other two methods. If you can build big sales volume, get growth when others decline, and achieve market leadership, you should be able to make a lot of money. But you might not make a million.

Why not? Because you'll always be number two to the man who can turn your big sales volume into profit. Sales volume alone, without profits, will leave you stranded when things turn down. But your profit-maker is off and flying somewhere else by then, because, even in sluggish markets, profit-makers can still make money.

ACTION PLAN IDEAS

1   Make out a long-term plan for yourself. What do you want: happiness; good health; good friends; respect of your peers; lots of money; and devoted family? Then work out how far your present work will get you there.
2   If you want to start your own business, then make some plans, well in advance. If you do not know what to do then start from your present skills and knowledge. Can you study in the evenings? Talk to friends? Can you prepare the ground two years or so before you move? When you move from your present company can you stay friends and still keep them perhaps as a customer of your new business? Negotiate the deal from the inside. Can you join another company first in your intended field of operation?
3   Talk to people who have set up and are running their own businesses now. They'll be pleased to help. Many of them have marvellous business ideas to start which they cannot do themselves but they might be pleased enough to help someone else get started with if they have a slice of the action. Join the local Chamber of Commerce, Rotary Club and Round Table.

4   Look for low capital-intensive businesses, with short manufacturing lead times, and good cash flows. If you have the reverse kind then you will find it difficult to retain control if things go wrong. In a new business you need flexibility. Things never turn out exactly as planned. Try to find a business which will bolt on to another existing business. Don't add to your complications by trying a radical new idea. Why not a management buy-out of part of your existing business?

5   If you still want a full-time salary and you also want to be part-independent, then think of businesses you can start and run part-time. The important thing is that these must be the kind of businesses which do not involve much of your time for the amount of money they make. That rules out freelance subjects like journalism, lecturing etc. But it brings in subjects such as property development and management. You can do this often at long-range with a minimum commitment of time. Start with a second home which you can re-furbish and re-sell at a profit. Grow from there. Certain kinds of mail-order business are quite good, too.

YOUR MIND MAP

YOUR ACTION PLAN

How are you going to develop your career for the rest of your working life? What has to be done?

HAVE YOU GOT WHAT IT TAKES TO DO YOUR OWN THING?

Most successful owner-drivers of businesses are type As. Ambitious and restless. Here is a test to show how much of a type A you might be. (Most successful owner-drivers claim that a part of their success is due to the fact that they worked at it night and day. This is unlikely to be the cause of success – not by itself. This restlessness is the product of their personality and it is a certain type of personality which gets to the top. Ambition to succeed, and the fear of failure are equally as important to these people as driving themselves hard. They would drive themselves whatever they did for a living.)

#							
1	You like to respond to events	1	2	3	4	5	You want to make things happen
2	You are not very premise	1	2	3	4	5	You watch the detail on those subjects which interest you
3	You do not use too many measures to check up on performance	1	2	3	4	5	You judge results by numbers
4	Work is just another thing you do in your life	1	2	3	4	5	You take work seriously. And bring it home, too
5	You don't usually set deadlines for yourself or others	1	2	3	4	5	Deadlines are important to you. You set them.
6	You will stay in one job for a long time	1	2	3	4	5	You are always ambitious for the next stage of development
7	All sorts of things interest you in many different fields	1	2	3	4	5	You become dedicated to things which interest you, such as work
8	You are sympathetic and will open up to others on your feelings	1	2	3	4	5	You hold your feelings in and control them well
9	You prefer to get things right	1	2	3	4	5	You'll cut corners to get your results
10	You do things slowly, in your own time	1	2	3	4	5	You do most things quickly particularly everyday things
11	You prefer to keep a low profile	1	2	3	4	5	Recognition and reputation is important to you

12	Generally you are not very pushy	1 2 3 4 5	You are fairly assertive for the things you want
13	You prefer doing one thing at a time and getting it right	1 2 3 4 5	You always have several things going at the same time
14	Never in a hurry even if the pressure is on	1 2 3 4 5	Always in a hurry
15	People think you are fairly quiet by nature	1 2 3 4 5	When you get going, you talk a lot
16	You take your time about things and will often leave tasks until later	1 2 3 4 5	You must keep on top of things and finish them quickly
17	You are relaxed about winning and losing	1 2 3 4 5	You always want to win
18	You will queue for a bus without tension	1 2 3 4 5	You hate queues and will go out of your way to avoid them
19	Your meetings often start late	1 2 3 4 5	You are irritated if people are not on time
20	On a motorway you drive in the centre or slow lane	1 2 3 4 5	On a motorway you drive in the fast lane most of the time

Circle the number which corresponds to your score. Add up your scores.

SCORES

80–100 points   Definitely Type A. You are the high achievers of this world. Fear of failure drives you on to new ambitions all the time. Take care with your health. Watch the diet carefully. Break up your work so you can relax sometimes. Take three, half-hour exercise periods a week. Cut smoking.

The problems occur late when your immune system starts to break down because of all the disturbance caused to your system by your hypercharged life. Take particular care if there is a history of heart attacks in your family.

But good luck. The future of the world depends upon you.

60–80 points	You are also type A but much more modest. The world also depends upon you, but you make less of a strain upon the health services.
40–60 points	You have a bit of A and a bit of B.
20–40 points	Type B. You make the world go round. You often spread happiness and light. You look in wonder at these mad Type A's always in a tearing hurry to the next goal. And you shake your head quietly as you think to yourself, 'I'm glad I do not run my own business. Who needs the worry of it?'

Part Two

Ten Marketing Management Tactics

6

The true and barely revealed secrets of marketing success

●

> The little known PIMS study holds the
> secrets of profitability – If you want to buy a
> business or re-structure one to make much
> more profit then there is one piece of
> continuous research you should study.

Q.1 *For making a great deal of money in your business, which of the following options are most important to you?*

    (a)   Being in a growth market.
    (b)   Having brilliant management with a past record of success.
    (c)   Having your product protected by patent.
    (d)   Having the biggest share of the market you serve.

Q.2 *To grow your market share you should think in terms of*

    (a)   Getting your costs down to lower your price.
    (b)   Increasing your sales force.
    (c)   Increasing your product quality relative to the competition.
    (d)   Using more effective marketing methods.

Q.3 *Your quality-control procedures should*

    (a)   Ensure that your production is meeting your specifications.
    (b)   Be linked to the customer's perception of the quality he is buying.
    (c)   Include your deliveries as well.
    (d)   Include a statistical analysis of all customer complaints.

ANSWERS

Q.1 (a) 3 points. The PIMS study shows that this is one
of the factors which make for profits.
But not the biggest factor.
   (b) 2 points. No correlation with profitability.
   (c) 3 points. PIMS also shows that pioneer products
in their market are very profitable when
their products are protected.
But it is not the biggest factor.
   (d) 5 points. Yup. (Notice the phrase, 'the market you
serve'. This might be different to your
standard definition of your total market.
It is the sector of the market in which
you choose to operate.)

Q.2 (a) 2 points. Many are the failures in this category. It
is not to do with price. It is to do with
relative product quality.
   (b) 2 points. It is not to do with the sales force. It is to
do with relative product quality.
   (c) 5 points. Yes.
   (d) 2 points. No. See (c).

Q.3   All the answers are right, you can have
2 points for each, but one answer is
different to the rest.
   (a) 2 points.
   (b) 5 points. The PIMS study shows this clearly. They
say that customers' views of quality
should be researched, and weighted.
Then a performance scale should be
produced for your company. Your
quality control should be measured
against that. They say that the trouble
with most quality control measures is
that they stop at the factory gate.
   (c) 2 points.
   (d) 2 points.

SCORES

11–15 points.   Give you a wide band here for top score.
Only one senior manager in 20, that I come

	across in seminars, knows about the PIMS data.
7–10 points.	Study back issues of *Harvard Business Review* for PIMS data, or buy Charles Carroll's book.
Up to 6 points.	It's anybody's guess if you have not studied the research on the subject. I sympathize.

● ● ●

NINE BIG PROFIT-BOOSTERS

I hereby acknowledge that I shall owe Charles Carroll a lot of money one day. Because four years ago Charles told me how to avoid stress, be happy and make much much more money. It's amazing how happy you can be and how little stress there is if you make money.

To be sure there was no deep counselling involved, no therapy. We had a chat over a fine meal in Dublin during the course of which he told me about the work he was doing for PIMS (or Profit Impact of Market Strategy). He told me that General Electric in the USA set up a think tank of business boffins a decade ago. Their job was to identify the factors in a business which make money. GE wanted to invest in companies and needed to have criteria laid down for those most likely to be profitable.

So they set about asking companies to report their results regularly and they analysed the differences. Being GE, when they get companies to report results they don't rely on just a few – they have thousands. The think tank identified about nine major variables which have the greatest impact upon profit results. There could be literally thousands of other factors which make for profit – the native skill and genius of the businessman, the length of time in business, being married to the daughter of the chairman of the biggest customer, all these are unidentified assets on the balance sheet.

Now all of this is the pretty dull stuff of which ordinary management books are made. But when Charles casually mentioned the key findings from the study, my life began to change and for the better.

PIMS NUMBER ONE

Of the nine most important things in a business, Charles said, relative market share could be identified as number one. It is not the only factor, mind you, and you could be very profitable indeed without being market leader. But you have a better chance of the shekels rolling in if you are. What you can't do, is to buy market share with extra vigorous marketing. That will lead you to a pauper's grave. You must box much more clever than that if you want to be number one.

Another PIMS finding is that businesses generally behave in a regular and fairly predictable pattern. How do they know this? Well, if you examined 15 000 bits of information about business activity and results over five years and you saw that the same patterns were being repeated in many different types of businesses and many different types of market – about 3000 different businesses actually – would you not tend to draw this conclusion?

PIMS NUMBER TWO

And the PIMS number two finding is that the laws of the market place determine about 80 per cent of the profit results. Being in the right business is 80 per cent of the story. Operating that business in a skilful or lucky way is 20 per cent of the story.

Let's put it all another way. Suppose you have a business with a weak market position. In a fit of sudden madness you put in a lot of expensive equipment – perhaps labour-saving equipment. I promise you one thing as a result – it's 'show me the way to the workhouse' time. You would do a lot better putting your money into a bank deposit account and letting inflation rot it away. Your money would last a lot longer. This is not an opinion. Fifteen thousand bits of information fed in to a computer regularly for at least five years can prove it.

WHAT BUSINESSMEN DON'T KNOW

The wonder is that this data is so little known to practising businessmen. To be sure, it is well known to academics, business school professors and marketing tutors in polytechnics. But beyond them – zilch.

I'm telling you about Charles Carroll because I feel I owe him something, and you also, come to that. After finding out about the study, I went away and re-hung one of our new business enterprises. It has got a low capital intensity (good on the PIMS rating), while not being high tech (also good), it is in a growth market (more PIMS plus points), needs very few people to operate it (PIMS rating now zooming up), it can maintain a high gross profit (extra plus points for having high added value), its relative price/quality offering is perceived by the market to be very good, it is different, it is innovative, and one part of it has a positive cash flow. Every one of these shafts digs deep into the bull of the PIMS target.

The only problem is that PIMS says that new business ventures take about six years or more to achieve reasonable profits and eight years or more to earn the PIMS rating. And I would like the money today. Charles Carroll has just put it all down in an excellent book you will not have heard of. It's all about Irish business and the way their economy relates to the PIMS findings. In Irish business and financial and government circles, he has upset a few established notions. The book is called *Building Ireland's Business* and you can get a copy from the Irish Management Institute in Dublin. It could turn out to be the best investment you ever made. It is certainly the best book on marketing I have read in the last ten years.

ACTION POINT IDEAS

1   What quality improvements can you make for the customer? Can you develop new second-generation products? Can you improve the value offering in some way?
2   Remember that a quality advantage over your competition is a wasting asset. Competitors constantly chip away at your edge. So you have to keep ahead of them all the time. Look at your long-standing, stable products. What can you do with them? What can you do with the packaging, the ordering system, the speed of service, the back up?
3   Can you get down your costs, so that you can lower your prices at the same time as putting up your relative quality? This will give you substantial value enhancement. But you must get down your product costs and your overheads.
4   If you are a market follower, then you will do better, according to the PIMS study if you enter a sector of the market where there is a demand for services.
5   Produce a quality profile for your market. Identify key non-price and non-product factors which are important to your customers. Give a weighting adding up to 100 for all these factors in order of priority. Then rate yourself and your leading competitors on each factor on a scale of 1 to 10. Now you have a good quality-control standard to improve upon.

YOUR MIND MAP

YOUR ACTION PLAN

How do you plan to become much more profitable in the long run?

CAN YOUR ORGANIZATION EVER MAKE IT AS A QUALITY PRODUCER?

The following table shows the results of a research study.

Your quality control standards		
Do your executives pay high attention to technicians' views when setting standards?	1 2 3 4 5	Do your executives pay high attention to customer benefits when setting standards?
Do you operate to tight tolerances in QC?	1 2 3 4 5	Do you measure real customer needs?
Is QC tied to manufacturing?	1 2 3 4 5	Have you got user-based QC?
Do you measure defects against manufacturing standards?	1 2 3 4 5	Does your QC cover all departmental functions?

This research by a multi-national company took two samples to compare with each other. One sample consisted of products which were recognized by their customers as offering high quality. The comparison was with the group of products perceived to be of low quality. The company then compared the quality control procedures. In most companies, QC is too narrow and measures the wrong thing.

7

There is only a weak correlation between good sales techniques and high company profits

●

> The marketing edge is more important than the selling edge – really good sales technique *should* lead to high profits. But you can get high profits from bad sales technique, too. So something else is the causal factor of high profits. It's called product positioning.

Q.1 *If you could make one thing excellent in your company, beyond all others, what should it be?*

   (a)   Collecting overdue accounts.
   (b)   The sales skills, and drive of your team.
   (c)   Your domination of a market sector.
   (d)   The opulence of your office.

Q.2 *You want to achieve low sales costs, and good results. What is most likely to achieve this for you?*

   (a)   Little competition.
   (b)   A high company reputation.
   (c)   Widescale advertising.
   (d)   Working your existing customer base.

Q.3 *Your market is very competitive. Everyone sells the same thing. In your sales operation which is going to be the most important factor?*

   (a)   A bigger sales force than anyone else.

    (b)   High commissions and incentives.
    (c)   Low overheads.
    (d)   Concentration upon target market sectors.

ANSWERS

Q.1 (a)   1 point.   Good to have accounts to collect at all.
        (b)   4 points.   Why not? This book is dedicated to this
                           idea.
        (c)   5 points.   But it is dedicated to this idea even
                           more.
        (d)   5 points   Just for your cheek.

Q.2 (a)   5 points   Big fish. Little pond.
        (b)   3 points   Reputation by itself does not guarantee
                           success. The *Titanic* was a great ship.
        (c)   1 point   It's no good without a decent product
                           that people want.
        (d)   5 points   Yes, they are cheaper to sell to. Your
                           conversion rate is high. Unless you have
                           been selling rubbish.

Q.3 (a)   1 point   No.
        (b)   3 points   Energy and ambition is a lot, but it is not
                           everything.
        (c)   4 points   Yes, because it enables you to have
                           sorts of options. Lower prices, for one.
                           Higher profits from smaller volume for
                           another.
        (d)   5 points   Even in a generalized commodity
                           market you must concentrate upon
                           something and do it better than anyone
                           else. Why not concentrate upon the
                           target?

SCORES

14–15 points   Easy to get high scores. And you read the
                    intro to the chapter before you did the ques-
                    tions anyway.
10–13 points   You should read the intro to the chapters.
                    They sometimes give you clues about how
                    to answer the questions.
Up to 9 points   Difficult to get a low score here.

● ● ●

I was advised by the locals to put an ad for the shed in the *Oban Times*. It was a biggish shed, too big for our garden, and in fair nick.

'Hello, *Oban Times*? Can I speak to classified ads?'
'What's it about?'
'I want to place an advertisement.'
'Do you know you'll have to pay in advance?'
'No.'
'Well, do you want to write in then?'
'No, I would like to speak to classified ads.'
'Oh, you still want to dictate it over the phone, though you'll have to pay in advance?'
'No. I want to find out how much it will cost, dictate it over the phone, then write a cheque and post it to you.'
'Oh, I see. Well she's busy at the moment. Can you ring back after four?'

Now, if you think this is an example of hot telesales technique then we do not inhabit the same business world as each other. After four I rang back. We went through the entire conversation again, stretching from the 'What's it about?' to the end, except that this time I got through.

They took the advertisement for the shed and agreed the date of insertion. They put the ad in a week too early, so when we got back to our home in Sussex the following Friday the telephone was already going as we opened the door. And it went again a few minutes later. And again. And again. We must have fielded eight enquiries that evening. So goodness knows how many calls we had received the previous day when the paper came out.

By 10.00 am the following morning the shed had been sold. In fact, I could have sold that shed ten times over – the calls were still coming in on Sunday. The point is that the paper has a monopoly in the area and is widely read. There was no other simple way of getting rid of the shed.

The *Oban Times* is the only newspaper I know that can have as its front-page lead a story about the lack of a gents' loo in Oban town, complete with a photograph of where a loo could be sited. Yet it is very popular and is stuffed full of ads every week.

WHEN YOUR SALES TECHNIQUE CAN BE PUTRID

When you have a product which does the job, when it has little or no competition, and when you do not want to grow, your sales technique can be as putrid as you like.

Conversely, when your product is in a very competitive market and where the competition has a lower price than you do and there is little to distinguish your product from alternatives, you will have to have a very hot sales technique indeed.

Take the finance industry, for example. Not so long ago, if you wanted to buy a car you went along to see your bank manager about getting a loan. He would quiz you about your income prospects, demand a few guarantees and lend you the money at a low rate of interest. You would have to go to see him, though. And he would grill you. For sure, he did not behave like a salesman.

Then the finance companies got their act together. One company, North West Securities, went from number nine in the industry league to number four in the space of six years through good sales technique, sales management, motivation and control. They set aggressive standards for selling what they call direct business to the man in the street. It has become a very sophisticated game now and North West could never offer low rates, not even very competitive rates. But they still did the business. Their salesmen are stolen by the other companies in the finance industry these days.

Their success has made the banks sit up and go for the business too. The banks thought they could just sit there and the loan requests would come in through the door, customers with cap in hand. A bit like the *Oban Times*. So now the banks make it easier to buy and they are more aggressive about selling. That is because they are in a competitive market and lack a very distinct edge. There are hundreds, indeed thousands, of companies and brokers who can compete, and if they sell aggressively and well, they will get the business.

As these examples show, while sales technique is of course important, the number one factor in business is the market and what it wants. Supply that with an effective service, and be the only people to supply that, and you will make a lot of money. So long as you do not actually upset people, you can afford for your selling effort to be a bit sloppy.

WHERE YOUR BEST PROFITS LIE

Have a look at those markets where you have a powerful share, with little competition. They might be quite small niches of big markets. That's where your selling is easiest and where the customer demands for discounts are fewest. Protect yourself with a patent, and don't tell too many people about your luck.

And if anyone can ship me a hundred garden sheds size 8 ft by 12 ft to a village on the west coast of Scotland for £100 each, then I can find just such a market for them. With the help of the *Oban Times*, of course. I'll mark the cost up by 100 per cent too.

ACTION POINT IDEAS

1   Try to get a clear focus upon your objectives in each different market sector and product you sell. Start with the main products first. What markets do they serve?
2   If you have a wide range, then can you pick out key market sectors to focus upon? Can these be measured in some way; their description, their buying habits, their numbers, the volume of their purchases.
3   Forget the small things you do. Forget the add-on products, the service items. Forget the small customers. Look for the core of the business. Don't measure everything.
4   In markets where you have little product edge, where you offer the same as the competition, have you jacked up your advertising and your selling to be better, more effective than the opposition? How do you know this?
5   Are there a number of markets you should not be in at all? Are there markets which will not form any part of your future? Can you profit strip them, run them down, and get out?

YOUR MIND MAP

YOUR ACTION PLAN

What action should you take to tighten up the definition of your core target markets, and your effectiveness within them?

HOW SHARP IS YOUR PRODUCT POSITIONING?

Take your principal product or service.

Score either 1, 2 or 3 points for each statement. Score 1 if the statement hardly applies to you at all, score 3 if the statement describes your situation very closely indeed. Otherwise score 2. Score 2 also if the statement is inappropriate for your company.

After you have scored each statement, then multiply your score by the weighting factor shown below.

This will give you an overall total.

Score 1, 2 or 3

(a)   You actually do define to your salespeople the kinds of customers you do not care about.   _____

(b)   You have a statement which describes your principal target market.   _____

(c)   Within your target market, your company is well known.   _____

(d)   Competitors find you difficult to beat in your target market.   _____

Now multiply your scores by the weighting factor below:
(a) times 1; (b) times 3; (c) times 2; (d) times 3.
18 is an average score (2 multiplied by the weighting factors). If you have less than this, then it is worthwhile thinking again about this whole issue.
A good starting point is to define the kind of business you do not want to waste time and effort on getting.
Have another think about your answer to (d) Is this an honest answer if you have given it 3 points? How do you know?

8

The secrets of sales success: get a really good accountant

●

> Product management for profit – This
> chapter is about calculating the profitability
> of different parts of the business; and
> keeping the business tightly controlled.

Q.1 *At a board meeting you are arguing about one of your poor profit lines. You have the following choices:*

    (a) Promote it, says the advertising manager, then it will become profitable through selling more.

    (b) Keep it, says the sales manager, because you need it to round out your range.

    (c) Chop it out, says the accountant. It is dragging us down.

    (d) Research the situation thoroughly, says the market researcher.

Q.2 *When is the best time to chop out products from your range?*

    (a) When you put new products on the list.

    (b) When your sales are going down.

    (c) When your profits are going down.

    (d) Review the range the whole time.

Q.3 *As a sales manager, what is the most important set of financial data for you to consider regularly?*

    (a) Comparison of actuals versus forecasts in the budget.

    (b) Profit and loss account, and balance sheets.

    (c) Cash-flow projections.

    (d) Product-line costings (showing profitability of the range you sell).

ANSWERS

Q.1	(a)	1 point	Promote success not failure.
	(b)	2 points	He may be right. I don't like this argument, personally, though it is the most widely used.
	(c)	2 points	He is right; but it is a pity to go to this final step without looking at alternatives.
	(d)	5 points	Your researcher may be a gentle chap, very quiet. But if only you all-action strivers would shut up a minute and listen to him you would hear him making sense. Your desire for instant solutions to every problem leads to some crass decisions. Don't do anything without more information.
Q2	(a)	3 points	I like this one.
	(b)	2 points	All action, no thought.
	(c)	2 points	All action, no thought.
	(d)	5 points	Yes, all the time. Keep the product range tight.
Q3	(a)	5 points	It's dull, and boring, but you've got this one right. But look at answer (d).
	(b)	1 point	Won't help you in sales much.
	(c)	2 points	Won't help you in sales much but it can keep your company alive. This can be the most dangerous index to watch – and your selling efforts affect it.
	(d)	4 points	You must plan around supporting the most profitable parts of your business.

SCORES

13–15 points	What's it like to be a trainee rich person?
10–12 points	Bit more number crunching needed.
Up to 9 points	If you are not doing it, then just make sure that someone is counting the profits.

●   ●   ●

GET A REALLY GOOD ACCOUNTANT

I am one of the few managers in the world whose business values were formed by a sausage roll.

We called it the Long Tom. It was bigger than the normal size and it had slices in the top so that you could see what filling was inside. We made it like that and we called it that, a name which had to pass a rather difficult board meeting during which anyone who questioned its sexual connotation was immediately denounced as having a dirty mind (this was the only way we could get the decision through), and we cut the slices in the top because research had indicated the need to do these three things.

Now I know that there are some who will be beginning to doubt the authenticity of this tale. Most men in their lives do serious things. They engineer things. They edit newspapers. They think of what one chemical can do to another, or of what a combination of chemicals can do to human beings – and we do know how serious this can be. But to imagine that there are other highly paid senior executives roaming around free, commissioning some of the most highly paid and expert market research talent to conduct a statistically valid survey, based upon the most up-to-date probability theory, with concept groups led by Freudian psychologists, to discuss the matter of how people think about sausage rolls, seems frankly daft.

THE SAUSAGE ROLL CRISIS IN OUR LIVES

The research also told us that there was a need for a bigger-sized sausage roll sold in the kind of catering outlets which we sold our products to, and the man in the street also told us, predictably, that he did not believe that there was enough filling inside the sausage roll, which was the reason for cutting the slits in the top. We had to prove the damn things had something inside.

You may consider that there ought to be a good reason for telling this story, and we are now coming to it. You see, the reason why it was so important to do all this laborious work on the sausage roll was because in our food manufacturing company, the sausage roll accounted for only 15 per cent of our sales, but it provided a full 35 per cent of our gross profit. Yes, you see now how important the wretched things were. Not only that, but business in sausage rolls was declining and at a rapid rate, and no one could make out why. And if sausage roll sales continued to droop the whole company would droop as well. So the sausage roll represented a crisis in our lives.

So now it is clear to you what this is all about. It is about management accounting. In the old days the financial accountant ruled. And in the way men organize these nasty little things he still holds a quite undeservedly high status in the hierarchy among different kinds of financial men. But in his relevance to business, the man who keeps the books neat and tidy, who watches the balance of assets and liabilities and examines the gearing of debt, is much less important than the management accountant.

True, in a time of high growth the financial accountant will give warning of cash-flow troubles – and how badly he does that from time to time. True it is nice to have a financial accountant who constructs matters so that more of the owners' money stays out of the pocket of the taxman.

PINPOINT WHAT'S MAKING YOU MONEY

But it is the management accountant who tells you what is making money in your business and what is not. The management accountant tells us what is going out of kilter in the plan against budget. The management accountant reconciles the stock. The management accountant tells you in advance of where nasty moguls lie in the path of the glissading businessman on the slippery piste of success. (Well, it is winter sports time as this is written.)

Piste or not, the business schools and the polytechnics are turning out a generation of graduates in business studies who are trained to observe the management acountant's every move. And they are right to do so. I learned from sausage rolls that you have to keep a business tight, really tight. You have to cut products off the range if you want to put new ones on. And you may have to take a few losses here and there.

What happened to the Long Tom? I'll tell you. We launched it in a blaze of publicity. Even the *Daily Mail* diary ran a story about these nutcase executives applying their Ph.D. brains to sexy sausage rolls. We copied the story and put it in every sausage roll pack we made. We gave out copies of the paper to all our customers. We advertised the story. We got some sausage rolls fresh from our ovens at Stratford in East London, wrapped them in beautiful beribboned boxes with aluminium foil to keep them fresh and hot and sent them by Securicor to Sainsbury's head office at Blackfriars. We had telegrammed their buying director to stand by for an important parcel. He did not know us from Adam then, but he was shortly to remedy this after he received the sausage rolls. He blasted us on the phone for our silly prank. Yes, we said, but did you like the sausage rolls, and did you see what the *Daily Mail* said, we asked. You'd better come round, he said. So we went round. And we landed an order that was to lead to a ten-year relationship worth £5 million of turnover a year. Not for sausage rolls. All for Sainsbury's own label steak and kidney puddings. But that's the way of the world.

ACTION POINT IDEAS

1   Do a skew analysis. Add up your products/services so their sales are 100. Add up the actual profit contribution from each so they add up to 100. Now identify those products which produce a high proportion of your profit contribution. Concentrate your plans on those.

2   Now look at the products which produce a lower proportion of your profit contribution than they should. If they are small products then consider how you can get rid of them.

3   Get rid of any small products which are difficult to produce, cost you excessive overhead, excessive customer queries or complaints, or cost you excessive service. You can afford all of these luxuries of cost only if the products concerned are big contributors to your overall profits.

4   Look at your distribution costs. Look at your advertising and promotion costs (discount costs, too if you like). See if any products are incurring a disproportionate amount of these costs.

5   Before taking any product off the range; see if you can strip it of all supporting cost and hack the price upwards, by a big amount. If it still sells, it may become profitable. If it does not then you lose nothing because you were going to take it off anyway.

6   Remember that you don't save any overheads merely by removing a theoretical cost associated with one product. You may have to take a whole group of products out of your range before you can get rid of the full overhead costs associated with them.

YOUR MIND MAP

YOUR ACTION PLAN

Write here the calculations you must make for *your* business. You will have to think about it seriously and adapt these generalized suggestions in this chapter to suit your own business. It does not take you long. Then make a plan to improve your overall profits. And identify what dead wood you can cut out safely.

SKEW ANALYSIS

List the products or services here	Your total sales		Your total gross profit contribution (after manufacturing costs)	
Put the biggest selling products at the top, and go down the range by size of product	£000	%	£000	%
_____	_____	_____	_____	_____
_____	_____	_____	_____	_____
_____	_____	_____	_____	_____
_____	_____	_____	_____	_____
_____	_____	_____	_____	_____
_____	_____	_____	_____	_____
_____	_____	_____	_____	_____
_____	_____	_____	_____	_____
_____	_____	_____	_____	_____
_____	_____	_____	_____	_____
_____	_____	_____	_____	_____
_____	_____	_____	_____	_____
	£	100	£	100

After you have done this with your products etc. then do the same thing with different markets you service; or different distribution areas; or different levels of advertising/promotion or discount support.

You can see quite easily from the table where your most profitable parts of the business lie; and where your potential loss-makers lie.

9

The judo strategy for new products

●

New products for business – So often new
products are dreamed up, launched and lost.
Most of them because there was no real
demand, or advantage in performance.

Q.1 *Four suppliers offer you new products. Which one would
you pick as a buyer?*

(a) The new product which reflects glory and prestige
upon your management.
(b) The new product which saves you significant costs.
(c) The new product which makes life easier, smoother
and happier for you and your staff.
(d) The new product which gives your own company a
unique and distinct competitive advantage in your
market.

Q.2 *What is the most worthwhile strategy for new product development?*

(a) To do the original research and development yourself.
(b) To constantly adapt and change your existing products.
(c) To copy other competitors' products, with variations,
quickly.
(d) To produce new products as and when the business
seems to need them.

Q.3 *When would you chop out a new product?*

(a) If it does not make profits immediately, within six
months.

(b) If it does not make profits within three years.

(c) You cannot make a general decision like this without knowing other factors.

(d) If you don't produce new products, then you are not saddled with the problem of chucking them out.

ANSWERS

Q.1 (a) 1 point   You are glorious enough.

(b) 4 points   Mean.

(c) 3 points   Compassionate.

(d) 5 points   Greedy, but right.

Q.2 (a) 5 points   But you must be a significant market leader to do this. This strategy is not open to most companies.

(b) 4 points   Absolutely, for maximum profitability, do this.

(c) 5 points   If you cannot do (a) then do this.

(d) 2 points   And you know it. You just want to find out what the comments are for a low score.

Q.3 (a) 3 points   If you buy your products in for re-sale, you might take this view, but it is too harsh for most.

(b) 3 points   It is a bit risky this. But with long lead times, this is right for some.

(c) 5 points

(d) 1 point   Heathen.

SCORES

13–15 points   Easy to score well. You are only allowed one small slip.

10–12 points   One slip too many.

Up to 9 points   Read the chapter twice.

● ● ●

My rate of success for new ventures is roughly the same as the average. It's about three failures for every success. But gradually a pattern is emerging about the difference between failure and success. It is beginning to dawn on me that innovation is a great idea, but it is not everything. I have always believed that in business you have to grow and that to grow you have to do new things – and if you can do things which others don't do then you will make money.

But there is something else I'm beginning to discover. In general, I am finding that it is better to sell the things that people want to buy. It's amazing, isn't it, how long it can take for a simple notion to penetrate a quarter-inch of human skull? The point is that I reckon that it is not too difficult to dream up new ideas – nor even to put them on the market. But the problem seems to be to fit them into what people want. You should move the way your customers are moving; fit your ideas into their scheme of things. It's the judo technique. Before you throw them, you have to pull them the way they are going. Then, when they are off-balance, you can throw them.

Small-screen television sets – I mean the tiny ones which Casio, Sony and Sinclair spent so much money on. Who on earth wanted to buy them? And the Sinclair C5 car, same question.

Now the Spectrum home computer, that was different. We were already used to calculators; some of us had computers at work, and most of us had kids with more or less idle brains at home and amusement arcade machines aspirations in the street. So the Spectrum sold beautifully.

Very often we get our new ideas as extensions of what we do now. In other words we try and persuade people to buy what we want to make. But should we not truly consider what customers want to buy first? I mean, our new product, how truly different is it? And what special needs does it fit? What are the real advantages for the customer in terms of service or product?

FOUR BIG QUESTIONS

Let us have a look at customers' needs. The first question is, what causes their demand? In the case of selling things to other companies, they are in competition too, for customers. If we can provide them with a competitive edge in their operation, then they will demand what we sell.

Of course, it's got to be sold to them at the highest level, and it will take a long time to penetrate into their brains that what we have got for them will give them a market edge. But if we can offer them a new idea for that purpose, then we are talking probably big money. Just let's take care that they don't manufacture for themselves, or get one of our rivals to produce it, too. Otherwise our advantage will be short-lived. Selling things to original equipment manufacturers is a tough game and they are expert at squeezing suppliers. But there is big volume in it at the end of the day.

The second question is, will it make them more money? To the extent that we can reduce their material costs, or save on their running costs, or save their labour costs, then we should be in with a fighting chance for our new idea. And we can price it nearly up to the point of break-even with their savings. Never mind our costs, what about their savings? Our selling price lies somewhere below that. This also takes a long time for such a new idea to be adopted. It is going to alter their routine; it will take time for them to make the changes. It will take time to convince them. And because several departments are likely to be affected, then their decision-making process will be complicated and slow. But there should be real money in it, in the long run, for us.

The third great question relates to making life easy for them. Everybody wants things to work smoothly. Everyone wants to employ a happy staff, well motivated and enjoying themselves provided that it is not at the boss's expense. So will your new idea help them to get things done? You might not be able to trace the savings but creating a general feeling of warmth and goodwill, or making people more interested in what they do, is worth something to them. And that should mean it is worth money to you.

But we are coming down the value scale, and it is going to be more difficult to sell new ideas without any of these three main questions being resolved. You might, however, get away with it if you can sell prestige and status to the right people. It is usually the boss men who respond to the executive time manager diaries; the BMW cars; or the architects' plans for using Italian marble in the reception. Such things might not give the customer a competitive edge. Neither do they save him any costs – indeed, where architects, lawyers or accountants are concerned, they will add to costs. Nor will they give his staff a feeling of warmth and happiness. But they are worth money because they give top management a feeling of warmth and happiness and since top managements control the budgets, you can make profit out of such things.

MODIFY EXISTING PRODUCTS

If I look around at the successes in this world, they have nearly always emerged after a lot of persistence. They are seldom the idea which was thought of in the first place. And someone nearly always had a lot of patience and faith to get them moving. And courage, too. You can have faith and patience in a weak idea which never sells at all, and you wear yourself out.

So perhaps the best thing is to modify the existing product or service range to fit in with the above questions. Can you modify what you do now and add to it so that customers can get an edge, or make more money, or have an easier life or greater prestige?

How does what we sell fit with what they want to buy? If we are trying to sell something which simply won't go, then can we attach it to something which does go? What do we have to do, to make our existing products more attractive to them? Getting a good answer to that question can lead to riches.

And what happens when three ideas fail for every one which succeeds? Ah – then, to avoid Armageddon, we have to learn the other lesson which has been known to the world's richest financiers down the ages. The first loss, they say, is the best loss. If the wretched thing is not going to work, then wrap it up. And the quicker you wrap it up and avoid further losses, the better.

You'll be throwing out some good ideas, of course. Some of them might have succeeded in the long run... or, if handled in a different way ... or, if marketed by someone else. But just play the odds. Get rid of losers fast.

ACTION POINT IDEAS

1 Have you made a serious study, with the help of some of your customers, as to the actual benefits provided by your products? Can you say, with confidence, how much profit they add for customers? Can you say, with confidence, how much money they save customers? It is well worth while taking out some specific calculations with friendly customers – you may be underselling yourself.

2 Take existing products. How about adding varieties to suit different sectors of the market, fragment the range? This should fatten up your sales and profits.

3 Take your main products. How far do you need second-generation versions? What are you doing about developing replacement products? This will give extension to the life of your product range.

4 How about new market applications for your existing products? Here test marketing is critical.

5 What can you do about basic R&D? If you have not got the funds to do it yourself, can you fund studies at universities? Can you buy-in product ideas from inventors? Can you make it known that you want new product ideas?

6 Can you become a fast follower? Can you copy your competitors' new developments quickly, efficiently and make improvements

upon what they do? Is your market intelligence so good that you know what they are up to within weeks of their launching, and you can track their successes/failures?

7 What new product ideas should you dump now? Either they are cluttering up your range and your management with poor selling products, or they are no-hopers for the long run. Get shot of them, quickly.

8 Can you sell some of your weak selling products to other companies? Other companies are smaller than you perhaps, and they might find them quite useful, while they do not add much to your business.

YOUR MIND MAP

YOUR ACTION PLAN

Does your product development work need organizing?

NEW PRODUCTS RISK CALCULATOR

The odds on success/failure.

Company entering new, unfamiliar markets.

New product.	1–20 against	New markets, unfamiliar to the company offer some of the greatest risks of all.
Existing product	1–10 against	

Company entering existing and familiar markets.

Radical new product, not seen previously	1–4 against	Needs test marketing carefully, to reduce odds.
Significant performance advantage, higher price	5–1 on	Offers potential success and big profits.
Marginal performance advantage, higher price	1–2 against	Evidence for high success here is not good.
Me-too performance, lower price	4–1 on	Success rates quite good, but often not much profit.
Me-too performance, same price	1–2 against	Odds improve if company is already a market leader.
Me-too performance, higher price	1–15 against	Only a dominant niche market operator selling this as an add-on to the range can succeed
Worse performance, same or higher price	1–30 against	Rip-off time.

There are many studies of new product success and failure rate. Much depends upon definitions. This table attempts to consolidate several studies to show the *relative* riskiness of different alternatives. Much depends upon the company's situation in its market. But most studies show that superior performance is everything – even beyond price.

10

Sharpen your competitive edge

●

> Applying quality control to your marketing effort – This chapter is about making certain that your sales, your service, your products, your marketing in general is ahead of the competition.

Q.1 *You are a printer, a good one. There are plenty of printers, good ones, around. Why do customers buy from you in the main?*

(a) Your printing quality.
(b) Your lower prices.
(c) Your service and reliability.
(d) Because you are nearby.

Q.2 *Why, as a buyer, do you prefer one particular technical salesman?*

(a) Because of his product knowledge.
(b) Because he sorts out your problems for you, with good advice.
(c) Because he gives you low prices.
(d) Because you can trust him.

Q.3 *You have a technical enquiry to make a phone call about. When you get irritated with suppliers, what is the most frequent cause?*

(a) They don't answer the telephone expertly.
(b) They put you through to the wrong people or people who cannot answer your questions.
(c) They don't return your calls.
(d) They don't treat you with respect.

ANSWERS

Q.1   (a)   3 points   But there are other good printers, too.

        (b)   2 points   Your prices are unlikely to be very low if your quality is good.

        (c)   5 points   It is the key factor if the print quality is high as well.

        (d)   2 points   This may possibly be a factor in terms of rapid service.

Q.2   (a)   3 points   But customer knowledge is even better. I accept that it all depends what you are buying.

        (b)   5 points   It really cannot be faulted if you think about it.

        (c)   2 points   Why think about the salesman when all you are after is a low price.

        (d)   4 points   Yes, very powerful point.

Q.3   There could be as many reasons as there are readers, and as there are suppliers, but if we are honest, the question asks about the most *frequent* factor.

        (a)   3 points   Very many firms do it well. Some do it appallingly.

        (b)   5 points   This is the most *frequent* problem. People who cannot handle technical enquiries. Try telephoning them at lunch time.

        (c)   3 points   Sometimes this happens.

        (d)   2 points   It is reasonably rare.

SCORES

13–15 points   You think about things. Service figures high in your regard.

10–12 points   Perhaps your industry is not so service intensive.

Up to 9 points   Service? What service?

● ● ●

It would be a foolhardy soul who said he was against the idea of quality control. It would be like being against the idea of motherhood. What idiot would not like to run an error-free business?

This idiot for one. I do not mind coming out and saying flatly that I am against quality control as it is now practised in industry. I am against trying to run an error-free business. I want, instead, 'inequality development'. I want to do things, make things and sell things which are different from my competitors'.

Not only that, but if I do try to run an error-free business then I'll take no chances, take no risks and make few of those decisions which are called courageous when they work and foolish when they don't. Of course, I want to keep the checks and measures in production which tell me that the product is being made to standard. Of course, of course. But I want more than that. I want much, much more.

If I am going to have proper quality control, then I must do it from the customer's point of view. Normal quality control just ensures that my standards are being met. But I want to meet my customers' standards – and they are far, far different from mine.

We were running a course in a medical company, a world-recognized name, a really good company. Every now and again in a training seminar, you needed to shake the group, to gain attention. So we set them on a piece of 'discovery learning' – that's the new-fangled name in education for the kind of story I am about to relate.

THEY WERE SHOCKED

I made them all go and telephone one competitor each. They were to make a vague enquiry about a technical product and see how well the call was handled. They had to report back on whether the telephone was answered well (how many rings), see if they were put through to someone who knew what they were talking about (only one-third did know what they were talking about), they were to try and get a price (some did get a price), and then they were to ask if the price could be reduced because it was outside their budget. (One-fifth of them got' price reductions immediately on the telephone – two of them being told how to buy it cheaply; and two were recommended to lower-priced competitors!)

We measured the results with a scoring system. My trainees were appalled. They decided that their market information could be updated through this method. They decided to test their own staff with their knowledge and co-operation, and they decided to monitor their own service. Now that's what I call 'inequality development'. I want to do things better than my competitors, and to do that I must measure what it is I do.

Whatever it is you make or offer, that alone is not entirely what customers buy. What you must measure in your quality control is what customers buy, and why they buy from you rather than from the competition. Now you have the start of an inequality development programme.

WHAT CUSTOMERS BUY FROM YOU

Let us take the issue logically. What do customers buy from you?

1 They buy your product, or service. Their alternative is to buy from your competition. Their measure is you versus your competition. Therefore, that must be your quality measure as well.
2 They buy your salesman. He gives them his knowledge. He should be an expert in his field and they want to deal with an expert. You must develop and measure the quality of your salesmen's expertise.
3 They buy your support and back-up. They want you to answer the telephone properly, with sensible answers to their questions. They want fast replies to their enquiries. They want you to make life easy for them. This is what you must put under your quality microscope.
4 They buy your reputation for reliability and honesty. So measure how you handle complaints, watch how you advertise and watch that you do not over-claim in selling to them. They want confidence and reassurance that you will treat them fairly.

So if all you control is the quality of production, you are controlling only a small part of what customers actually buy.

Instead you want a quality control routine which will:

• Show you how well you are doing against competition.
• Show you what customers think of you.
• Show your competitors' weaknesses.
• Show you where to develop your strengths.

TEST YOUR PRODUCT

Get hold of your principal competitors' products or services and test them. We sometimes get friends in the industry to ask competitors for quotes, and the data is sent on to us. Test their products in your laboratory against your own product. Not all your competitors need to be tested, just the ones closest to you and the market leader. (A small tip here: get the balance sheet and company accounts of your principal competitors once a year and have a good look through. Very interesting are the things you will read therein: very useful titbits to be applied in the market-place.)

Run a test of your own product among customers. Send them a questionnaire after they have bought it and used it. Telephone them and ask them what they think. Do a large enough sample, draw up the questions first and then run the check. Let them tell you honestly what they think of you versus the competition.

Now you have got the semblance of real quality control on the product. (We do all of this. We get reports when our clients attend a training course, and get feedback from them for three months afterwards. How on earth would we know if we were doing any good if we did not do this?)

TEST YOUR SALESMEN

Now this is more difficult. People do what they are inspected to do, not what they are expected to do. And sales people change, so you may have to start the training process over and over again. Of course, you must train them properly first in your product knowledge and in your application knowledge. Rank Xerox sales engineers can take apart their competitors' machines as easily as they can handle their own. They know everything it is necessary to know about their products. No one can kid them. Their customers depend upon them absolutely.

Question: is every one of your salesmen really top-notch at knowing the products, knowing the applications, knowing the competition, and knowing the customers? Of course not – we all have weaknesses here, my outfit included. We are trying hard to get better but it takes time and patience.

I know a sales manager who asks his salesmen a technical question each time he speaks to them, and they must give him the right answer each time, because he will not answer their queries if they don't. He makes it fun.

TEST YOUR SERVICE

You can telephone your competitors. You can telephone your own offices. You can send for literature. Record and score them all, on a regular basis.

I know one life assurance company who stopped the work in the office one day, while the manager's secretary went around and simply measured all the paper on the desks. Measured the time the paper was received in, that is. They then produced a chart showing the 'age' of the paperwork on the desks. They pushed this around the office staff and told everyone that they would run another check the following Tuesday. On Monday, everyone worked late, some worked very late. The Tuesday chart showed an improvement on the previous one. Every month now, they run a check. The staff try and get the paperwork out quickly. They feel good if they can beat the previous month's check. It's not a perfect system. But it is better than nothing. And it makes everyone efficiency-conscious.

Nowadays, in this particular company, the life assurance salesmen use the charts to prove to customers how efficient they are at handling the paperwork. They have the highest reputation for speed in the industry. Could you run a check on your deliveries, for example? Could you find out the average time; check on what was promised; check on the percentage which was delivered before the promised date, on the promised date, and after the promised date? This is one great big area of weakness in so much of British industry.

All you have to do then is to make sure that your salesmen do not over-promise. And if this means lengthening your delivery promises then so be it. Better to know what the situation is and tell the truth about it than to lie unwittingly, and wait until the customer complains.

TEST YOUR REPUTATION

Now this is a lovely test for which you will need a little professional help from someone who knows what he is doing in market research. Try the Market Research Society in London for help if you want to get professionals on the job. Or try the marketing tutor at your local technical college. He might set up the study for you.

Identify your target customers. Run a survey among them either by mail or telephone or a personal survey. (You do need expert help here to choose the sample and the correct method with the proper checks.) Identify the job function of the key executive you want to survey. Don't disclose you are the company doing the survey. Set up a questionnaire to tell you whether he ever buys in your category of goods, what he buys and who from. Ask him what he thinks of the suppliers.

Ask him to rate suppliers on various factors such as quality of salesmen, quality of service, friendliness/helpfulness etc, and to score these against competitors. You can also ask him what publications he normally reads (good for telling you which publications to advertise in) and how he normally hears of new products. With other questions this will give you the most valuable quality-control material ever.

This is what I call proper quality control. Not that production quality nonsense.

ACTION POINT IDEAS

1 Telephone your own offices, those of your competitors. Get your competitors to send sample literature. Measure their speed. Measure your own performance.

2 Take a sample of 500 of your customers. Mail them with a questionnaire about your products. Give them a bottle of wine if they fill in the questionnaire. Pilot test the questonnaire first on a sample of ten friends, then correct the questions. (It is always wrong the first time.) About 10 per cent will respond to your questions. Ring up 20 of those who do not respond and get the answers over the phone. Check them out against the totals from your mailing. (You may get a skewed response from your mailed test.)

3 Identify the critical factors in service which makes buyers select a particular supplier. Go and visit ten buyers just in order to ask these questions – not to sell them anything. Ask them what they think of you, your operation. Ask them the same thing about your competition. It is not a valid research exercise – but it will give you valuable insight into how you are regarded and where you may have to tighten up.

4 What *is* your competitive edge? How do you measure it? How do you know the buyers want it? How do you know they recognize you for it?

YOUR MIND MAP

.

YOUR ACTION PLAN

How are you going to start to push your competitive edge even further into your opposition?

THE UHQ SCALE *(ultra high quality)*

These are unusual things to test and measure, yet they are all factors which affect your customer support and service. Answer honestly. How high a priority do you give to quality controlling *these* factors in your business?

	Not much			*A great deal*	
	We don't think of it	We worry about it a bit	We take checks now and then	We set standards	We run statistically valid samples
The quality of the letters you send. Typing, prose, spelling	1	2	3	4	5	6	7
The speed of your correspondence with customers	1	2	3	4	5	6	7
Your telephone answering routine	1	2	3	4	5	6	7
Product tests with customers *after* they have bought	1	2	3	4	5	6	7
New product tests with customers before they have bought	1	2	3	4	5	6	7
The reputation of your sales force compared to competition	1	2	3	4	5	6	7
Your company/product reputation against competition	1	2	3	4	5	6	7
Your deliveries/reliability	1	2	3	4	5	6	7
Your salesmen's promises	1	2	3	4	5	6	7
Your customer complaints, criticisms of all kinds	1	2	3	4	5	6	7

Add up your total scores; divide by 10. It is very difficult to score more than 2.5. If one factor does not apply to you then just drop it out and divide by one less number.

11

Fight the flab in sales management

●

> Getting your figures into trim – This chapter
> is about how you control your selling and
> marketing effort. Which measures to watch
> in order to plan better for the future.

Q.1 *What is your sales management style? Pick the most effective.*

(a) Hire good people, pay them well, trust them and they'll get you good results.

(b) Hire cheaper people, push them out to sink or swim, run them hard all the time. The good ones will always perform.

(c) Good communications to and fro, a human style of management, let them all become involved, they set their targets, general all-round democracy.

(d) Hard-driving, demanding, relentless when things are going either very well, or very badly, and a looser style at other times, always pushing them for targets.

Q.2 *How do you truly know when they are doing well?*

(a) You set up independent information channels.

(b) You discuss things with them.

(c) They give you reports and figures.

(d) It does not matter, because you always want more.

Q.3 *How do you know how good your sales force is?*

(a) You take independent research checks versus competitors.

(b) You look at their figures and compare to previous periods.

(c) You ask customers what they think of your people.
(d) You watch how well they handle themselves at meetings.

ANSWERS

Q.1 (a) 1 point   We are miles apart you and I. Let us agree to disagree. You are a nice chap and I'm a cynic.

(b) 1 point   You and I also do not agree. You will only be as good as your people allow you to be. The good ones will either leave or come after your job.

(c) 3 points   You'll have politics all round, too. Democracy in sales is bad, bad news. They'll skin you.

(d) 5 points   Evidence shows, both empirical and researched data on performance that this style – or combination of styles depending upon the circumstances – works best. It might not be you, and actually it is not me either, but I'm not the best manager ever made.

Q.2 (a) 5 points   Make sure the source of your information is independent of the folks affected by it.

(b) 3 points   Of course.

(c) 2 points   Of course they do; but they put the best light on this data.

(d) 4 points   It *does* matter, but you can always ask for more just the same.

Q.3 (a) 5 points   Great idea, pity so few large sales forces are measured by research. Some are, though.

(b) 4 points   But you are not getting a competitive measure, merely a measure against themselves. (The market might be growing furiously so their improved figures could be nothing to do with them at all.)

| (c) | 4 points | Provided that it is done informally, and related to the company's general standard of service, then this is a legitimate question to ask. Asking about individuals specifically is not right at all. |
| (d) | 2 points | We can always spot the 'meeting' star or the 'training course' star. They are not the same as sales stars though. |

SCORES

13–15 points	Difficult to score well on the first question, but you can't really miss on question 3.
9–11 points	Fair enough. Should you put a bit more suspicion into your style? They could be leading you a dance.
Up to 8 points	Your sales force is leading you a dance. Unless they are paid only by commission, in which case they'll be grafting hard without you bothering to watch.

●   ●   ●

FIGHT THE FLAB IN SALES MANAGEMENT

Get your figures in trim

There are a lot of flabby managers around. Flabby managers simply *trust* their salespeople to produce results. Of course, there is a place for trust in managing salespeople. But trust alone will not do it. What we need is a bit of data. It is amazing how many people do not identify the proper controls they need to know what is happening. How can they make any plans if they do not have the figures to work on? Every company needs controls which are suited to itself. Here is a selection. Which ones are vital to you?

Calls per day, per week, perhaps

What is the actual sales work rate? How is it divided up between existing accounts and new prospects? How many of the calls are genuine prospects being dug out by the salesperson? How well, how quickly, are your sales leads being followed up? Can you correlate work rate with success?

Conversion rate of orders to calls

What's the strike rate? How does it vary between salespeople? What is the recall rate: i.e. how many calls does the salesperson make before a particular customer is landed? What does this tell you about the salespeople? Is one messing around far too long on old prospects, are others just trying to hit and run?

The sales value per order

What sales value does each person bring in over a period and what is the value per order? Why do some people get a large number of small orders while some get a few large ones? Can you relate this success to the other figures? What is the difference between the best salesperson's way of working compared to the worst?

What is the profit on the business?

What products are some salesmen selling compared to others; what discounts and giveaways are being traded? What is the profitability of the salespeople? Have you got a league table of performance? Do the salespeople know when they give away too much in discount – are the best people praised for their performance, the worst made to feel guilty?

How good is your sales force?

How good is your sales force compared to the rest of the industry? Can you run a research study to find out which salespeople from which company your customers have met? What do they think of them? How about their product or industry knowledge? Are your salesmen rated better, worse, as good as other companies' salesmen?

How about your advertising?

How many customer prospects know about your company? Where have they got this information from, advertising, exhibitions, magazines, word-of-mouth or what? How do they hear about new products?

How about your customers?

Have you identified your target market? Where is the most fertile geographical area? Which type of customer is best as a target for big sales? Do you need a lot of new customers or do you have huge repeat business? Which is the core of your market, can you identify it and prepare your salesmen to attack it?

How about the buying decisions?

Who, in your target customer's company initiates the decision to change suppliers, and why? Who then searches for and screens possible suppliers? Who evaluates propositions and clears them on technical grounds? Who evaluates the budgetary decision? Who is most likely to give the go ahead? How long does this process take? Is there a change agent in your customer's organization and who is it?

How about your admin. and your delivery?

If you were a buyer, would you find it difficult to buy from you? How quickly are orders processed? What is the average lead time in getting out quotes? What is your actual delivery time, how reliable is it, what times are your salesmen promising? What about your complaints; what kind are they, how frequent, is there data circulated around the company about them? Is a log maintained? Is there a plan for improvement? Is there feedback to the responsible department/person?

How good is your telephone?

Do your staff have a standard number of rings on the phone before it is answered (two minimum, three maximum, is the rule). Do they always give the company name and their own name? Do they know who to put the caller through to? Does *this* person have the knowledge to answer the query? Is he or she properly trained? Does he or she give their own name, and get the name and number of the caller? Is there back-up for this person during the lunch break, for holidays? Can this person describe benefits, can he or she obtain information about customers' needs? Can he or she close business, make appointments for salespeople? Are these people of yours checked on regularly, with dummy telephone calls?

How about your products?

How well do customers like them? Have they been compared to your competition? Have you done proper post sales tests? Have you got sound reliable evidence of the benefits you offer?

How about your direct mail?

What is the cost per thousand? What is the advertising cost versus sales, and per order? Which lists pull best? Start with your own current customers, that will be the best, next will be your past customers, then will come the people who know you but have not bought from you yet, after that you are on your own. How do you test your lists, your advertising literature? Do you code everything you send out and measure the return? Do letters pull better than leaflets? Do personalized lists pull better than job function lists; long copy better than short; two mailshots better than one? Once we have the critical parts of this data then we can put it together in a plan.

But the flabby sales manager will never do it. Fighting the flab means using just a few measurements which will give you a clue as to what is happening and make your results more exciting.

ACTION POINT IDEAS

1 Look at your selling process. What is the most important factor? Is it new customers? Is it selling more to old customers? Is it the product mix you sell, or is it price, perhaps? Whatever is the critical factor in your business, the one which can make or break you, then get a grip on the numbers. Measure it, monitor it, analyse success, do more of the right things, less of the wrong things. Don't fly by the seat of your pants in the critical areas.

2 Measure carefully the advance-warning indicators. What about your new business leads; your conversion rates? Is your advertising pulling? It is your job to know when things are going wrong before they hit the profit and sales figures. If you just look at sales figures, it's too late, because they are past history.

3   Get even further into understanding the market yourself. Get
    down the line, out with the salesmen, talk to small customers, go
    into the field. Develop that vital, vital touch or feel for the market.
    It will give you a firm personal grip on the situation and lead you to
    a sound understanding and to good decisions. Get off your chair,
    out of the office and go look for yourself.
4   More even than that. Sometimes do unusual things. Take time to
    see important people. Talk with competitors. Talk with advisers,
    consultants, editors. Create opportunities for yourself to learn.
    Not so much about what is going on, but to give you good creative
    ideas about your future business moves. There is no such thing as
    'luck'. The 'lucky' people are those who keep thinking, keep
    learning, keep talking, keep listening. They create circumstances
    when lucky things can happen to them.
5   Never ever be satisfied. Always want more. Always keep a bit of
    change going. Don't let folks become grooved. Don't let systems
    run people. So don't get control happy either. Having too many
    controls is the sign of a sick organization.

YOUR MIND MAP

YOUR ACTION PLAN

What are we missing that we should measure? Does everyone have the data they should have, and do they use it? What can you do for a personal action plan to learn more at grassroots level?

HOW DO OTHER PEOPLE SEE YOU?

People spend a lot of time and attention on what interests them. Other people can easily see where their interest lies, both from their attitude and their behaviour. *If your colleagues in business were to rate your interests, how do you think the ones who know you would score you?*

	They would say that . . .						
	Your interest is very low					Your interest is very high	
Numbers, data, forecasts, budgets, figures	1	2	3	4	5	6	7
People skills, listening, communicating, leading by consent	1	2	3	4	5	6	7
Driving, ambitious, results oriented, demanding on others	1	2	3	4	5	6	7
Interest in ideas, things, theories	1	2	3	4	5	6	7
Perfectionism, effectiveness, getting things right	1	2	3	4	5	6	7
Caution, thoughtfulness, care, planner, organized	1	2	3	4	5	6	7
Curious, inventive, creative, full of ideas, open to ideas	1	2	3	4	5	6	7

This is generally the image you are trying to present to the world; this is the feedback you get from everyone. Is it the real you? What is quite interesting to do now are three more things. Take some colour pencils and just plot some more scores, after thinking about them quite carefully.

1 Plot the 'real' you. Are there any differences do you think?
2 Plot what you think the job truly demands. Does your score deviate in any way from the ideal job score?

3   Now plot the company 'culture'. Most companies encourage or discourage these aspects of style and personality. Do you fit your culture well, or is there a misfit?

Where there is a serious misfit between you and the job, then you should make sure that your closest appointment, your secretary or your assistant should be able to fill in for your gaps.

12

Cold turkey for fast growth addicts

●

Controlling the dangers of fast growth –
Here we look at the problems caused by
success coming too quickly. How growth can
cause problems in the company operation,
and how finances can be hit. We look at
control measures to watch carefully during
the company's expansion period.

Q.1 *Things are very exciting for you. Your sales are growing very fast indeed. New orders are flooding in. New customers are ringing you up. You've hit a winner. At this rate of growth you will soon be profitable. You have run out of product for the time being. What do you do?*

(a) Sub-contract for extra supplies.
(b) Put in more staff to do the work.
(c) Pay big rises and overtime for your present staff.
(d) Trim back on sales.

Q.2 *Why do companies go bust?*

(a) They are unprofitable.
(b) They overtrade and run out of cash.
(c) They overprice their products.
(d) They underprice their products.

Q.3 *Which department in your company affects your cash flow more than any other?*

(a) Your accounts department.
(b) Your production department.
(c) Your research and development department.
(d) Your sales department.

ANSWERS

Q.1 (a) 3 points As long as you maintain quality and the sub-contractor cannot pinch your market from you, then this is fairly safe. Secure long credit.

(b) 2 points You want to cool the growth down a bit to bed-in the new staff. Nasty on your cash flow.

(c) 2 points Short termism. You are stocking up trouble for the future in exchange for profits now.

(d) 4 points The key to this is the notion that the company is not yet profitable. In fast growth you run out of money. Therefore to be safe not sorry, you might consider cutting back on any customer who is taking a long time to pay, in exchange for servicing those who pay quickly. No decision here is totally healthy and I don't like this one any more than you do, but sometimes you must take another look at your customer base.

Q.2 (a) 5 points 50 per cent go bust when unprofitable.

(b) 5 points The other 50 per cent go bust when they run out of money even though they may be profitable.

(c) 2 points It's practically impossible to do. The market won't buy until you lower your price.

(d) 2 points Some may do, but this just leads to answer (a) which is the more elegant.

Q.3 (a) 3 points Credit control may be bad.

(b) 2 points Poor products/service may lead to customer complaints and poor payments.

(c) 1 point Never heard of this.

(d) 5 points The sales department have more effect upon cash flow than any other. They sell to the customers. They are in a position to judge the creditworthiness. If they negotiate the terms badly or not at all, you'll have bad cash flow.

SCORES

12–14 points	Good controller, you are.
9–11 points	Work at it.
Up to 9 points	Don't go into accountancy for a living.

●   ●   ●

COLD TURKEY FOR FAST GROWTH ADDICTS

Next time you go to a Post House or Holiday Inn around coffee time, watch the telephones. In any fifteen-minute period, there will be three fresh eager young lads, area managers usually, telephoning their offices for the previous day's sales figures.

It's their morning fix. It's what gives them their high. The sales are up on budget, up on a year ago, the big order has come in – and there is nothing as exhilarating as this. Well, nothing which happens in a public phone booth, anyway. But you know what happens with drug addicts. Acquiring the habit might be quite pleasant but what happens when you need too much? Disintegration. And the same thing can happen with companies.

One of your problems with salesmen who are born and bred into the job is that all their confidence, all their rewards, come from sales increases. They get promoted because of them. They get sales incentives because of them. And there is a dangerous tendency for them to forget that sales growth by itself brings big problems to other parts of the business.

HOW TO GO BUST THROUGH GROWTH

We had some heady days at the Buxted Chicken company when I started there twenty-two years ago. Sales more than doubled every year – they trebled. We went public and the city fathers beamed. Some of them watched our success and set out to spend the odd few thousand on a chicken broiler house of their own. It was a fancy stockbroker's investment at one time – not now!

In those days, no one ever knew what cash flow was – some technical accounting problem, nothing to do with us. And, chumps that we were, the trebling of our sales in a year wasn't enough of a fix for us – we wanted more. We bought up the next two biggest companies in the business. And we did this at the same time as the market became flooded with cheap chickens. Oh, calamity! Board resignation. City uproar.

Suppliers having to buy into the company to save it. I was one of the 200 or so who had to go. It is what made me determined never to allow a company to become a mother figure for me again. For me the road of independence started at Buxted in Sussex. What was our sales result? We grew from a £2.5 million turnover to £12 million turnover in under three years. We were doomed by our addiction to sales growth.

I come across the same thing a lot, even now. People get into a growth sector of the market. They push their teams to get sales and the sales are got. And they run out of money. Please don't misunderstand. I like a fix as much as the next man. But I want slow growth if I have to pay for it myself. If I have a parent company with lots of boodle to spend then I'll go for medium-paced growth. And I'm not saying that fast growth is always going to spell doom. But you must, must, must be careful to control it.

FIVE RULES FOR FAST GROWTH

Here are five rules for controlling fast sales growth.

Rule 1: Get your finances right. Make sure your parent board is told, long before your dash for growth, that they will have to stump up a lot of cash for you and that profits might be thin in the meantime. It's very, very difficult to be very profitable and fast-growing at the same time. It can be done, but it's rare.

If you are financed by the bank then try to get two accounts running so you don't offer yourself as a hostage to fortune. Use a finance company to fund your fixed assets – and make sure it is not a subsidiary of your company bank. Clients in difficulty have been known to be the subject of the occasional telephone debate between bank manager and their sister finance company manager before now. Would your bank manager be willing to give you an extra loan so you could pay off your arrears on the finance agreement?

Rule 2: Get your cash flow right. Try to get customers to fund your growth. Not too easy at first sight but you'll never make it unless you try. Try to get split payments so that the development work on contracts is funded up-front. In a fast growth market, the seller is strong and the buyer is relatively weak, so you might try selling without credit! (I know, I know, that's impossible in your market. That's not the point. The point is to think about using every means possible to improve your cash flow, without damaging your profits.) Can you bank the cheques quicker? Can you ask personal favours of customer friends to pay you, personally, on the nail?

Rule 3: Get your admin. right. Now this gets really boring. If your organization is going to undergo strain because of fast growth you must be able to handle the business efficiently. Everything must work well and be able to cope with extra surges of pressure – from stock control, through to sales office, credit control and management accounts. It's no good putting sales on at one end if the profits are being mopped up by crisis management at the other.

Rule 4: Make sure your people are good. One big problem with fast growth is that more people are needed in management. There is no time to train them. The demands are on them to produce immediately. So new people from outside are not given enough time to bed themselves in. Or to avoid the problem and speed up the process you promote from within. You might even promote people whom you otherwise would not. It's good news for them, but no good for you if they can't do the job.

Rule 5: Watch the figures. Watch every measure. Watch the pipeline sales leads, the orders in progress. Watch the profitability on the monthly management accounts. Watch the mix of business, watch the customer mix. Watch the bad debtors – normally you call them customers – and hammer them to pay on time.

All of these rules cover the boring part of growth. For us in sales, it's always someone else's problem. Listen to the area manager on the telephone when his secretary tells him that production cannot meet the deadline. 'Tell them to pull their fingers out. They're always complaining.' And if he's told the company is not profitable, what does he say? 'What are they doing upstairs, then? I'm getting them all these sales increases and they still can't make it profitable. They're a bunch of bunglers.'

And away he goes to get his next fix. As if that will solve the problem.

ACTION POINT IDEAS

If you have a fast moving market to service; or if you have *any* cash-flow problems (such as taking a long lead time between manufacture and sale) then think of:

1   Working out a good trading forecast for the short-term business. What business is due to come in this month, next month, etc. How much do we need. Then convert this to a cash-flow statement. Then you will know for a certainty where your dangerous cash levels are.
2   Do everything you can think of to improve your cash flow. First, sell your customers properly. Make sure that every sale is made with the terms of business implanted in the customer's mind. Get

your salesmen to call in on the financial controllers. You yourself, as the chief, should look after the payments by the big accounts. Do not delegate this. If these big ones don't pay you on time, your company may be dead. Work on friends, people you know, to pay you early. Stop business with those who pay you late.

3   Next, negotiate longer terms with your suppliers. Don't steal the credit from them; negotiate it and make sure you honour your side of the deal. You'll be surprised how long some will agree to if your sales are growing fast.

4   Bank the cheques faster. Do it daily.

5   Keep your admin. and accounts department stable. Don't make sweeping changes here. Subcontract the overflow work. Do not over promote and add too many new staff too quickly.

6   Don't let the sales force over-commit you on orders, or deliveries or servicing, and definitely not on credit.

YOUR MIND MAP

YOUR ACTION PLAN

Write down here where you think your operation might be a little
slack. Make a plan to improve things.

IF YOU WERE THE CHIEF EXECUTIVE WHAT WOULD
BE THE MOST IMPORTANT THING IN YOUR
WORKING LIFE?

Score each item in order of importance for you	Not at all important for you		Of average importance for you	Very important for you	
(a) Working very hard indeed	1	2	3	4	5
(b) Growing the company	1	2	3	4	5
(c) Making the company safe	1	2	3	4	5
(d) Generating maximum profits	1	2	3	4	5
(e) Achieving your aims	1	2	3	4	5
(f) Enjoying yourself	1	2	3	4	5
(g) Being very efficient	1	2	3	4	5
(h) Being respected in the business community	1	2	3	4	5

There is no right and wrong answer here. This just gives you a profile of your attitude. Your style will flow from this so will your strengths and your weaknesses.

Most chief executives play down (a), (f) and (g). They say they play down (h), but I for one don't believe them. (c) scores pretty high, (making the company safe), and so does (e) achieving your aims.

13

Communication: the unoriginal sin

●

> Increasing the power of your communication
> – Most communication with customers is
> boring. Make it come alive. And know who
> you are communicating with.

Q.1 *You want your message to be effective. Pick the worst sin out of the following.*

(a) Giving them far too much technical information.
(b) Giving them too little information.
(c) Making the information boring.
(d) Writing to them instead of talking face to face.

Q.2 *You want to make your message interesting to the customer. Which technique would you use?*

(a) Picture of topless girl.
(b) Big picture of the customer himself.
(c) Wrong spilling in the massage.
(d) Big picture of you yourself.

Q.3 *To get your prospect to respond to direct mail, out of all the following techniques, pick the best.*

(a) Use a personal handwritten letter.
(b) Use an offer with a closing date for reply.
(c) Give something with the mailing.
(d) Use a well designed brochure.

ANSWERS

Q.1 (a) 5 points It's called information overload. Long copy can be very useful in direct mail – but this is mostly about benefits, and not technical features.

(b) 3 points It can be bad, but for effective communication you want simplicity.

(c) 3 points It might be all right if he is a boring customer. No accounting for tastes. Some people do not like hype. They are not likely to be reading books about tactics, either.

(d) 4 points Cannot say this for sure. Generally better to be face to face, but I can think of exceptions.

Q.2 (a) 3 points You'll sell a few people.

(b) 5 points Try not to be interested in any mailing which sends you a picture of yourself. Perhaps combined with (a).

(c) 4 points Made you think twice didn't it?

(d) 1 point Oh come on. (I do it all the time in leaflets but it is not making the message more interesting. It has a separate purpose.)

Q.3 (a) 5 points Yes. Try it some time.

(b) 5 points Of course.

(c) 2 points He's got it. Why should he reply?

(d) 1 point Lowest response rate of all.

SCORES

13–15 points Lucky I gave you three marks for question one even if you got the wrong answer.

9–12 points You only missed getting in to the top bracket because your business is different from everyone else's.

Up to 8 points Never mind.

●   ●   ●

The most complex system known in the universe weighs only three and a half pounds. Despite its complexity, we only use about 1 per cent of its total potential. This system can recognize one person's face out of thousands in three-hundredths of a second. It will use visual data, sound and smell to analyse the face, interpret feelings, decide on courses of action, and start intricate combinations of muscle processes throughout the body, all in one-quarter of a second. The variables involved are calculated at 30 000 distinct alternative patterns. The results of such actions may be an outstretched hand, a warm smile, and the face saying 'Hiya George, nice to see you.'

We are talking about the human brain. The human brain belonging to other people is what you try and influence when you sell things to them. And yet we pay so little attention to it. Here is a list of unoriginal sins in sales communication. Are you guilty of any of these?

TELLING THEM TOO MUCH

What a problem this is! The brain can memorize only about seven things at a time, plus or minus two. Yet salesmen stuff people's brains with fact after fact after fact. A man called Ebbinghaus once ran an experiment which qualifies as the most boring bit of science in the world. He spent six years of arduous hard work memorizing nonsense syllables all in the cause of studying the brain. He was trying to discover how quickly the brain forgets and how frequently one must repeat data for it to become memorized effectively.

He discovered that of information learned by rote – in the way teachers used to teach tables to trainee football hooligans when they were very young – 50 per cent is forgotten within one hour. Within nine hours, 60 per cent is forgotten, and within one month 80 per cent is forgotten. The decay in information storage is frightening unless we do something to reinforce it. Try, one day, getting a buyer to repeat back what the salesman has just told him about the product and see how accurate is the data. You'll be shocked. Is this what is costing you £20,000 per annum in on-the-road costs, with car and supervision, plus national insurance?

NOT TARGETING THE MESSAGE

Do you specify the target audience? Is it described factually? Who are the decision-influencers behind the scenes who help get you the business or help lose it for you, but whom your salesmen never see? These people are often called managing directors, general managers, finance directors and so on.

If you sell products to caterers, then you know there are approximately 100 000 buying points in the UK. There are two big trade publications in the industry. If you take advertising in both of these and if you add a couple more smaller catering publications, you will find that the total readership is about 80 000 in all. That's enough you might say, to cover your potential audience.

You would be wrong, wrong, wrong, though. Because many buyers take both magazines. If you advertise in both you will only reach 50 000 buyers but some of them many times over. And even if you take *all* the catering magazines you will still reach less than 60 per cent of your total potential market. Because nearly one half of the market never reads a catering magazine!

You will never find this out unless you do a survey amongst buyers. Don't tell them it is your company behind the survey, let a research company do it. You could ask buyers what companies they know of in your field. What do they think of them? You can use scales to measure your reputation relative to competitors. You can ask them what they think of your products, of your service, of your salesmen, all compared to competition. Since they will not know it is you behind the survey they will not tell too many lies.

You can ask them how they hear of new products, whether they go to trade exhibitions and which one, who the decision-makers are. You can also ask them what publications they read regularly and what they read occasionally. Then, when you have asked such questions, and only then, can you say you have identified your target audience and you can build your campaign plan around it.

WARNING

Bad research is very damaging to your health. Information which is wrong is worse than no information at all, because you believe it. Otherwise you use common sense. Common sense is poor but tolerable. Better to have good market information. Market research is a specialized job. Drawing up the right samples, constructing and piloting the right questionnaire is a job for experts. So do not try to do any major study yourself. You can do small, simple studies, but here it pays you to examine the principles of market research yourself.

REACHING THE RIGHT SIDE OF THE BRAIN

You are reading this with the left-hand side of your brain. Figures, logic, analysis, facts – all these things you do with the left side. It is a dull boring side. The other side of your brain is much more fun. It's the part where you have an emotional, creative response, it's the side which makes you laugh.

Use your advertising to appeal equally to the right side of peoples' brains. Look how memorable things are when they use the right side. What are Pirelli tyres known for? You are right, the Pirelli Calendar. How much other brand tyre advertising can you recall?

For your message to be effective it should have the following characters:

- It should be *memorable*. Do something to make people remember your name, remember your product. Associate it with something in their imagination.
- It should be *unique*. Find something to say, or some way of saying it which is different to your competitors.
- It should be creative and *interactive*. Do you offer a free trip, free holiday, free something exciting if they reply to your ad? You should. The more people can get involved with you the better. That's a big advantage of running company seminars or exhibitions. People interact with you. It should be *sensory*. It should appeal to their visual instincts, or their auditory instincts, or their kinesthetic instincts – the way they feel about something. Don't let the message go just to left-sided brains. If you can exaggerate, exaggerate, EXAGGERATE, E.X.A.G.G.E.R.A.T.E, then so much the better.
- It should be *simple*. Keep it simple. Remember, people can remember in the short term, only seven things.

And if you can do all that and include benefits matched to needs as well, then you are a communications genius.

ACTION POINT IDEAS

In none of the following ideas can you reveal your own company name.

1   Run some of your advertisements (leaflets, mailing shots etc.) before a test group of people. Ask them to read the material first and say afterwards what they thought your message was.

2   Run a telephone survey amongst your target group of customers. Test their knowledge of you and your competitors, their reaction to your salespeople and the competition, their opinions of your products, how they receive messages about your industry (i.e. what journals do they read, exhibitions do they attend etc.). Do not reveal that it is your company carrying out the survey.

3   Test a sample of customers with this information against a sample

of non-customers. Test a third group – those prospects to whom you have made unsuccessful sales presentations. Find out why some people never buy from you. Find out why some people prefer to buy from competition.

4 Run a penetration test. Find out how many people amongst your target decision-making group know of your name, plus those who have bought from you in the past, are buying now etc. Run them through the same questions for your leading competitors.

5 Use a market research company. Or read a do-it-yourself market research book and follow its instructions explicitly. (Do not draw up a questionnaire yourself if you are not an expert.) Get your local evening college lecturer to advise you. Look in the *Yellow Pages* for market research interviewers. They'll help you.

6 Use a discussion group. Get five or six of your target prospects together for a discussion on the subject which interests you. Tape record it. Do not lead them in their views. Be absolutely neutral. Raise topics, but let them do all the talking between themselves, only probing where it interests you.

YOUR MIND MAP

YOUR ACTION PLAN

What work must you do to find out your true position and reputation
in your market's mind?

THE THREE STEP COMMUNICATIONS TEST WHICH MOST COMPANIES FAIL

Only a few companies can pass this test. They are usually the rich and famous. Most companies can score high on one or two counts, but rare is the company which can score high on all three. That's the test. You must score high on everything. 4 or 5.

		Poor rating	Average rating	Good rating
			'We think about it'	
1	You know by testing or researching how your *target audience* receives its messages, which publications they read, how they hear about new products etc.	1 2 3	4	5
2	You know through research what your company image is, versus the competition, and what the market thinks of your sales force, service etc. compared to competition.	1 2 3	4	5
3	You research your critical communications through pre-testing, or post-testing or by couponing direct mail or split running press ads to see that you are understood by your market and your message is clear.	1 2 3	4	5

The information does not have to be recent, nor continuously monitored. It's enough to have some feedback that is a reasonable signal to you of how the market is hearing you. Believe me, the top companies, the household names do actually have this information. For branded products it is essential. Most industrial companies do not have this information.

14

Try a short course of death

•

Cutting back on your marketing operation –
To achieve high profitability you must keep
the whole operation tight and slim – That
means getting rid of things.

Q.1 *You are a highly stressed sales person. You must unload some of your work. Which customers are you going to cut out?*

(a) The nasty ones.
(b) The unprofitable ones.
(c) The ones who are far away.
(d) A mixture of all these types.

Q.2 *You are a highly stressed financial controller. The bank has told you your profitability is not good enough. What action will you take to improve your return on capital?*

(a) Slash the workforce.
(b) Sell off some of your assets, reduce your capital base.
(c) Find a new job.
(d) Put up your prices.

Q.3 *You are a highly stressed marketing manager in a multi-product company. Your sales and profits have gone ex-growth. What action will you take?*

(a) Argue with the managing director less often.
(b) Increase your advertising budget.
(c) Re-train your sales force.
(d) Strip out the range to force the good products.

ANSWERS

Q.1 (a) 2 points Take care if they are also the big ones.
(b) 4 points But measuring profitability of individual accounts is very difficult.
(c) 3 points There may be some big and profitable accounts there too.
(d) 5 points You need to keep the whole lot pruned for effectiveness the whole time.

Q.2 (a) 3 points Bit of a panic reaction.
(b) 5 points Brilliant idea. Called asset stripping. Some of the world's finest businessmen have made careers on it. This way, they can acquire companies out of the acquired companies' own money.
(c) 1 point Come on. Having arguments with bank managers is everyday stuff.
(d) 2 points Cannot tell on this evidence if this is right.

Q.3 (a) 3 points Yes. Give him the stress instead.
(b) 1 point The ruin of many a marketing manager.
(c) 1 point 'Buy a bit of training to see if it works'. Uh?
(d) 5 points Concentrate upon your strengths.

SCORES

13–15 points Fantastic. How do you do it all the time?
10–12 points I don't see how you can fail to get top score with this. Keep trying.
Up to 9 points Don't bother trying.

● ● ●

DITCH YOUR KILLER CUSTOMERS

For most of your adult life you'll spend about 150 000 hours at home, with your family, on holiday and enjoying yourself. You'll be having fun. For the other 100 000 adult waking hours in your life you will be travelling to, thinking about, or at, work. That should be even more fun. If it's not, then there is something wrong.

I met a nice man at a conference last month. 'Used to own a television and video business', he told me, 'but it went bust.'

'My bank manager told me not to chase turnover but I didn't know what he meant. So I went after the sales. I thought I had to beat competition, so whenever I could steal some business with a bit of deft price-cutting I did so.' He is quite happy now, working as a sales manager for another company. He was very ill for a time though.

There are some customers you don't want to win. If you win these you'll lose.

How can you become very very profitable? What you are about to read now is more than startling. It may shock you. It will certainly surprise you. It may even offend you – particularly if you are conducting the wrong strategy. What you are about to read will not be popular in government circles. The government, for reasons of its own re-election, has been trying to persuade you to do the wrong thing for years. All governments give you the wrong advice whatever their political complexion because they all want to be re-elected. They all tell you to invest more heavily. And that is wrong. If you want to be in social service and to help people, then do what governments tell you. And I, for one, shall admire and respect you. But you will not be rich. When did you last meet a millionaire social worker? No, without any fear, I advise that you do the opposite.

The key to becoming very very profitable is to *disinvest*. That's right, to get out of things which do not make you money. The quickest way for man to increase his return on capital is to lower the base of capital. Shock, even horror, may be your reaction – but I plead with you to give us a hearing. Please keep an open mind for another 1000 words.

For example, don't win customers who haven't got any money. No, I'm serious, if you want to have a bad time try selling to someone who has no resources. First, he complains about your price. However low, it won't be low enough for him. And then he'll complain about your product and your service. This is to avoid paying the bill. Finally, he'll stall and stall paying the bill. My honest advice is, don't operate at the low-cost, cowboy end of the market. There's a lot of heart attacks down there and not many millionaires.

Next, don't sell to small customers who give you a lot of trouble. The ones who squeeze you, or make heavy demands on your time or service. If they're big then you can afford some hassle but chop off the small troublesome ones. Of course, if most of your customers give you hassle (I'm sure they don't!) look somewhere else for the solution to the problem. I would look inside myself. I would say 'If I were a customer, would I be happy buying from me?'

The third kind of customer you don't want is the very big one who squeezes you on price until the pips squeak and who then forces you to commit new capital to his business. This is as dangerous as committing yourself to a new venture which, if it goes wrong, will bring the business down. It's tempting to do the business but taking on thin margin large accounts which dominate your business is no way to have those peaceful, dreamless nights which are your just reward for a hard day's work.

If you want to build a base of more profitable customers, then cut out the unprofitable ones. Take out the tiddlers, take out the remote ones, take out the ones which squeeze you too hard on margins, take out the nasty ones. Then you will have invested more heavily in the ones which make you money. You can afford to look after them, nurse them, improve your service to them. You will get more of them. They will grow, and so will your reputation.

I was with an industrial carpet company the other day – a first-class organization which had a star salesman. He made fewer calls than the other salesmen. He landed fewer new accounts than the others. But his figures were remarkable. Luck, was it? A more favourable territory? Not at all. What he was doing was to screen out the leads early on by the telephone. Out of twelve leads he could land ten appointments just as the other salesmen did. But some of these prospects would turn out to be window shopping for new suppliers; others were too small; and yet others had notions about the cost of carpets which were a long way removed from reality. So the star salesman qualified the leads properly on the phone. He went to elaborate lengths, making several telephone calls to establish what they might want, what the competition was, how the decision would be made and generally assessing privately his chances of making a profitable deal. Having sussed out the good prospects then he would go for them ruthlessly.

He would research them properly, he would secure meetings at a high level, he would assess their needs properly with a survey. And he could afford to do all this because he knew that at the end of it he would have an 80 per cent chance of landing big and profitable business. The point is, that he could only afford to do this if he did not waste his time on long shots or tiddlers. He *dis*invested in poor sales prospects.

DITCH YOUR KILLER MARKETS

Examine the markets you serve. Apply yourself to those where you are not in a strong market position; where there are no prospects of you ever getting in to a strong market position. Sort out those where you have little in the way of a product quality advantage which would earn you a premium price. And if such products do not pass the test of strong position or quality, then pull out. Forget all those bits of products that you carry in order to 'round out the range' or 'give the salesmen a chance' or whatever. Dump them all. They are cluttering up your production, cluttering your stocks, cluttering your sales-men's time, cluttering your administration and severely damaging your profits. Your accountants may tell you that you earn a high percentage margin on such items. Don't believe it. Because of the way accountants allocate overheads these little cannibal products eat up your expenses.

Dump those nonsense markets which lie outside your main market. They eat up your selling time, management time, and stop you from becoming very rich. Stop wasting money on things which will never make you any.

Cut down your investment in machinery. A high fixed investment cost relative to added value is a killer for profits. Get flexible with your machinery, lease it so you can change it later for a new model – don't buy it. Lower your fixed capital. Don't let extra profits drag you into exotic equipment. (Let extra profits go into your personal pension fund. A payment of £6000 a year for 15 years until you retire will build you a fund of well over half a million pounds. What would you rather have at retirement date, clapped out machinery or half a million pounds?)

CUT BACK ON YOUR AREAS

Trim the area markets you service. Your most profitable markets will nearly always be the ones closest to you. Develop your market share in those. Come out of those bits of sales you get in Maubuland, the Channel Islands and Inverness. How on earth can the Inverness market make you rich? They are all Scotsmen up there. Inverness can only make Scotsmen rich. Why do you think Hadrian built his wall? To stop chaps like you wasting your money in the deserts of the north, that's why.

So you do want to be very, very profitable? Then just build up the quality of the product and the service you offer so that customers will tell you it is significantly better than your opposition. Force down the unit costs as low as possible. Let your salesmen force you into the market vigorously, very vigorously indeed, with all the power you can command, but going for the big profitable customers. And you will gain that vital market share. And the profits which go with it.

ACTION POINT IDEAS

Here is Dr Winkler's six-point health plan for a prolonged, active business life.

1　Aim to be the biggest. Being the biggest in your particular market is a very good way of making money and having a nice time. But remember only one company can do it. There are no prizes for being fourth. You've got to do something different from everyone else and do it very vigorously. And the market must prefer what you do to what the others do. If you do the same thing as everyone else then that's a good way to become average. You don't get to be market leader or number two by accident.

2　If you cannot be the biggest, then aim to be the best. Do everything superbly well. Train everyone thoroughly. Set high standards for everything, particularly service, delivery and customer attention. Become the expert in your field, make customers dependent on you. Look after them all and trust them as friends. And price what you sell very high – much higher than the competition.

3　Get to be very profitable. Keep your fixed cost investment low. Really low. The easiest way to improve the return on capital in most companies is to strip out the capital. Employ few people – sub-contract, but control it properly. Don't buy machines. Don't spend on non-productive assets such as fancy office blocks. Keep the operation small and tight.

4　Have fun! Get into growth markets. People in recession-hit or declining markets have a tendency to be miserable. There's a lot of flak flying about. Avoid these people. Happy people are those whose figures go up by 20 per cent a year without really trying. Try a growth market for a change and see how happy it can make you. But watch out for the drain on your cash flow.

5　Avoid stress. Get out of those thin margin lines. Try finding products to sell which have an 80 per cent gross profit on them after variable costs. If you look hard enough, they'll be there. They might be add-ons to your existing range, they might be services for which you charge. If you think it's impossible to find them, then it always will be until you start looking. They are there, all right, but the people selling them do not boast about it.

6　How to sleep nights. Cash flow. Make sure that if possible your money comes in before it is paid out. A positive cash flow means that your customers will finance any expansion you like to dream up. If you've got a long negative cash flow that's a sure way of driving your expansion decisions to your bank manager.

That's all. You can't do them all of course. But you might do some. Now where have my headache pills gone?

YOUR MIND MAP

YOUR ACTION PLAN

Where exactly are you going to prune this lovely rose you call your organization?

YOUR PERSONAL RISK EVALUATOR

Score the correct rating for the way you feel on each issue.

You would feel safer running a wide product range.	1 2 3 4 5	You would be happy being dedicated to a single product.
You feel better with a wide spread of customers.	1 2 3 4 5	You do not mind if all your business is with one major account.
You would rather work for a big multi-national corporation.	1 2 3 4 5	You would prefer to be in a small outfit.
You like well organized large markets to serve.	1 2 3 4 5	You like the small, specialized ventures.
You want a big salary, if you are selling things.	1 2 3 4 5	You would prefer a big commission rate or go self-employed.
You will be on someone else's payroll throughout your career.	1 2 3 4 5	You will, one day, set up your own operation, and go it alone.

There is evidence, surprisingly, that those people who run their own business do so more because they find the constraints of working for others are too heavy. They are not necessarily risk-takers. It has been said that big companies sometimes take more risks than small ones do, because they make more decisions in groups (called by psychologists the 'risky shift' it indicates a phenomenon that groups will often take substantially more risks than any of the individuals in the group would take). Also they are playing with other people's money.

Entrepreneurs are often risk-aversive. Having made their capital in the first few years, they tend later on to conserve it. Most people score around three on most of these issues above. But you know yourself without having to take the test.

15

It can pay to keep a low profile

•

> Keep your marketing secrets away from
> competition – The fastest way to grow
> competition for yourself is to blast out your
> advertising for everyone to see, and then
> boast about the profits you make.
> Don't do it.

Q.1 *You do not want your competition to find out what you are up to. How will you market your product for maximum security?*

   (a)   Give sole supply to past customers.
   (b)   Just sell it face to face through your own sales force.
   (c)   Advertise it through private exhibitions.
   (d)   Use selective direct mail.

Q.2 *You want to find out what the competition is up to. How do you set about it?*

   (a)   Ring them up and pretend to be a customer prospect of theirs.
   (b)   Watch their advertising carefully.
   (c)   Get one of your customers to order their new product.
   (d)   Ask one of their people when you meet casually.

Q.3 *How would you copy one of the competition's new product ideas?*

   (a)   By head hunting and hiring their technical development manager.
   (b)   By buying their products, and examining them technically.
   (c)   You can't. It is illegal and unethical to copy.
   (d)   Try to develop your own version from scratch.

ANSWERS

Q.1 (a) 5 points Maximum security. Well, short of not putting it on the market at all.

(b) 4 points Pretty good. You can control who sees it.

(c) 3 points They can infiltrate your exhibition if they are really determined.

(d) 3 points Sooner or later you'll make a mistake with your list and the word will get out. But you can keep your secret for a long time this way.

Q.2 (a) 5 points Yes, most effective if you can get away with it. You think it is not done? It is done all the time.

(b) 3 points Yes.

(c) 5 points Make sure you know your customer well though. He might switch to the opposition! This is the most common way it is done.

(d) 4 points You would be absolutely amazed at what people will tell you if you just ask them casually, when they are relaxed.

Q.3 (a) 5 points This is exactly what we did at one company where I was marketing director. He came complete with product formulations and saved us three years of technical development.

(b) 4 points Bit obvious lads, but maybe there is no other way.

(c) 1 point It may be illegal and unethical but it *is* done. It is called capitalism.

(d) 3 points Takes too long.

SCORES

13–15 points We expect high scorers at this stage. You are getting good.

10–12 points Could you try a bit harder? Any chance of asking you to finish off reading all the alternatives before you rush to an answer? Perhaps not.

Up to 9 points Any chance of asking you to read *any* of the answers before you pick 'em with your pin?

● ● ●

WHY IT PAYS TO KEEP A LOW PROFILE

Do you need secrecy? Do you have a few little foibles that you would rather other people did not know about? I'm not talking about the little lapse of memory you had last April when you filled in the 'other income' section on your income tax return. Nor will we raise the question of that other little lapse at the Christmas party.

No, we are talking about business secrets. The great new product which you want to keep away from the competition, or the marketing idea which works like a dream. It can lose you a fortune if the news gets out.

Boasting about your success can make you feel good, but it can also cripple you. I was marketing manager once at a company which grew very quickly and made a lot of money. The board hired a major public relations outfit to publicize our greatness. Every business page of the national press carried stories of adulation; personal profiles in the weekend magazines and appearances on television made our top people walk tall. People recognized them in hotels; their neighbours gave them new respect.

The problem was that the formula which they had found for success could be easily copied. Within six months there was massive new investment being put into the industry. The giants moved in, the market became over-supplied and within a year prices crashed. The company was sold. We all disappeared into obscurity. Ever since then I've been wary of boasting about success. Because there are a lot of people out there who are looking for your ideas and who want a slice of the action you have so carefully built up.

What is your net profit on sales? Is it 10 per cent or around 5 per cent? I'm not talking about the net profit which shows on your profit and loss account at the end of your financial year – that's the one which you and your accountants fix about three months before the year-end. No, we are talking about the real net profit on sales you earn before you start mucking about with the figures. Do you realize that some companies earn as much as 30 per cent or even as high as 40 per cent or more? Yes, 40 per cent net profit as a percentage of sales. Do you think they boast about it? No, they most certainly do not. You have to look up their accounts in Companies House to find out. And these are not necessarily small companies either. They can be quite sizeable.

Most of us have a few secrets we want to keep from the competition. For a start, if you are a small company making big profits get your accountants to send only a shortened form of your accounts to Companies House. We take out the accounts of our top twenty competitors every year, and very interesting reading they make, some of them. But the ones we really want to know about keep their figures disguised.

KEEPING SECRETS: TWO THINGS TO AVOID

1   *Avoid mass advertising.* The important thing is to use selective media which reach your target market directly. If you use press ads, radio, technical journals or public exhibitions, your competition will know immediately. They will get their friends to send off for your literature. They might even get someone to call in one of your reps. They will telephone your office with their 'technical enquiry'. You'll never get any business from them but they will get your information from you.

2   *Avoid press and public relations.* When your information gets into the trade and technical press through public relations work, the journalists will gobble up the information. For them it's news, but for you it's your competition being made aware of your secrets. Your first priority is to get your product firmly established in the market before you release the news publicly.

KEEPING SECRETS DARK:
THREE THINGS YOU CAN DO

1   *Use direct mail to your target audience.* There are problems with using direct mail, such as the difficulty of finding good lists, but the one thing which is important to you is that you can control it quite tightly. If you want to stretch the market for your new idea into the long term, use selective marketing and just market it to your previous customers and your existing accounts.

2   *Use personal selling.* Provided you are not in the habit of losing your salesmen to the opposition, you can keep things under wraps for a long time by using telephone sales or personal selling. Try and avoid cold calling on accounts held by your rivals, particularly where the industry is full of supplier loyalty or where the competition has sole supply, because the first thing your prospect will do will be to turn your information over to his existing supplier and you will lose control.

3   *Make use of private exhibitions, private shows, demonstrations and videos.* You have total control over what you say and whom you invite. Making a video of your new product presentation is all the rage these days. Even making specialized videos for particular customer

prospects is not uncommon. But you must be careful not to let your video go out of your hands, or your film may be copied and within days your rivals will be watching it.

With any new product idea you have a choice of two strategies: creeping it into the market or blasting it out all at one go. You can extend the market for quite a long time if you creep into it. It might not be so glamorous and you might never get your photograph on the back page of the *Sunday Times* business news, but you might get something more valuable to you in the long run. More profit.

ACTION POINT IDEAS

You want tight security, we will assume, over a part of your production process, or your marketing methods or your new product.

1 Production process. Don't let *anyone* near it, even most of your own staff, and be particularly careful of your suppliers. Having supplied a key part of the system to you, their sales engineers are off round the rest of the industry swanking about the results they've got for you. Use several suppliers and give them only a bit each to do. Let no one have the whole system to build.

2 Site the plant in Korea. Have you ever seen a Korean security man?

3 Security over your marketing method. This is much more difficult because by nature it must be visible to someone. Try using careful face to face selling, but concentrated in the hands of only a few top salesmen who have been with you a long time and who are getting on in years. Competition will find them difficult to poach.

4 Use direct mail, but carefully compile your own list. Do not use cold lists (you get poor results anyway, compared to using your own). Have someone pick the list through name by name, with security in mind. Avoid those major customers who might be more pally with your opposition.

5 Use private exhibitions and shows. Use videos on customers' premises, but take them away afterwards.

6 Your big customers may easily be the biggest source of security leak you can have for your new product idea. Times without number, major buyers – particularly in fast moving retail trades or in OEM businesses – will take the supplier's unique product and then deliberately give it to a competitor to copy. This gives them two suppliers and they can squeeze them against each other. Don't deal with anybody who cannot be totally trusted. And I'm talking about some world-famous names here. In the *Times*' 1000 and *Fortunes*' top 500.

7   To get information yourself pick up copies of your competitors' accounts at Companies House. You will be amazed at what some competitors reveal. Then get someone to telephone them for their product details and literature. Use a press cutting service if you want to pick up copies of their press stories, get a major and friendly customer of yours to buy one of their products. Just keep digging. You'll get everything you need in the end, if you search hard enough.

YOUR MIND MAP

YOUR ACTION PLAN

What are you going to do about security? Can you extend the life of your secrets in any way?

THE PERILS OF NICHE MARKETING

Niche marketing, where you position yourself in a specialist sector of the market and dominate it, is probably the single most profitable way for a small company to operate. But it can go wrong.

Rank these hazards in order of danger to you.

	Ranking order of danger to you 1 (safe) – 6 (dangerous)
(a) Your market sector grows so that it attracts the attention and entry of the major market leader.	_____
(b) Your profits are so substantial, you attract in other small suppliers to your sector.	_____
(c) Your niche market customers start to produce for themselves.	_____
(d) Technology overtakes the specialist market sector and your product becomes obsolete.	_____
(e) You fail to consolidate your hold on the market by not broadening the product range and application.	_____
(f) The number two in the niche market sector takes over leadership through improved product performance.	_____

We cannot speak for your market, where special factors will apply, but (a) is the most common threat to the niche market operator. The business starts off small, but grows in applications until the giant comes in.

(b) is quite common, particularly if niche market players boast about their profits. There is research evidence to show that 25 per cent of market leaders lose their position every eight years. Of the new market leaders, half of them come from nowhere with new technology and the other half come from the previous number two in the market just overtaking the leader. So answers (d) and (f) are also very common. If you have a secure niche market – keep quiet about it.

Part Three

Six Tactics to Get the Price You Want

16

Pricing: four do's and five don'ts

●

> Pricing decisions – Here we are looking
> at the general principles of
> price setting.

Q.1 *The critical factor in pricing is:*

- (a) Finding out what the market will pay.
- (b) Calculating the costings properly.
- (c) Asking the buyers for their views.
- (d) Checking out the competition.

Q.2 *To make selling your price easy, you should, if you can:*

- (a) Employ top sales people.
- (b) Advertise a lot.
- (c) Get your costs down below the competition.
- (d) Sell to everyone you can.

Q.3 *To get better prices you should:*

- (a) Sell to customers who have money.
- (b) Sell much better products than competition.
- (c) Get the business first and price it up later.
- (d) Sell truly specialist products.

ANSWERS

Q.1 (a) 5 points — Difficult to do, it involves guessing, but vital, all the same.

(b) 2 points — Yes, but it's not the place to start.

(c) 0 points — Whatever your price, the buyers will tell you it's too high.

(d) 4 points — Yes, but it is not absolutely everything.

Q.2 (a) 4 points — Well, good people will make a better job of it than others.

(b) 3 points — It can be true sometimes, but not in every case. If it's a poor product, it will not sell however much you advertise it.

(c) 5 points — Catch question. The reason is that if your costs are low enough, then you can afford to take *any* price. If your costs are high, then you *must* get a high price.

(d) 1 point — No, you must lose some customers on price otherwise your prices are too low.

Q.3 (a) 5 points — Try selling to customers who haven't any money then.

(b) 5 points — Got to be right.

(c) 1 point — Terrible idea, in *most* cases. I *can* think of the occasional exception however.

(d) 5 points — Easy question to score 5 points on, isn't it?

SCORES

13–15 points	You are a pricing specialist
11–13 points	It is OK. You didn't quite get the hang of the questions, I know.
Up to 11 points	Did you try to get the hang of the questions?

●   ●   ●

Most businesses can make more money than they do, simply by raising the price of some of their products and services. But which prices can be raised in safety, where do you look for price increases? Don't let anyone kid you that pricing is a science. They'll say that you can examine cost data and extrapolate trends to set prices, and it's all bunkum.

Pricing is an art – some of the finest management judgement I know is used by the owner-driver of a business who has all the facts at his fingertips. His customer asks for the price, and the personal micro-computer lodged between his ears makes a set of calculations based upon how strongly the customer needs what he is selling, how much he can afford to pay, what the customer's alternative choices are, how far the customer is prepared to shop around, what he, the small busi-nessman himself, needs to cover his costs and what contribution the deal will make to his profits. Leaving himself with a bit of bargaining room up he comes with the right price. The whole process takes about two-fifths of a second. That's what pricing is about. It's an art form, not a science.

Don't let anyone tell you that you can leave pricing to the account-ants. The accountants will tell you the costs all right – and even here there is a lot of guesswork involved. But they'll not tell you what the market will pay. And the market is a far more powerful determinant of selling prices than costs ever have been or ever will be.

Don't let the buyers frighten you to death. Every buyer worth his salt has a stab at getting the supplier's price down. 'Never accept the first price' – it's an old maxim of buying. And the easiest way of frightening the supplier is to kid him he is not going to get the business because someone else's price is lower. You use the trick yourself a dozen times a week if you run a business. And it works nine-tenths of the time. So why should you worry too much when your buyer puts the pressure on?

MAXIMIZE PROFITS, NOT SALES

Don't believe that the right price will win all of the business all of the time. If you don't lose some business on price then the chances are your prices are too low. You are probably giving away a lot of net profit. There's an old saying that my old grandmother taught me as I was bouncing on her knee. She used to say, 'Son, when 10 per cent of your customers threaten to take their business away because your prices are too high, and when 2 per cent of them do take the business away because of it, then that's when your prices are about right.' But you'd better have another look at your pricing if 10 per cent of them take their business away.

Do believe that your product and your service have something to do with the price you get. For example, if 10 per cent of customers really are taking business away because of your prices, then have a look at your product and service first. You must either reduce your price, or better still, develop a better product or a more reliable service, or give them more of what they want to buy and less of what you want to produce.

Don't give yourself a sales problem. Make selling easy. How do you give yourself a sales problem? All you have to do is to allow your production costs to rise so high that you have to demand a premium price for your product in order to survive. That's a nasty sales problem. Make selling easy. Get the costs down so low that you can make a lot of profit, whatever price you sell at. If you want to take a premium price on top, and if you can get it because the market wants what you've got and no one else makes it, then take the premium price. And cart the money to your bank in security vans because there'll be a lot of profit.

WHEN TO GIVE WAY ON PRICE

Do be flexible with your price. You will have to go easy a bit with your largest customers. You will have to go even easier if your market is very competitive and the product you make is much the same as everyone else's. Go easy when your product is selling to an OEM (original equipment manufacturer) and it's a big part of his own production cost. Remember he makes his money by screwing down his suppliers and he dual-sources. He uses two or three suppliers in competition with each other. Go easy if you want to develop a new market – don't create a price umbrella for your competitors to shelter under. Go easy if you have a minor market share and not much clout in the market.

Do go for the big prices when you can, though. Some customers have very profitable businesses. When they've got a lot of money they'll pay more. When you have a specialist product and a high market share, then go for the big money. When there is a lot of added value, and few people produce what you do, then go for the money.

Do be careful of the oldest trick in the book. The tactic which sends more businesses to oblivion than any other. The one pricing tactic which the businessman bereft of any other idea about what to do with his business always turns to. It's called 'buy it and cook it'. It's the pricing tactic which makes you take the order at a knock-down, loss-making price, because you know (you hope) that there will be variations later to the contract. You know (you hope) that something will turn up to make the job profitable later. The problem is that sometimes we are left with just hope. And the business goes crunch because the profit doesn't come in.

ACTION POINT IDEAS

1   Do a pricing audit of your products and services. See what you can increase in price. Look for products with a difference which competitors do not produce.
2   Look for products which sell irregularly – only occasionally to a particular customer. If it is only bought now and again then the customer pricing reference point is lost and it can sometimes stand a higher price.
3   Look for products where you have a high market share, and take a small premium on those products.
4   Look for products which are specified by technical staff or others who basically tell the buyers what to buy. They'll be more difficult for the buyer to get the price down. This includes products which are sold to end users. Products sold to distributors and agents are often held down on price because your middleman has to take a margin to earn his living. And he feels more comfortable selling lower-price products.
5   Balance out your prices. If you have to take a low margin on one product, make sure that you sell the customer on a high margin product as well.
6   Take price increases frequently, make your prices flexible, get customers used to the fact that you are always likely to be putting up some prices and putting down others. If you get locked in to a regular timetable on price changes, this works to the buyer's advantage, and against yours.

YOUR MIND MAP

YOUR ACTION PLAN

Write down some products which you know you can put up in price soon. Write down how you are going to do this, and when. Arrange to do a pricing audit of all your products. Think of your big customers. What can you do to raise their prices? Even a little tiny bit can help. Or can you reduce your costs in servicing their business? Or can you sell them a more profitable product as well as your usual products to make their business more profitable?

Also note here the products which need to be held in price for the time being. Write down when you are going to review these again.

PRICE SETTING: HOW GOOD ARE YOUR CONTROLS?

There are different levels of pricing authority down your organization	1	2	3	4	5	6	7	Prices are fixed by one person, more or less
There is a lot of difference between your net selling price and your gross selling price before discounts, rebates, deals etc.	1	2	3	4	5	6	7	One price sticks throughout the organization
There are demands made for special deal prices	1	2	3	4	5	6	7	Never any special prices given away. All discounts are published
You are not completely sure what the market price is at any one time	1	2	3	4	5	6	7	You know the market prices all the time
You rarely lose customers on price	1	2	3	4	5	6	7	Some customers do not buy from you because your prices are higher than they can afford

Add up your score

You want 20 points or more on this table. If you score low, then try and improve on one of these control factors. Knowing the market price perhaps; or reducing the amount of price freedom people have down the line.

17

Surviving in the heart attack pricing market

●

> Meeting low price competition – In this
> chapter we show you some ways of meeting
> low price competition. We show the softer
> areas of the market.

Q.1 *Your dealer/distributor comes to you to ask you to reduce
your price to him so he can compete with lower price
competition. Is your likely response:*

(a) Tell him it is nothing to do with you. He must drop his
own price out of his margin.

(b) Give him a lower price but ensure that he chips in
some of his margin too.

(c) Get really price aggressive and knock out the
competition.

(d) Tell him to leave it for a while until things settle down.

Q.2 *You plan to open a shop selling antique dolls. There are four
possible sites for it:*

(a) The Portobello Road open market in London selling
from trestles and stalls.

(b) A shop in the smart West End area of London.

(c) A shop in the very smart country town of Chelmsford
where they have no shops like this at all.

(d) A shop in the middle of all the antique dealers and
wholesalers in a town outside London and renowned
for its antique market.

Q.3 *Competition on price is very very tough in your market. Many people go bust. How can you survive?*

    (a)   By selling to your past customers.

    (b)   By turning away really low price deals even if it sacrifices sales volume.

    (c)   By presenting your price message very carefully.

    (d)   By using selective discounting.

ANSWERS

Q.1 (a) 2 points Only where you have a really strong position in the market and where you are wanting to find a new distributor anyway.

    (b) 5 points The more he chips in from his own money the more incentive he'll have to make it work. You'll have trouble selling it to him, though.

    (c) 1 point Only when you have the resources of Fort Knox, and where you have 60 per cent share of the market you are trying to protect and where you are trying to defeat the opposition before they land on the beaches. Even then, think ten times before doing it.

    (d) 2 points OK but you may need to watch things carefully. If it is a price war and you are losing volume, then you will have to respond sooner or later.

Q.2 (a) 3 points OK for gaining you experience. There *is* a market here. But not many millionaires are there. (Oh, I don't know though . . .)

    (b) 4 points Fish where the rich fish are. But the overheads will kill you – very dangerous until you have built up your experience and a sound customer base to work on.

    (c) 1 point Lots of you pick this. Good luck, that is all I can say. Takes a long time to educate a market all by yourself. And some markets are so thick they'll never get educated. Wear yourself out trying, you will.

	(d)	5 points	Love it. Go for the fast stock-turn. Dump your loss-makers quickly. Buy from stock holdings nearby. Gain experience. These people know the game. Go join them.

Q.3	(a)	5 points	Best future customer base you will ever build.
	(b)	3 points	You must turn some people away. Some people are so mean you must tell them to hang on to their money. They'll bankrupt you, while they complain about your service.
	(c)	4 points	Yes, very carefully.
	(d)	3 points	Yes, keep light on your feet with special deals.

SCORES

13–15 points	Great. You are a winner again.
10–12 points	What was it? Temporary dyslexia?
Up to 9 points	Perhaps you didn't understand the questions?

● ● ●

'We want you to speak at this big conference', they say. 'And we want you to tell our dealers/customers how to stop chopping each other to bits on price competition on our product.'

I had three requests like that last year, and three more requests of much the same kind have come in during the last two months alone. There are a lot of manufacturers out there who don't care too much if the end-users pay more for their product. And there are a lot of end-users who don't care too much about the price, if they want the product. So who is causing this price-cutting problem? The people who believe that the only way to compete with someone else is to match his price, or drop below it. They're the ones causing the problem. It's called heart attack pricing.

But then, look around you. There are plenty of people who make a good living even in the price-cutters' market. How? They're prepared to see some low-price business walk out of their door rather than chop their prices. They certainly don't advertise low prices. That's because they don't offer them. So how do they survive?

AVOID HEART ATTACK PRICING

First of all, they avoid heart attack pricing. They do not share the common view that the only way to win in business is to beat the other person's price. They tell themselves, 'Pricing is critical to my profits. My profits are critical to my living longer, living happier, keeping my marriage and making much more money. Therefore I must do everything I can to prop up my prices.' And they proceed from there.

Second, they position themselves in market sectors which are less fiercely competitive on price. If they are antique dealers they open up in Bond Street rather than Portobello Road. And if they cannot afford the rent and rates of Bond Street then they'll find other quality customers, selling to rich visitors in Brighton's Lanes, perhaps. This way they are in a rich market, but with low overheads.

Third, they advertise their unique qualities. They carefully nurse their existing customer list, the people who have bought from them in the past. This way, they will find easier selling situations and they differentiate themselves from the competition.

What they don't do is to go out and advertise the fact that they trade on price. They'll have a 'special deal', perhaps, just to show that they can be competitive, too. Part of the trick about price competition is the presentation of the price message itself. You can offer low price or high price, but you have to be careful about the way you present the message.

THE RICH ARE DIFFERENT

Heart specialists love price cutters for another reason. Low prices attract people who do not have much money. People who have a lot of money care less about price. They argue about it, of course; they try and get the price down, of course. That's maybe how they got to have so much money in the first place. But, by definition, they cannot care so much about the price as people who need the product desperately but who have not got enough money. That *is* desperate.

So try marketing the product to sectors of the market which themselves are fairly rich. Sell to customers who are already profitable. Sell to bigger organizations, perhaps, to whom the expense is petty cash. Sell to companies not individuals. People who buy things using other people's money are always a bit easier on price than people who buy things using their own money.

Get to the technical specialists, behind the buyer. Get to your customers' directors for a decision. Get to the people who will use your product. If they like it they will specify it. And they won't care so much about the price. Who will care about the price? The professional buyer will care. He has got to spend the money on it, so he wants the price down low. So don't sell to the buyer. Pre-sell to the technicians behind the scenes – or the people who are going to be affected by using the product.

Don't sell the same things as everyone else. That makes it easier for others to compare your prices. Sell something different. Something unusual. Do it in an unusual way. Add better services. Change the specifications. Find a specialist niche in the market and produce for it. Sell it hard and keep selling it. But price it up.

I'm not saying all this is easy, you understand. It's just that doing it the other way is even more difficult. And, finally, how high can your price be? Well, with one or two exceptions for people who sell things such as life-support drugs, your price can be as high as the market can bear. And sometimes that is very, very high.

Question one: How high does a price have to be before it is immoral?

Question two: Is it therefore more moral to price things so low that you make losses, fire staff and have heart attacks? 'Nuff said.

ACTION POINT IDEAS

1   Look at the *people* in your organization who always bring in low prices. Think about the *people* in your company who always ask for special prices and deals. The people who always seem to need the boss to handle the final stages of the awkward customers for them. Ask yourself, why are they not confident? Is it product knowledge, customer knowledge, inexperience, lack of training, neglect by their boss, or plain straightforward fear? Do something about it.

2   Look at the customers who give you low prices or who always get special treatment. *How* do they negotiate this with you? How were the deals set up in the first place? What can you do to prevent *more* deals being set up in the same way in the future? Is it always one type of customer or one type of market which gives you trouble?

3   Look at the high margins you earn from other customers. What are the characteristics of their business? How can you get and develop more of this business?

4   Work your past customers again. Sell to the ones who have stopped using you. (Yes, they will still be easier to sell to than cold prospects, if your service was any good.) Develop business with existing high margin accounts.

5   Sell hard on the customer's problem. Get to the customer's needs and stay there all the time. Make him see your benefits. Make him see that you can give him things which other people cannot give him. He'll pay the price.

YOUR MIND MAP

YOUR ACTION PLAN

Start by analysing your thin margin markets. Look at the business you do in these competitive situations. Now some of it will be at higher margins than the rest. Identify this core cluster. And make a plan to swing round some of your very low margin business to this slightly higher margin business. In other words, change the customer mix. What are you going to do?

VERY PRICE COMPETITIVE MARKETS: SORTING YOUR PRIORITIES

To improve your profitability in your most competitive market which five of the following actions would you rank in order?

	Most important	Not applicable	Least important
Lowering your product and service costs	_____	_____	_____
Getting more sales	_____	_____	_____
Improving the prices	_____	_____	_____
Finding better-quality customers	_____	_____	_____
Finding easier markets	_____	_____	_____
Selling to users, and technical people, not professional buyers, agents or distributors	_____	_____	_____
Improving your sales force skills	_____	_____	_____
Adding better quality to your product	_____	_____	_____
Matching buyers needs more effectively	_____	_____	_____
Reducing your sales or distribution costs	_____	_____	_____
Reducing your overheads	_____	_____	_____
Selling your maximum capacity	_____	_____	_____
Selling a balanced range of profitable products	_____	_____	_____

Then cross out those which do not apply and then mark out the five *least* important factors.

Have a look at any factors you have not scored at all. Do you want to have another think about those? (The reason is that you are always chasing hard on your top five priorities. But these others also represent opportunities for improving your profits, too.)

18

The verdict on the boss is: guilty

●

> Restructing discounts – In this chapter we
> look at how you structure your special prices
> and deals.

Q.1 *You are the buyer. The salesman is refusing to give you the
lower price you want. You demand to see his boss. Why?*

(a) You just want a chat about the old days.

(b) The boss can lower the price down to the bare bones.

(c) You want to complain about the salesman.

(d) You want to ask him why he does not let his salesmen
give lower prices.

Q.2 *There are some people you should never give discounts to:*

(a) The people who are small customers and very nasty.

(b) The very big customers.

(c) The ones who will want a mile if you give them a yard.
(Or if you are in Europe, a metre if you give them a
centimetre. Or if you are a Common Market farmer, a
litre if you give them a millilitre.)

(d) Customers who will use your discounts to cut their
own prices and screw up the rest of the market for you.

Q.3 *To re-structure your discounts, you should:*

(a) Put a time limit on all deals.

(b) Stop calling them discounts; break them up in small
bits.

(c) Change them overnight, without warning.

(d) Not bother to try because it is too dangerous.

ANSWERS

Q.1 (a) 1 point   What a pushover you'd be as a buyer.
　　 (b) 5 points What's the point of being the boss if you
　　　　　　　 cannot show how important you are by
　　　　　　　 giving money to customers?
　　 (c) 1 point   The boss will fight you tooth and nail
　　　　　　　 and later on will fight the salesman.
　　 (d) 3 points Well, if you like. It seems pretty paltry to
　　　　　　　 me.

Q.2 (a) 5 points As a customer you have the right to be
　　　　　　　 small, if you are nice. Or you can be
　　　　　　　 nasty if you are big. But woe betide you
　　　　　　　 if you are small and nasty.
　　 (b) 2 points If you are going to give discounts away
　　　　　　　 at all, and hopefully you are not, then let
　　　　　　　 the monkeys be big ones if they are to
　　　　　　　 get hold of your nuts.
　　 (c) 3 points Some people are like this. Hold out
　　　　　　　 against them for as long as you can.
　　 (d) 5 points Frontal lobotomy job, this one.

Q.3 (a) 5 points Yes, yes, yes.
　　 (b) 5 points And yes, again.
　　 (c) 1 point   Good way to get rid of your customers.
　　 (d) 2 points Yes, it is dangerous. But yes, you should
　　　　　　　 try it. But not if you have only five years
　　　　　　　 to go before retirement.

SCORES

15 points	You must get all three right to get top score. Well, you've got five chances out of twelve.
11–14 points	You missed your chances.
up to 10 points	You could have done better picking with a pin.

● 　 ● 　 ●

'THE VERDICT ON THE BOSS IS: GUILTY'

Only two sales managers in ten can allow their sales executives to read
this. Because the other eight are guilty. It's a brave man who writes like

this. I'm going to be very unpopular – but as my old granny used to say, 'There are no medals for being popular, son'. So here goes.

The first rule of buying is *find out if the salesman has got any price discretion*. Which means that buyers probe, attack, wheedle, and whine to see if they can get your price down. The motto of the Royal Institute of Chartered Buyers and Manipulators is 'Never accept the sales rep's first price'. So they hammer your sales executives to see if they'll drop the price.

The second rule of buying is *get the discretion from him. All of it*. So the more the sales executive shows signs of giving way on price and offering up new discount ideas, the more the buyer tries to get extra. When your sales executive gives in to price pressure, it doesn't reduce the pressure. It makes it worse. Every time the buyer sees the sales executive, he has another go to get a bit more.

Then, when he sees the sales executive coming to the end of his discretionary limit on price, he brings the third rule of buying into play: *when you've got all the salesperson can give you, then get hold of his boss, because he can give you more*.

ARE YOU GUILTY?

Now you see what I mean about being not very popular with this chapter. Because if you are one of those managers who gives the buyer more discount than your sales executive is authorized to give him, then you come under the heading of guilty.

You have cut the arms and legs off your sales executive. You have made the buyer want to deal with *you* when it comes to money. And he will insist on seeing *you* whenever he has a big deal in tow. So how is this going to train your salesmen to handle big deals? What does your sales executive think of you, if you always land the business by giving more away? He thinks you are a chump. And how will you improve your golf handicap if you've got all these wretched buyers asking for you all the time?

(You and I both know that you, yourself, are not the guilty one. But I must tell you in confidence that there are other readers who feel very sensitive on this subject.) I don't know of many subjects which are trickier to handle in sales management than the control of discounts. How should you handle severe competitive pressure without giving way? How do you shore up the confidence of your salespeople?

TIDDLERS: TWO CHOICES

First, it's a good idea to work out what business you do not want to do. The bad payers. The nasty people who hammer you all the time and demand extra service. The small tiddly accounts. The people who keep you screwed down to providing unprofitable business. There's two things to do with this lot and one thing not to do. Do get rid of them if they are unprofitable. Or do put up their prices. And don't under any circumstances give in to their pricing or discount pressure. There, you feel better already. That's my number one rule about discounting. Don't give discounts to people who don't do nice business. Life's too short.

Don't give people long-term discounts. That is, don't give them a discount which will stay in forever and ever. Because it will cost you a fortune over the years. I know you have been doing just this for years. That does not make it any better, does it? And maybe all the competition does it, too. But when 3000 people do a silly thing, it still stays a silly thing. Don't do it.

Set all discounts with a time limit. Make sure that you leave yourself in control. And you do this if you limit the discount to a specific time or period. Not too long, either. Three months is fine. One year is too long.

STOP CALLING THEM 'DISCOUNTS'

Mix up the discounts. Break your discount into two. Call part of it something else. Be inventive, be imaginative. Call it a bonus. Call it a support incentive. Call it an overrider. Call it a seasonal promotion. Anything you like, but stop calling it a discount.

This is because you want to bring your discounts under your control. So you have to get the buyers used to the fact that your discounts are negotiable. And then the buyers get used to the fact that they are expected to do something for the extra bonus. Like taking more product. Or giving you extra volume. Or providing promotional effort. Or taking a new product. Anything you like so long as you trade it. If you give them something, they must give you something back.

So, if you usually give them a 5 per cent discount, then try to split this with a special campaign into a 3 per cent discount plus a 2 per cent support allowance. They won't know what that means but you will. (What it means is that you won't be giving it to them in future unless they play fair with you, like giving you all their business.)

Try breaking away from a percentage discount, particularly if you sell high-value products or service. Try setting an overall budget, breaking it into cash amounts and then offering cash bonus incentives.

Do this instead of offering percentage discounts. Or mix up your present discount by reducing the percentage but giving away a cash bonus as well. The total money can be the same, of course, but cash looks so much better to them. And you will have the right to alter the terms of the deal later, when the time limit is up.

SQUEEZING OUT EXTRA SALES

All of this is designed to put you back in control of your discounts and take the control away from the buyers. It's in their interests that they go for the long term. They try to get a commitment from you now, on a particular deal, which they can point to later and use as a precedent. Then they've got you hooked. So you go just for the short term, not the long. Try to give bonus or discount away only for their doing extra for you. Don't give it away on the normal business they do anyway.

For example, suppose you are thinking of increasing their annual rebate from 1 per cent to 2 per cent if they do more than £1 000 000 a year with you. Well, this might raise them from their present volume of say, £800 000 to just over the million. (They have no good incentive to go much higher.) For that extra £200 000 you have given away an extra £10,000 which is 5 per cent. Why not give them instead a 1 per cent rebate on everything up to £1 000 000 and thereafter give them $7\frac{1}{2}$ per cent? The cost to you is less up to £1 million of sales, but they have a marvellous incentive to go well beyond that figure. Make sure you set a time limit on it, though, so it can be re-negotiated.

SAY NO SOMETIMES

Controlling discounts is absolutely beastly. Even if you allow some limited discretion to your salesmen, and keep more to yourself, which is what most people do, there will always be some sales executives who will keep coming to you for special prices. You must say no sometimes. Because if you don't ever say no, and always tell them to land the business, you'll end up losing your control. The sales executive will always be giving it away, because he knows you are a soft touch.

P.S. What should you do when the buyer calls you, the boss, in for extra money? What you must do is to play the heavy at the meeting. Refuse to give in, but let your own sales executive persuade you in the end. So make sure the customer sees that it is your sales executive who is his best friend, not you. But you must appear to fight him. It takes a bit of rehearsal and practice. But keep at it. Because your golf handicap will improve when you get it right. The buyers won't want to see you so often.

ACTION POINT IDEAS

1 Identify all the discounts you offer. Separate the special bonuses, the promotional deals. Measure the cost of special low prices which you negotiate with the big customers. Identify all these costs, compare them to your standard prices and see what the total amount of money is.

2 Now calculate as far as you can, what extra business these special prices are bringing back for you. Work out how you can still get all this extra business but without giving so much money away. Make a long-term plan, over two/three years to re-structure your discounts.

3 As a first step in this long-term plan, simply put a time limit on all your discounts and special prices. Explain that they will be re-negotiated before the final date. Then offer customers the same amount of money as before but break up the deals into special prices, not regular discounts. Put a new time limit on these special prices. Ensure that where you can you reduce someone's discount, or else you try and trade in more product for the money you give away.

4 The next time change the routine again. Put in a special promotion or support fund but reduce your basic discount. Start to mix things up, but always with a time limit set. Be highly creative with your promotional discounts – to force up the volume.

5 Get them off percentages and on to cash.

6 Always measure the total of your discounts. Compare the total giveaway to your gross sales figure. Ensure that over time you improve upon this figure, giving less and less discount away over-all, and getting more and more back in exchange. Soon you will increase your net profits by 50 per cent. You watch.

YOUR MIND MAP

YOUR ACTION PLAN

List here the specific actions you will have to take in your company in order to improve your discount figures. What meetings will you have to have, with whom and when? What action is needed to get the analysis started? What sort of project team will you need? How will you get the sales force involved?

DISCOUNTING DIFFICULTIES ANALYSIS

	Score yourself out of 5 5 = total agreement 1 2 3 4 5
1 You take time to think about discounts; you plan them very carefully indeed; you are never rushed into a discount decision.	_____
2 Your special deals and discounts are very flexible. You can change them at a moment's notice. You are always in control of them.	_____
3 Sometimes you give away extra product; free service; or do your deals as cash reductions. You rarely present your discounts as a percentage off.	_____
4 Your sales people are totally confident of refusing demands for extra discounts. They are trained to handle this pressure.	_____
5 When your sales people do ask you for special prices for customers, they know you are likely to refuse them.	_____

You want to be scoring 15 or more on this table. If you don't score this then you *must* train the sales force and agree your special price policy with them.

19

Dumping your sales problem

●

> Selling excess product below cost – In this chapter we look at marginal pricing. How to sell below full cost without it wrecking your business. Marginal pricing is one of the most dangerous techniques of all.

Q.1 *You are a major international airline. Here is a low-price competitor, ripping out all his overheads to punch the price down really low. He is getting all the publicity and taking a lot of business away from you. You have a lot of spare capacity. What action will you take?*

(a) Cut prices down to the floor and take the competition out altogether even if it means you make big losses in so doing.

(b) Give up the low-price sector of the market, cut back on your capacity and trade up for regular flyers and business people.

(c) Get together with your competitors quietly to see if you can all join together to 'get' the cut pricer, yet protect your most profitable sectors of business at the same time.

(d) Do nothing on the grounds that the cut pricer is likely to go out of business.

Q.2 *You have a second grade of product, a by-product of your main line which you must get rid of. Any price will do. Will you:*

(a) Sell it at normal prices.

(b) Sell it through an agent into the market.

(c) Dump it into a market a long way away from your present customers.

159

(d)   Sell it to selected non-customers of yours so as to damage the health of your competitors' business and to put them under pressure.

Q.3   *Here are some things you can do, if you want to dump spare product at low price. Pick the best.*

(a)   Sell it to existing big customers.
(b)   Back it with capital investment.
(c)   Strip out all the costs, make it profitable, sell it cash up front.
(d)   Advertise it widely.

ANSWERS

Q.1   (a)   2 points   Big losses usually mean a restructuring of the board of management. You may have to do this, but remember you are likely to lose your job in the process.

(b)   1 point   Bad move to give up market share if you are a market leader. They'll go for your main business after they get to be profitable, you see.

(c)   5 points   I love it. It is illegal in most markets, but just cover your tracks well. Never meet in public. No letters. No records. If you don't get caught you'll keep your job. If it goes wrong you lose your job and *could* go to prison. Well, get some nasty publicity anyway, until someone fixes you up with a non-executive directorship somewhere else.

(d)   2 points   You mean let someone else kill them off? Oh well, in that case I like it. The strategy called 'Yugo First' seems to be called for here.

Q.2   (a)   2 points   If you can do this then surely you can get a bigger price for your main A grade product?

(b)   3 points   OK but it might spread back to damage you.

	(c)	5 points	Brilliant. You are a genius.
	(d)	5 points	You are a genius, too.
Q.3	(a)	1 point	Awful.
	(b)	1 point	Dreadful.
	(c)	5 points	Great, 'specially the cash up front bit.
	(d)	1 point	Wait a minute, you not only want to sell it at a big loss, you want to advertise it with your hard earned money, too. What's your name – Rothschild?

SCORES

11–15 points	Difficult to get a really high score here. If you don't pick right you get few points.
8–10 points	You didn't pick right.
Up to 7 points	You definitely didn't pick right.

●   ●   ●

DUMPING YOUR SALES PROBLEM

Here's a dangerous game you can play. It's called 'selling below full-cost'.

It's dangerous because the penalty for playing outside the rules can lose you your business. When Sir Freddie Laker was trying to get his low-cost Skytrain service to the USA approved by the aviation authorities, he told a meeting of the Marketing Society that once he got going with low-cost fares, the major airlines would never be able to fight back, handicapped as they were by their heavy overheads. Sir Freddie believed he was on to a winner. But he got the rules wrong and look what happened. The big boys ganged up on him and his business was destroyed.

So why play the game at all if the penalty for losing is so high? The truth is that few people play it out of choice: most are forced into it.

Once, when Sir Michael Edwardes was sorting out BL cars, he found himself with a little financial problem. His yards and car parks were stuffed full of outdated models which the market did not want. The government refused to lend more money. So his cash flow was jammed solid and he found himself facing the prospect of being unable to meet his wages bill. Does this story sound familiar to you, in your business? So he loaded up his dealers, offered huge deals, sold below cost and thereby knocked some money back into his bank. He solved one problem but created another. Even though Ford tried to hold off the price war, they finally gave in. The car market has never been quite the same since.

Sure, they've made profits and sold cars. But they have also created a market of car buyers who now shop around for the best deals. There always was dealing in the car market, but never was it so widespread across all cars as it is today. So although there is one good reason for selling below cost – to generate cash – it is usually a bad move if the price cutting spreads into your normal market.

OFFLOAD YOUR 'SECONDS'

Here is another good reason for dumping – second-quality goods. But it is even more important to keep these out of your normal markets. The humble frozen chicken, for example, can sometimes become a bit bruised and battered as it is processed. These blemishes show up badly on the shop counters. So the wholesalers put them into plain bags and sell them off cheaply to catering outlets, hotels, cafes and the like. Now that makes sense and maintains standards in the retail sector of the market.

Shops themselves have this problem with their annual sales. The shop groups take 'seconds' from manufacturers, and they knock out their year-old stocks and their ends of ranges which have not sold. They discount at prices up to 25 per cent off normal. Menswear shops merchandise their sales windows by 'call birds', as they are prettily called in the trade. These items are discounted very heavily indeed but they are often of an exceptional size, so people are drawn into the shops but they find the call-bird does not fit them.

Shops find there are two distinct markets they serve. One is the normal everyday market for normal-price up-to-date goods. This is often quite separate from the bargain hunters who save their clothes purchases until January. Multiple shop groups have this dumping down to a fine art. They always keep the sale going in one shop longer than the rest. They keep the annual sales open for a very short time in their prestige high-street sites and towards the end of the sales they move out all their unsold goods into one or two shops in poorer markets. This way, they avoid contaminating their normal markets for too long with low prices.

If you do plan to dump then put in conditions of trade which make it difficult for normal customers to switch to your low margin items. Airlines offer stand-by tickets which businessmen cannot reasonably use. 'Away-day' tickets always start after the rail commuter rush is over.

DISGUISE IT, EXPORT IT

A chemical company supplying factories with cleaning products has a low-grade by-product which would be in great demand if it got into the normal markets. So they put a different name on the drum and sell it cheaply through a couple of distributors. They strip it of all service and all technical back-up and the distributors find low-cost markets for it, some overseas. In this way the company does not find its own low-cost product competing with its major brands.

A meat products manufacturer finds it economical to buy whole pigs on the market. It gets the best buying price this way. But the company does not need the whole pig for its production. So the company employs one specialist salesman to knock out its excess product to the wholesale market. It could use its own sales force to do this but it does not want to in case the salesmen begin to sell the cheap by-product too vigorously. So if the pressures are on you to dump your sales problems then here is a summary of the rules:

1 Get it out of the normal price markets as far as you can.
2 Don't deal on low price with existing customers who pay full price
    – they'll want low prices all the time.
3 Don't put in any long-term commitment and certainly invest no
    capital in a project which sells below full cost.
4 Profit-strip the deal, and try to get cash up-front from the cus-
    tomers. Why give long credit terms as well as low prices?
5 Only do it when you have spare capacity; and don't guarantee
    future supplies.

Perhaps we should have mentioned all this to Sir Freddie.

ACTION POINTS IDEAS

1 How do you get rid of excess product? Can you find a profitable
    way to turn it into cash, but avoid selling it to your regular
    accounts? Can you use it to promote other lines? Can you use it to
    put competitors under pressure?
2 Do you have any second-grade product? Or should you deliber-
    ately develop a second-grade product of lower quality to run out
    against your low-price competitors? Can you make sure you keep
    this away from most of your own product sales? Can you sell
    something where the unit selling price is half of what you normally
    sell at? Can you do it by using up spare capacity in your existing
    plant? But it must hurt the competition, not your own sales.

3   Would it pay to have an annual sale? How about a special collection of your products – at the end of your usual selling season perhaps, sold at low prices. Could you move this sale around the country, from market to market?

4   Before you make a decision to extend your manufacturing plant, or other facilities, can you see if it is possible to take out some low-price, low-margin item from your production to clear the space for high margin lines? Sometimes people say they need new plant, when they are carrying loss-making products on the old line.

5   When you give special low prices, well below the norm, can you change your credit terms so they pay cash up front?

YOUR MIND MAP

YOUR ACTION PLAN

Go through your very low-price deals, one by one. Analyse them and see if you can improve them. Are you sure they are not doing harm to your other business? You are not giving them added service as well, are you? Then think hard; where is there some sales potential for really low-price products, perhaps at very low specification? Is it worth going for some of this business?

SELLING BELOW FULL COST: PROBLEM ANALYSIS

You sell a lot of business at low prices	1	2	3	4	5	6	7	You hardly sell anything at low prices
Your overall margins are always under pressure	1	2	3	4	5	6	7	You maintain high gross profit margins always
Profitability is a struggle for you	1	2	3	4	5	6	7	You are usually awash with profits
Cash flow is a problem for you	1	2	3	4	5	6	7	You are awash with cash
Big deals disrupt your production process	1	2	3	4	5	6	7	You can fit in any size of deal easily

Add up your scores. You want to have high scores here if you can. You really want 24 plus. Below this, watch these marginal deals really closely.

20

'Don't bother me with details, just tell me your price'

●

> Personally selling your price – This chapter is about how and why buyers so often put the pressure on price. How they often bluff. What you should be wary about.

Q.1 *You need the business badly. It is a competitive market. The buyer says that the deal will turn on price. He leaves the room and you can see a competitor's quote on his desk which is 5 per cent cheaper than your lowest price. Do you:*

    (a) Think how you can get your price down by reducing some of the package you offer.

    (b) Drop by 6 per cent to land the business.

    (c) Hold on to your price and ignore the competition.

    (d) Ask the buyer to compare your specifications with the competition.

Q.2 *The buyer has a warm manner and smiles a lot. You have not met him before. Is this:*

    (a) A good sign.

    (b) A bad sign.

    (c) Part of a softening up treatment.

    (d) A signal that you have got the business.

Q.3 *The buyer wants to see your boss. Is this because:*

    (a) He wants to meet the man who can manage a genius like you.

    (b) He wants to complain about your incompetence.

    (c) He is a snob.

    (d) He wants to meet a person who can give him a lot of money.

ANSWERS

Q.1   It's all tricky, whatever you do.

(a)   4 points   You need this as a fallback move.

(b)   0 points   Oh, come on, man or mouse are you?

(c)   3 points   Fortune favours the brave. Sometimes.

(d)   5 points   The buyer has left it for you to see the price. But you must compare apples with apples. The other quote might be for rotten apples. Go for it.

Q.2   (a)   4 points   Take it at face value. He might be a happy idiot.

(b)   3 points   Could be he is just using you. Not enough evidence yet.

(c)   2 points   Bit unlikely, but you never know.

(d)   1 point   Could be. But on the other hand, you could be the happy idiot.

Q.3   (a)   4 points   You know what you are worth.

(b)   4 points   You know what you are worth.

(c)   0 points   He can't be a snob. He wants to meet *your* boss?

(d)   5 points   Bosses give away more money than anyone else. I'm not being cynical. This is a statement of fact.

SCORES

12 points plus	You have a nice blend of cynicism and hope.
9–11 points	Best to play with other people's money, not your own.
Up to 8 points	Why bother?

●   ●   ●

This friend of mine called Dick Norton was the managing director of an electronics company. He has a gentle, open manner. He could make Attila the Hun sound like Billy Graham. He has room for only one tiny bit of wickedness. And it's the same kind of wickedness which, if not recognized and carefully countered, takes you and your salesmen straight to the cleaners every time. Never mind caveat emptor: let the seller beware, too. Especially if the seller has discretion on price, so he can reduce his price.

Like most ideas which earn you a fortune, Dick came upon his by accident. He once listened to a very powerful presentation from a strong and competent sales engineer. Knew his stuff this chap did. All the technical knowledge at his fingertips. He put forward his proposition and told Dick what the price was. Now Dick is not slow, but he wanted a bit of time to think. Having nothing else to say, he just murmured, 'Can't you do a bit better than that?' He said it with a big smile. He was kidding really. He had actually made up his mind to buy.

You can guess the answer, probably. The engineer became a little agitated and mumbled that he could drop the price by 10 per cent. Just to pull his leg, Dick grinned and told him he had budgeted for less than that. So the salesman knocked off another 5 per cent. Having a heart of gold, Dick let him off then. And he has been using the same technique with the same smile ever since. And he has been putting the percentages away on four deals out of five. People love dealing with Dick. He is so amiable. Very polite, very trustworthy. His word is good. He has just got this one streak of wickedness.

HOW THEY'LL GET YOU SHAVING THE PRICE

He has to vary the technique, of course. He can't use the same line on the same person all the time. A salesman gets caught like that once, then he is on his guard. So Dick plays variants on his theme. Before now, he has been known to pop out of the room, leaving a competitor's quote for a salesman to see. Or he asks for a quote for half the quantity, then squeezes the extra discount for the full total. Sometimes he offers a fake trade. 'Look, if you can do something for me on price, then I'm prepared to place the order with you today' is one of his favourites.

On one notable occasion a finance company executive was astonished to hear Dick presenting the proposition to his company chairman over the phone and getting bawled out by his boss. Putting his hand over the telephone he said to the representative: 'Just a bit of verbal GBH. Sorry old boy, you can see how I'm placed. The chairman says we've got to do it through a bank loan.' That bit of gameplay was worth $1^{1}/_{2}$ per cent on a £60,000 deal over three years. The chairman played his agreed role with relish. The bank had already refused facilities! The technique is very common, of course, among professionals that is. But so many amateurs play it with a nasty manner. They use aggression and the seller is forewarned. 'If they look nasty they probably are nasty, so be on your guard' is the rule to follow.

Dick's technique is as old as the hills. Every antique dealer gets it from customers all the time. Every car dealer gets his share of the tyre kickers. 'How much will you take for this, then?' sneers the buyer. And although the technique is commonplace – you yourself probably use it all the time, with a smile I hope – it is nevertheless true that the majority of antiques are sold to people who do not question the price. And a large number of cars are sold to people who are too nervous to ask if the price can be reduced. So you might think that the moral of this story is intended to point you in the direction of the amateurs in your business who take the seller's price without argument.

THE BUYER'S THREE LAWS

Actually the moral of this story is not about Dick. No, the point of this story is about the salesman who sells things to Dick. The technical chap who knows his stuff but is put under pressure by his own sales boss to do the deal. The sales engineer who knows that his boss will let him agree to a lower price. The point of the story is to highlight the problem caused to their companies by salesmen who have discretion to negotiate prices and who get taken to the cleaners by skilful buyers. Buyers who smile a lot. Buyers who bluff them with tiny lies about not having enough in the budget, or tell them that a competitor is cheaper. When all the time they are going to buy anyway.

This story is about the salesman who gives it away without really trying, without getting anything back in exchange. It's about the salesman who hasn't been trained in negotiation. Luckily, you don't have any of these chaps working for you. Do you?

ACTION POINT IDEAS

1   Have you got a higher priced competitor in mind to compare with yourself? The buyer is going to take you down in price to a lower competitor. So you must take him up in price to a higher priced one.
2   Work out what is your distinct edge for each buyer. Something that he wants, but which no one else can give him. Sell him that edge hard. He will pay a little bit more for it. You can then point out what he will be losing if he goes to a competitor.
3   Have a fallback position. Give him his low price at the end if you have to but cut back on the service and the specification. That will make him come back to trade with you.

4   Do not give in on your core price if you can help it. But give in on
    the peripherals. You will have to give him a hard time on price and
    make him face the prospect that you will not be able to reduce it.
    Then give him a little something right at the end. If you give in
    early, then he will fight you on price every time. *Courage, mon
    brave.*

5   Are you sure, are you quite quite sure that you are not the cause of
    some of your price difficulties? Do you ever give in too quickly, too
    easily? Do you usually assume you have to give money away? Do
    you hesitate too long before answering? Are you uncertain of what
    to do when faced with a demand for a reduced price? If so, you will
    cause some of the price pressure yourself.

YOUR MIND MAP

YOUR ACTION PLAN

Think of individual buyers who give you a hard time on price. Name three of them. Write down here a specific technique you are going to use to stop them from beating you down next time.

MONITORING BUYER BEHAVIOUR

Go into a market this coming Saturday. Watch the buyers. Monitor how they behave. Watch them walk up, inspect the goods, think, clarify, talk to the stallholders. Watch how they deal on price. Make notes. Did you notice any of these things?

	You noticed	You did not notice
All buyers behave differently from each other.		
The same buyer tends to behave in a consistent fashion in various situations.		
Some are nice, some are nasty, most are neutral.		
All buyers feel they are more important than the salesmen.		
Some buyers are arrogant – so are some salesmen.		
Some buyers try to get the price down – not all buyers do this, though.		
Some buyers look for cheapness, others pick through quality items.		
The buyers who go for cheapness often argue about the price more.		
Some salespeople give it away with the suggestion of offers straight away. They use price reductions as their principal appeal.		
Some buyers are inept and awkward.		
Some salespeople are poor on product knowledge; or lack attention. Some salespeople don't care.		
Some salespeople are in the wrong job.		

There are no rights and wrongs in this table. It is just a means of sensitizing us to the fact that every selling situation, every buyer, every seller, is different. The styles in the market are rich, colourful and hugely varied.

P.S. What were the principal characteristics of the stall which had the most attention; the most customers?

21

The fear factor in selling your price

●

> Debating your price – In this chapter we
> look at how you can play a few games to
> handle the buyer who is putting you under
> price pressure. What can you say to him
> when he says your price is too high?

Q.1 *Just for a moment you be the buyer. The salesman questions you about your problems and needs for his product. You want his best price. Do you:*

    (a) Answer his questions letting him dictate the conversation.

    (b) Stop him and ask him questions.

    (c) Tell him the deal will turn on price.

    (d) Be aggressive.

Q.2 *Still be the buyer. Is it in your interests to:*

    (a) Be nasty to him.

    (b) Be nice to him.

    (c) Tell him what you want.

    (d) Know all about the competition first.

Q.3 *Normally, when you yourself buy things, do you:*

    (a) Always search for the lowest price every time.

    (b) Sometimes pay a very low price.

    (c) Always pay the normal price.

    (d) Always pay a top price.

ANSWERS

Q.1　(a)　1 point　　He'll roll over you.

　　　　(b)　3 points　　Pretty good.

　　　　(c)　4 points　　It will stop him from getting too confident.

　　　　(d)　2 points　　Usually there is little point in doing this without a specific purpose.

Q.2　(a)　1 point　　Why be nasty now? You can save it up for later.

　　　　(b)　3 points　　Better. Still got your options open.

　　　　(c)　2 points　　Tell him later, not too early. The full story, that is.

　　　　(d)　5 points　　Yes, bring your chosen supplier in last, after you have full information from everyone else.

Q.3　(a)　1 point　　A few people, very few people do this.

　　　　(b)　5 points　　If you don't do this sometimes then you are not negotiating hard enough or searching hard enough.

　　　　(c)　3 points　　Bit too easy going, this.

　　　　(d)　2 points　　You are probably paying with other people's money.

SCORES

12–14 points	Great; nice sense of wariness about you.
9–11 points	All right, let us just agree to differ.
Up to 8 points	Maybe the world *should* be like your world.

● ● ●

The finest pricer in the world is the small businessman. He uses a computer made of blood and tissue, two cubic inches of it, portable. Faced with a customer he can assess the profitability of the order. He can calculate his costs, judge his spare capacity and consider his work programme all in a split second. Nothing works as fast on prices as the computer in a small businessman's head. It is a really slick machine when it works well. The trouble is, it's the only computer in the world which can get scared. It's the only computer which can be frightened by the thought of competition for the deal. It's the only machine which lies awake at night worrying.

So when you sell things and the buyer quibbles about the price, it might pay you to remember some of these nine specific questions used by highly experienced and well trained sellers. First of all, avoid the price pressure and try and find out your own strength. Try to establish what the buyer likes about you. So ask directly, 'Why have you put us on your short list?' Don't be afraid of it – most buyers will tell you the truth. This will help you shore up your pricing arguments.

ISOLATE THE PRICE FACTOR

Next, clarify the issue. Isolate the price factor – you don't want to start dropping the price only to find the prospect coming up with another objection which might force you down further. So you should identify his objection, then say, 'Apart from that (price etc.) would we get the business from you?' The buyer is caught. If he says yes, then if you solve the problem for him you will get the business. If he says no, then you will find out the other problems before you commit yourself to dropping the price. Another way of getting to the same information is to ask, 'Is it purely price which is stopping you from giving us the business?' He will now tell you what else he is looking for from you – very useful information before you come to the final crunch.

Now let us say your prospect is putting you up seriously against competition. He shows you their quotation which is lower than yours and asks you to come down to their price. Here you must do two things. First you must know your competitors. Find something you do which they don't, or a benefit in your specification which is not in theirs. You must compare like for like. Don't rush it. Stay calm. Go through the competitor's specification point by point. Remember the customer is buying reliability and truthfulness as well as buying products. Ask him, without knocking the competition, 'What have they left out to get their price that low?'

If there is something about your service – if your delivery is faster, if your premises are nearer to the customer, if you yourself are an expert – then try this. Ask: 'Would ... (fast delivery etc.) ... be a benefit to you?' Or 'Would it make a difference if I personally supervised your account?'

CLARIFY THE DEADLINE

Now let us say that you are getting towards the end of the debate. Perhaps you have decided that you may have to drop the price a bit to land the deal, but you do not want to drop it much. The first and absolutely vital thing to do is to clarify that he is going to make a decision, yes or no, now, depending upon what you say. If he is going to go away and 'think about it', then he will call in the competition, tell them your new low quote and they will drop their price below yours. When you quote your best price, you must do it when the prospect is hard up against the decision and after all the competition has quoted. It is not easy to do, but whoever said that selling in a competitive market was easy?

So ask him, before quoting, 'Are you going to decide today?' If he says 'Yes' then you can battle for the deal now. Don't leave his office without it. If he says 'No' then you have to try for a re-bid. Give him only a ball park figure now. An outline figure, a figure for budgeting purposes. Ask him in what range his budget lies. Tell him that you will come back with a firm quote just before he is ready to do the deal and you expect this quote to be very good for him indeed. Then come back close to his deadline.

If he says that your price is too high, ask him, 'How high is too high?' That will tell you whether you are a long way out or just a little. Don't expect him to tell you the truth, but watch his reaction carefully and you will be able to guess shrewdly. Then you can ask him directly, without equivocation, 'What are you seeking to pay?' Or, at the end of a long argument, you can say, 'What do we have to do to get the business?'

Again, he will try and chisel more than he hopes to get if he is tough. If he is not tough, then he will tell you straight. But – whatever he says – even if you are willing to sell at his price, you must react by shaking your head slowly. You just infer that this will not be possible. Don't hurry it. You've got plenty of time. You can always find a way of meeting his demands later. Meanwhile, you may find he is willing to come up to you a bit. You will find out if he is bluffing.

But if you agree too early, he will think he has not tried hard enough and next time will force the price lower still. And, being in the business of selling, we always like to deliver more than we promised. So here is a free bonus question to add to the other nine we promised. Politely ask your prospects, 'Do you always buy the lowest price or do you buy the best value for money?' It never fails to unsettle them.

ACTION POINT IDEAS

1   Develop a little process for your price negotiations. Tighten it up. You should record every meeting when you had to make a price concession, and work out how you could have got more. Think of specific things to say, phrases to use. Practise it. Rehearse it. And

use it often. Your prices will go up I promise you. No one can do it for you. You have to work on it yourself.

2   Watch your timing carefully. Don't let price come into it early. Play around with it until you get close to the deadline. You must find out about his deadline and that becomes the time when you go firm.

3   Find out what he likes about your proposition. Just ask him. Ask him to criticize it, tell you what's wrong, what he would like to see improved. If you have done a good job then you can be firmer on price. But always remember he is likely to be a game player. He'll be saving a bit of pressure for the end.

4   Don't get caught out by the unexpected. Sometimes the buyer will just jump you. He will get you off your guard. He will suddenly attack or threaten. Always be prepared for the unexpected.

5   The most important thing in price debating is to have confidence. Be proud of the fact your price is higher than competition because your product and service is better in some way. Competitive knowledge will give you confidence. Remember you win deals on competitive quality, seldom on price. So whatever quality edge you are going to sell him on – make sure it is one he wants.

YOUR MIND MAP

YOUR ACTION PLAN

Dream up some questions which will put pressure back on the buyers
when it comes to price. Don't be nasty when you do it. Ask them what
they think of your product. Ask them if they are looking only for the
lowest price. Ask them what their budget is. Ask them to show you in
detail the competitive quote they are talking about. Ask them when the
decision will be taken. Look them straight in the eye and watch their
reactions – (an easy manner will help you). These are all difficult
questions for them and you will level off the price pressure if you ask
them. Make a list of good questions here.

DEBATING THE PRICE: YOUR SELF-ASSESSMENT

	Nearly always	Some-times	Rarely
Be absolutely honest:	_____	_____	_____
You are nervous of the moment when price is raised as an issue	_____	_____	_____
You have a really good routine worked out for handling buyers' price pressure	_____	_____	_____
Self-control is your strong point, even in the toughest situations	_____	_____	_____
You give in on the price, or on extras, or giveaways quite often	_____	_____	_____
You suggest that you can lower the price to him, sometimes by mistake	_____	_____	_____
You can beat all the other sales people in your team when it comes to price arguments	_____	_____	_____

Think about this: are you telling yourself that you can improve somewhere or is what you do really and truly good, say, nine times out of ten. (Nobody is expecting you to be brilliant all the time.)

Part Four

Ten Sales Management Tactics

22

Gung-ho sales management

●

> Spot the company wreckers amongst your
> sales managers – This chapter highlights the
> problems of an over-confident, over-zealous
> sales management team.

Q.1 *You have just been appointed as general sales manager.*
Your initial action is:

(a) Walk the job quietly, talk to people high and low, think
and plan before taking action.
(b) Set up a sales conference to announce your action.
(c) Read the market figures, study competition, talk with
customers, analyse sales data.
(d) Can't answer the question at this stage.

Q.2 *Your new product is a sure-fire winner, you believe. It will*
lift the company's sales and profits enormously. How will
you launch it?

(a) Big blast advertising campaign, public relations
launch, motivational sales campaign.
(b) Careful test market, waiting for results.
(c) Mixture of several kinds of approach for the first period
to find out which works best.
(d) See the biggest customers about it first.

Q.3 *What is your attitude to personal publicity?*

(a) Useful if targeted against specific goals.
(b) Any publicity is good publicity.
(c) Keep your head down low.
(d) Better that you promote the publicity of your key
people.

ANSWERS

Q.1 (a) 4 points — I've given you four points, but it's a bit cool and level headed. Where is the sparkle? (OK, OK, don't blame me, I've given you four points, haven't I?)

(b) 1 point — Gung ho, lad. If you get fed up leading sales conferences, try the Royal Shakespeare Theatre Company at Stratford.

(c) 3 points — Blimey. You cerebral thing you.

(d) 5 points — Think about it. How the devil do you know what you are going to do without having an idea of the problem? (All right, so it's a cop-out answer. But I honestly don't think there is one style which will suit all occasions, that's why I'm copping out.)

Q.2 (a) 1 point — You might not score many marks from me, but you'll feel good. For the first few weeks, anyway.

(b) 5 points — Goodness knows how many new products I've put on the market over all these years, and I still cannot be sure about them before they start selling. The older I get the more I want to test things out first.

(c) 5 points — Sometimes it is very difficult to set up a proper test. But you can have full marks for trying out several approaches at the same time. I want to test the marketing and selling methods as much as the product itself.

(d) 4 points — Yes, in some fields, I will accept that the reaction of the biggest customers to the new idea may be the most critical element in the process.

Q.3 (a) 5 points — Sure, it can be. So long as you always remember who wrote the copy in the first place.

(b) 2 points — Up to a point it may be true. Well, up to two points actually.

(c) 4 points Depends upon the field of activity you have chosen.

(d) 3 points I really want to have a good reason first from you. Highly publicized staff often become well-known competitors sooner or later.

SCORES

13–15 points Very good. High scores are easy to get here.

10–12 points All right, we won't argue about it. It is a value judgement area, and your view is as good as mine.

Up to 9 points Let's just say we disagree about style.

● ● ●

Here's a three year career plan for a Super Sales Megastar.

YEAR ONE

1   He searches for a top sales-management job in a growth market. Makes a presentation to the board on the subject of going for market share growth. Uses data to support the argument that market leaders make more money than anyone else. Lands the job. Hires a top-flight PR outfit for a marketing communications assignment of which personal publicity forms a major part. Sends out a press release about his appointment. (*Note*: Megastar's opposite number is Unsung Profitmaker. He knows that market leadership does provide more profit than anything else – only just – but the cost of getting there may be horrendous.)

2   Megastar hires a lot more salesmen. Tracks down the high-flyers in other companies, pays them to join him complete with their customer lists if possible. He doubles or trebles the sales force size. He goes for big presentations to big accounts. He runs competitions: 'Sales are the name of the game'. Pays rewards for new customers. Rings salesmen every day for their figures. Rings them at home. Runs sales meetings at weekends. (*Note*: Unsung Profitmaker knows that the new recruits who bring their old customers with them when they arrive are the people who'll take them away when they leave. He carefully calculates the cost and returns he gets from his salesmen, analyses the markets carefully, and puts new salesmen on after careful training and supervision, just one at a time. He's boring, reckons Megastar.)

3   Super Sales Megastar then pays his sales force a hefty commission rate on sales turnover. He really whacks the figures up high for very high returns. This will secure their devotion to the job, particularly if the lowest producers are fired. (*Note*: Old Unsung pays out his commissions on the basis of the gross profits earned by the salesmen – not on turnover. He reckons that profits are the name of the game, not sales. He's wall-to-wall boring, says Megastar.)

4   Megastar's sales go up beyond forecast. Production runs out of supply. Megastar sends out press stories about the sales successes, uses the evidence of production shortage to 'prove' how successful he has been. Also, the production shortage can now be blamed for the very poor profits being earned. (*Note*: Unsung ties in his sales plan with production. Real rigor mortis, he is. He even talks to production people sometimes.)

YEAR TWO

5   Now Megastar has got extra production, he must shift it. He gets a big burst of life from heavy advertising. This gives the whole sales force a great lift and produces many new enquiries which will have the sales force charging round all over the place chasing up tiny prospects. (*Note*: Unsung is not into this game. Megastar has left him for dead.)

6   Later in the year, Megastar gives the sales force the freedom to discount if they have to. Megastar does not put heavy constraints on this otherwise the salesmen will be de-motivated. Nothing should stop them from their purpose in life, which is to give the company's money away to buyers.

7   The company runs out of product again. Megastar now sends out more press releases, plus radio interviews and personal features about his success. He has new personal photographs prepared and tries to get into the City pages. He is now thinking of his new job. Production are again blamed for the financial losses but he is himself getting serious opposition at board meetings.

YEAR THREE

8   Megastar has one shot left in his locker. The prices of the competition have come down now because of the discounting. So Megastar launches his final throw. Called 'Match the Competition', it is an attempt to win business, any business, away from competition at any price.

9   Finally the company cannot stand it. They pay Megastar whatever it takes to get rid of him – the first £25 000 is tax-free. On the back of

his self-publicity some loons in other companies will hire him for their dash to growth, and the cycle will start all over again. And if you think I'm being unduly cynical, let me list here the occasions which I can call to mind in the next five minutes where exactly this process has occurred.

- *Chickens*: one chap went on to do two other companies in different industries in the same way.
- *Consumer goods*: three big, very big, pay-offs from different companies. (Salesmen in one of them went around the accounts after a computer program had been installed asking customers if they owed the company any money!)
- *Videos*: small company story. Chap had heart attack.
- *Men's clothing*: company went into receivership.
- *Transportation*: Paints. Home computers (enough said).
- *Cheap airlines*: (Definitely enough said).

ACTION POINT IDEAS

1   Think about the people you employ. How effective are their styles? There is room for many different styles of management, but is their style appropriate for the job they do? Have you got studied, measured calm where you should have attack? Have you got too much personality projection where you should have analysis, and controlled delegation?

2   How *thorough* are your sales managers when they recruit, train and supervise new staff? Do they nurse them in quite carefully, or have you a 'sink or swim' attitude in your team?

3   In a company life-cycle, and in a product life-cycle, there are a number of distinct phases. Before we start, we need fairly careful research and testing, looking at various approaches. Once that is out of the way, we need full scale launch and commitment with all our guns blazing. We need cash for this stage because it is very expensive. Then we need a period of profit consolidation. Trim out the waste, make the money; then blast off again with sales drive. This process will crash out the market share for us without destroying the company. Work out which products and services are at which stage of this cycle. *Question*: have you got too much consolidation, too much control, not enough sparkle? Or are you all drive and energy and little profit?

4   Think of the role which personal publicity and public relations can play. It is a very powerful tool if directed at specific targets. These need to be marketing and sales targets. What press publicity do

you receive and do your customers see it? If it's just for massaging the ego, then that is ludicrous. But if it is for putting across the company and product message, then that is a laudable objective. How are you going to improve the publicity?

YOUR MIND MAP

YOUR ACTION PLAN

The balance which you need between the spectacular drive and the careful control. Have you got it right? Where do you need to apply more of one and less of another?

THE VOLUMITIS TEST

Are you in any danger of catching the volumitis disease? This table will show if you are in the risk area.

Record how far you agree with each statement. Be sincere.	Total dis-agreement	Neither agree nor disagree	Total agreement
When the chips are down, sales are the name of the game in most businesses	1 2 3	4 5	6 7
You must hit the competition hard, very hard, so they cannot fight back	1 2 3	4 5	6 7
The market place is all about winning, and winners	1 2 3	4 5	6 7
It's stupid to lose a big order on which you can make money just because you will not give way on price	1 2 3	4 5	6 7
Paying the sales force a big commission on their sales results is the best way to get them properly motivated	1 2 3	4 5	6 7

Add up your scores. 20 is a borderline case. Above this score I should get a check up. Above 26 book into a health farm, keep reading the *Daily Telegraph* job advertisements.
19 or less. Clean bill of health.

23

Recruit more McEnroes

●

> Recruiting sales staff – You will never do
> better than the quality of your sales team will
> allow. You *must* get the right people to start
> with.

Q.1 *A salesman has just left one of your key territories. He was looking after important key accounts. How do you recruit another?*

(a) By advertising quickly in the local paper.

(b) By telling the area manager to get on with recruiting quickly, sending the shortlist candidates to you.

(c) By asking around the headhunters and job agencies.

(d) By getting someone to look after the territory from your organization while you sort it out.

Q.2 *You had few replies to your first ad. You have increased your budget so you now have many replies, but all the shortlist candidates were fairly poor. There was one candidate who seemed a bit better than the others. The territory has been uncovered for a long time, and your temporary man in there must return home. What do you do?*

(a) Turn them all down and start again, all over.

(b) Take the best candidate on trial to see if he works out well.

(c) Look around for an internal candidate for promotion to the job.

(d) Leave the decision to the area manager.

Q.3 *What attributes do you look for in a candidate?*

(a) Smart, well turned out.

(b) Wife, two children, mortgage commitments.

(c) Ex Jehovah's Witness.
(d) Pushy.

ANSWERS

Q.1   (a), (b), (c)   Recruitment needs care and attention.
        3 points each   Our nature is to make quick decisions;
                         we are urgent people. But the first three
        5 points   options, which I would be inclined to do
                         too, are not as good as the (d) option.
When recruiting, you need to buy
yourself time. The haste toward a quick
decision rather than the right decision
can cripple the quality of the sales force.

Q.2   (a)   5 points   Yes it's tedious but it *must* be done.
        (b)   3 points   If you take this chap the danger is not
that he is going to be no good. You will
probably fire him if he is no good. The
danger is that his performance will be
very ordinary. It is compromises like this
which get you an ordinary sales force.
And an ordinary sales force is not good
enough.
        (c)   3 points   Should have done it before.
        (d)   2 points   Cop out.

Q.3   (a)   4 points   If he does not look good when selling
himself, how will he look when he sells
for you?
        (b)   3 points   The hungry salesmen make the best
salesmen, uh? You want to drive people
by fear? I know a lot of people with
commitments up to their eyeballs and
they'd never sell a lifeboat to a
drowning man.
        (c)   5 points   Funnily enough, I'm fairly serious. Once
had a client telephone to ask me where I
could get him five Jehovah's Witnesses.
He had recruited one who produced
marvellous results for him and wanted

more. Not afraid of rejection, and very persistent, you see.

(d) 3 points   Obvious pushiness can't be good. But quiet persistence seems pretty good to me.

SCORES

12–15 points   We could all disagree together about this. It depends very much upon the nature of your selling operation and the work they have to do.

8–11 points   So we disagree. You are probably right in your particular field. I'm not going to argue.

Up to 7 points   I'm going to argue.

●   ●   ●

For about one million minutes of his life, John McEnroe has thought about tennis. He has spent about 100 000 minutes or so playing matches and winning the vast majority of them. The number of minutes the man spent losing matches isn't worth calculating.

Being rather longer in the tooth than John the Intense, I can claim to have spent rather more minutes in thinking about a subject I love. The subject is sales. How to get them. How to get more of them. How to get more profitable ones. I reckon to have spent just over three million minutes, one way or another, in thinking about sales.

Not all of it has been intense. There has been the occasional cup of coffee and social chit-chat. The first million or so minutes were spent in thinking how my clients could get more sales – I worked in some fairly slick advertising agencies, working with copywriters who dreamed up immortal slogans such as: 'Veet hair removing cream. Remember, even in winter it's always summer under your arms.' (I kid you not. It sold tons of the stuff.)

The second million or so of my minutes were spent in thinking of how my own sales could go up and up and up. Since I moved to work in marketing and selling on the clients' side, I developed a vital interest in my own sales graph and the sales graphs of others. We noticed a strange phenomenon at the time. This was that some salesmen always seem to outsell others. And it was always difficult to say why the same people always sold more.

SKILL ISN'T ENOUGH

The latest million minutes or so have been spent in examining this phenomenon at close quarters. I am concerned in the training of such people and I tell you it is a fascinating business. You would expect that a person would have some fairly firm views after three million minutes of thinking about a subject.

You would expect that with that experience a person should be able to walk into a roomful of sales people and spot the star immediately. Well, some people might be able to, but I can't. Perhaps there should be some clue in the stars' selling skill level? Well, apart from the fact that stars are generally very knowledgeable on their subject and they get their customers to rely upon them a lot, I must tell you that a lot of sales people I know are very skilful and they don't achieve stardom. Are stars more tough, arrogant, pushy, then? Yes, some are. But just as many are not, perhaps more.

Does all this matter, you might ask? Well, three million minutes of thinking about sales and things to do with sales have convinced me of one thing above all others. I am not half as firm in my views about selling as I was when I had not thought about it so much. But on one subject my views have become a lot harder: if you want better sales, then you must, must, must recruit the potential stars to start with.

Now you see the relevance of the problem. The difficulty is that you can't easily spot the best people in the crowd. They look, sound, talk and behave like normal people. However, there is one little thread which runs through them all. All the stars, all the winners, from John McEnroe downwards, share one thing in common. They all want results badly. They are all high achievers. And the top ones want it more than most.

Think about it for a minute. Is it just the money alone which drives John McEnroe? Unless you are devoted to cynicism you would probably admit that the laddie still went on playing, making come-back after come-back long after he had as much money as he was able to use sensibly for the rest of his life. But he still went on, and on, and on. Why? Because he could not bear to lose. He wanted to see how far he could go. He was devoted to success for its own sake.

THEY WANT RESULTS BADLY

Now I have noticed this in stars. They want results badly. Perhaps you can notice this in yourself. Why are you the boss when most people are not? Does it happen by accident? Did someone place you there in that comfortable slot and do you now say, 'Good, now I can take it easy'. I bet you say no to that. I would even believe you if you said that now you are the boss you work even harder.

Are you a high achiever, too? Do you buy this book because you, too, want results badly and it is this hunger which has got you into the position you are in now? I'll take a bet that a very high proportion of the readers are in this category. So my advice is to look at your recruiting policy for salespeople. It's nice to have degree-level qualifications but not if they are attached to a personality which is merely theoretical and reflective. Give me the active pragmatist with drive every time.

There is one other thing about winners. They train hard. They get a lot of coaching. The higher up they go, the more they get trained. John McEnroe might have spent 100 000 minutes playing matches. But behind all that there was another 400 000 minutes he spent in training. Everyone needs training. Stars and dumbheads alike – all can improve. To look at him you would never think that John McEnroe enjoys his tennis. Don't you believe it. He enjoys winning. It's when he faces the possibility of playing badly – that's when he gets angry.

SEVEN WAYS TO GET A TERRIBLE SALES FORCE

Ask yourself, if you had a sales force who were all as good as your best sales executive, how much could you get in extra sales? If your best salesman outsells the average by 20 per cent – and that is a conservative figure for many companies – then that is up to 20 per cent extra sales you could get for your company as a whole if you could recruit only those with star potential. That shows you how important it is to choose the right people to start with.

Now ask yourself again, if all your salespeople were as bad as the worst, how much would you lose in sales volume? You could easily lose enough to put yourself out of business, couldn't you? That's the price you pay for recruiting badly. To get a good sales team, you must train them. You must motivate them. You must control them. You must inspire them. But you will never, never, never do better than the quality of people you recruit will allow you to do. All of these things work well, when you have good people to start with.

I've been recruiting people for years, and the years have taught me that there are people who are much better at it than I am. So, these days I get specialists in my management team to do the interviewing and to make recommendations to me. Sure, I'll see the candidates and talk with them, but for the past three years I have always accepted my team's recommendation even when I might not agree with it. And our appointments in this time have all been good.

Rushing it kills your sales force quality

So what goes wrong? The first and most important thing is not to rush the decision just because you have a space to fill. I used to work with a production director in a large food company who thought nothing of interviewing lists of candidates, turning them all down and advertising again if he had not found the right person.

It used to send us potty, working with him, because projects would be held up, developments put on ice, delays caused all along the line because he had not got his executive in place. But, I tell you, when he got his man, it was worth waiting for. My friend was a pretty grim production director, but later he became a superb vice-president of personnel for a multinational organization based in New York. Me? I'll take the best of the bunch and hope he or she turns out OK. If you think that's stupid, you're right. But that doesn't stop me doing it when left to myself.

No preparation, that's a killer

This is not my problem, but I have seen others make the mistake. There may be no job specification, the application form has gone adrift or hasn't been read, there are constant interruptions to the discussion – and all of this recruits us a bad sales force, especially if there are no plans for the job and no profile of the qualities we are looking for in the candidate. We draw five-point scales on four or five key factors we want in the candidate including experience and personality factors, and this device works well for us.

Frighten them, and they'll clam up

Some sales managers intimidate the candidates. They don't look up, they go on writing. They bark out questions and pick on answers. If they walk behind the candidate and snap a sudden question at him just when he has a mouthful of the biscuit they've just given him, they are not going to get a lot of sense out of him. I know he has to stand up to pressure in the field, but they are going to deter the best candidates from joining. They'll only get the ones who are prepared to be sub-servient, or the ones who can't get a job with a company which has a sensible boss.

Help them too much and they'll roll over you

But the opposite is true as well. Some interviewers try to help the candidate too much. They nod their heads, agree with every statement, finish off candidates' sentences for them and sell them the job. It is very common to find that the interviewer spends all his time trying to persuade the candidate to join. Now you may want to do that with the right candidate, but not with every one.

Don't throw in red herrings

Some interviewers are too discursive. They wander off the point and discuss irrelevancies. They tell personal anecdotes. This makes the candidate wonder if he should join in with the reminiscences, so both of them spend a happy hour talking about the time they spent in Hong Kong, or camping in the Ardennes, or some other nonsense. It's a good way of making friends, but not of recruiting key executives. You might need to probe their background for evidence of qualities which could be useful in the job you have to offer, and to see if they display useful attributes in their private life, but that's all.

Boasting will damage recruits

Some interviewers tell of their own success. They dress up their own achievements, they boast about the company, they show what wonderful individuals they are. No good salesman with an ego of his own is going to have much respect for a boss who is clearly going to take personal credit for all the team's successes. You must, of course, sell them the company, the job and yourself if you want them to join. But going over the top is no way to do it.

Good listeners get good people

Not listening is one of the critical signs of a bad interviewer. Selecting only the bits you want to hear without listening to the whole story is a sure way of recruiting the wrong people. The candidate must be watched, too. The really skilled interviewer watches for the fudged answer, he looks for the element of discomfort and probes gently and skilfully. If there is a weakness, he will find it – but he must listen and observe all the time.

ACTION POINT IDEAS

1 For sales people, give them a psychometrics test to start with. Give them *your* company application form to fill in. Both of these tell you a lot about a candidate before you ever see him. Having to write out an application just for you, giving reasons for wanting the job, can be very revealing. It also eliminates many time wasters who will not bother.

2 At shortlist stage, run a group discussion. Take a morning. Put three of you on a panel, bring in all the five candidates together. Tell them to talk about anything they want for the first five minutes. Then give them a subject to talk about related to the industry, or related to selling practice. Then give them a mildly ethical problem to discuss. Watch and observe, the jurors should not join in at all. You'll pick out the leaders, the thick ones, the compromisers, the ones who do not shine.

3 Then bring them back in to see you, the panel, one by one. Ask them how they enjoyed it. Ask them if they were you, who would they pick out of the group as the best candidate. Then ask them why you should pick them as against the best candidate they have nominated. Prepare any other questions for them. If you do the first three things, you will get very revealing results – your opinions will change, I promise. It's fair – they are salesmen aren't they? And the most important product they'll ever have to sell is themselves.

4 Get your candidate to talk with some of your staff, and another manager. Not to be interviewed, but just to see how they relate to others. Collect the views together.

5 Watch them all in their fourth month of employment. That's when they feel they have the job cracked. They know the people by then. They have been trying hard up until that time, watching their step all the way. They start levelling off to their usual habits around month four. Don't let them get sloppy at this time.

YOUR MIND MAP

YOUR ACTION PLAN

TEST YOUR RECRUITMENT PHILOSOPHY

You like recruiting youngsters because you can mould them your way

You need fully trained, experienced people to join you

    1   2   3   4   5

You want hard-driving, ambitious sales people, with energy

You want thoroughness, care, technical ability, and service

    1   2   3   4   5

You set detailed personal sales goals, and use strong control methods

Your sales people act more like advisers and consultants

    1   2   3   4   5

You want 10 per cent to leave every year so you can promote others and keep your sales force fresh

You like people to establish strong connections in their areas and maintain stability

    1   2   3   4   5

You want McEnroes

You want Billy Grahams

    1   2   3   4   5

You pay a high commissionable element

You pay straight salaries

    1   2   3   4   5

One person makes the decision to employ

A group advises on the decision to employ

    1   2   3   4   5

Comment

It is common to find a reasonable consistency in the profile. All the scores tend to be mostly high, or mostly low. If you have got an erratic profile with scores swinging from one side to the other, I wonder if you have thought through the sales task properly, and what you are trying to achieve. Has this been translated into a type of person you need? Of course it *is* true that we need a mixture of different qualities at different levels of management and in different jobs but it is less true when everyone is doing roughly the same job.

Extreme profiles (mostly 1s and 5s) are a little dangerous. There may be tunnel vision at work? (Maybe not. Don't be offended. It's just worth a question mark.)

24

The abominable no men

●

Selling to the decision makers – Buyers tell
salesmen deals are lost on quality, or price
factors. But most *makeable* deals are lost
because there is an abominable no man
behind the scenes. And he is a powerful
animal.

Q.1 *You, the salesman, are rarely there, at the meeting, when
the sale is made. How true is this, for most salesmen?*

(a) Very true.
(b) Quite true.
(c) Not true in general.
(e) Not at all true.

Q.2 *The best champion for your product behind the scenes if
you can convince him is the customer's*

(a) Managing director.
(b) The technical manager or head of the section which
will be concerned with using the product.
(c) The buyer, purchasing officer.
(d) Champions vary.

Q.3 *To find out the decision making unit in your prospect's
company, you should*

(a) Ask the buyer if he makes the decision.
(b) Ask the buyer who makes the decision.
(c) Ask everyone who makes the decision.
(d) Ask the managing director's secretary who makes the
decision.

ANSWERS

Q.1 Catch question. First it applies 'for most salesmen', not necessarily you, yourself. Second it requires you to calculate the truth about a negative. 'You are rarely there . . .

(a)	5 points	Most buying decisions are taken behind the scenes between
(b)	4 points	various people. They make the decision and leave it to
(c)	3 points	the buyer to negotiate. So the buyer often negotiaties the
(d)	2 points	price and terms even when he has a mandate to buy. Only he is not going to let the salesman know that. So when the decision is actually taken, earlier on, subject to final clarification, the salesman is rarely present.

Q.2

(a)	3 points	All of them are important sometimes. But the truth is that
(b)	5 points	Champions vary depending upon the company structure and the
(c)	3 points	type of product you are selling. But you want to make your
(d)	5 points	pitch to the senior person whose section would be most affected by using the product. The decision-making group in most companies will definitely listen to them. Try selling a word processor or fancy typewriter to the managing director – he'll pass it pretty sharpish to his secretary for evaluation. In front of you, or when your back is turned. And he will not go against her view.

Q.3

(a)	2 points	He'll say he does.
(b)	1 point	He will say he does and be offended with you.
(c)	4 points	Provided you do it with skill, a lightness of touch and with care, why not? Well, not everyone – just most people you meet.

(d)   4 points   She knows. Get on with her and she will
                         mark your card for you. Why is there no
                         award of 5 points for the best answer.
                         Because the best answer was not
                         included. It is dull and boring. The
                         correct answer is – it depends. But if we
                         put that, then you would all get it right.
                         And you've been scoring too high
                         recently anyway.

SCORES

12–14 points   Clever dick.
6–11 points   Not quite so clever dick.
Up to 5 points   Dick.

●   ●   ●

Don't show this to your salesmen if you want a quiet life. If you do, they'll argue like fury. They'll tell you I don't know what I'm talking about. Or they'll say that your business is different from everyone else's. They'll say they know their customers best and I don't understand. The best arguments always come out of the sales force when they are explaining to the boss why the sale was lost.

When a sale is lost, then nine times out of ten they'll say it's because the price is too high, or because the quality is not good enough. And they will continue to believe either or both of these things until the cows come home. Why do they believe this so rigidly? Because it is what the buyers tell them. And – this much is true – these are the things the buyers tell them when they lose a piece of business.

So why do they really lose business? Research evidence shows that 60 per cent of the business which could be landed but is lost, is because someone behind the scenes swung it to another supplier. In other words, when the decision came down to the last two or three shortlisted suppliers, someone, usually the boss, but sometimes a technical manager, made the final choice in favour of a supplier he knew and he swung the decision.

Now in this circumstance the buyer is not going to say 'I thought your proposition was the best but someone overruled me.' He has got his ego to protect. And a statement like this will make your salesman go scurrying off after the Powerful One next time, instead of the buyer. No, he's going to fob you off with an excuse. He's going to tell your salesman that a competitor put in a better price. Or a competitor's quality was better for their purpose. So, back at the ranch, your salesman reports what he has been told, that you lost the deal on price or quality.

MAKEABLE DEALS LOST

But it may well not be so. On most occasions you lost makeable deals – notice the important qualification – because your salesman failed to see and certainly failed to convince someone powerful behind the scenes. Rarely does a salesman come back to you to report that the deal was lost because he was seeing the wrong person! Remember, he has an ego to protect as well. It is easier for him to believe that the price is too high rather than there is a deficiency in his technique. That makes it your fault rather than his.

I say that some salesmen do not research behind the scenes thoroughly enough to find out how decisions are made before making their sales pitch. Far too many think that the buyer's job is to buy and that if they convince him enough they have done the job. And this is patently not so. For salesmen, here is a simple way around the problem to start with. Don't say to the buyer, 'Do you make the decision?' The buyer is going to say he does. Don't say to the buyer, 'Does the managing director make the decision?' Because the buyer will be offended.

Instead, get around the problem by asking, 'Who, apart from yourself, will be involved in the decision to buy?' This will crack the issue, if you ask the question early on in the discussion. And then go on to ask the same question of all the other people you meet when you see them, senior and junior. This will flush out all the names of the people involved in the decision-making and will establish their pecking order.

REACHING THE YES LEVEL

The salesman must then find time to speak to those decision-influencers. There is no point in him calling upon the many people who only have the power to say 'no'. He must, must, must get to the 'yes' level. For the salesman, the way around the problem is to get the approach right to start with. Make the initial contact high up in the customer's organization somehow or other. You can do it by telephoning them first to ask their advice. Don't try and sell things to senior people because they will turn you over to their buyer. But ask for their advice and you are home and dry, because they love giving advice.

Ask them how they think your important message should be made to their company, who to approach initially and who afterwards, and how do they think you could get all their people together. At the end, ask them if they would like to be kept informed of your progress on this very important issue which affects their responsibility. Many of them will say yes to this, and ask you to keep them copied.

You can now contact the people they have named and can quote your powerful person as a reference if you want to. Do it gently to avoid causing offence. You are also free to go back upstairs to them if you run into difficulties with their juniors. Why? Because they have asked to be kept informed. Don't forget that there are several stages in their buying procedures which will mean different people being involved. Initially they use a screening process of possible suppliers so your first objective must be to get on to the shortlist. Who is responsible for the screening, and for the searching of potential suppliers? Later, there will be technical evaluation, and different people become involved here. After this there will be financial considerations and again different people may be involved. Price and quality may be critical considerations, but they are not the only ones. People are just as important. Reaching the right people will gain you a number of deals.

ACTION POINT IDEAS

1   Analyse a sample of your most recent new major accounts. Draw a chart showing who was the influencer at each stage. Identify the following people:

- The initiator of the enquiry.
- The influencers.
- The users.
- The purchaser or negotiator.
- The deciders.

Look at the job function of each person; and their level of authority. You now have a pattern of your decision-making unit and can plan your sales and advertising accordingly.

2   Find out if your sales force is tempted to call initially upon the easy person to contact or the most obvious person (such as the purchasing officer). Have a general discussion with them at a meeting. Now find out if your top producing salespeople – including yourself, are doing it a different way perhaps and trying to approach the account through different people.

We have evidence drawn from our own business that both of these analyses (1) and (2) are very revealing and they show us that our competitors are often approaching prospects through the wrong people.

3 Once you have selected your key influencer then you may find that their reaction to your proposition falls into one of four different categories. Their answer may be: no; don't care; maybe; yes.

Even if their answer is 'yes' to you, it does not guarantee the deal because there are others with an opinion behind the scene. If their answer is likely to be either 'no' or 'don't care' then you should ask their permission to do a survey, or get information from others. Then you should go searching for a suitable 'champion'. This person, who may not necessarily be the boss but who must be quite powerful in their organization, will be the one to get your proposition through. You need the champion to say 'yes' or at least 'maybe'.

4 See if you can get everyone on your side, particularly the users. And, in your major existing accounts, make sure they stay on your side.

5 Give your 'champion' all the sales aids he needs to carry your case through his colleagues. Not just literature, give him a survey report, an analysis of his needs, a summary of your benefits, a copy of the meeting report. He is going to sell your deal for you. Make it easy for him.

YOUR MIND MAP

YOUR ACTION PLAN

How do your customers make decisions? What can you do to help your salesmen get to the right people?

IDENTIFYING THE POWERFUL PERSON IN YOUR CUSTOMER'S DECISION-MAKING GROUP

How far do you agree/disagree with the following statements

	Total agreement	Sometimes right sometimes wrong		Total dis-agreement	
Power is the personal ability to cause other people to alter their behaviour	1	2	3	4	5
Power is not the function of a position or a title. Its true source is the action of other people towards it	1	2	3	4	5
Other people are inconvenienced more than the powerful person	1	2	3	4	5
Power is not static, but it must be sought, defended, and increased	1	2	3	4	5
Powerful people tend to be authoritarian, less-powerful people more persuasive	1	2	3	4	5
Powerful people do not necessarily need the goodwill of others, they can risk being disliked	1	2	3	4	5

The more you agree, the more you understand power. Look for these signs of power within your customer's organization.

25

Inner salesman deprivation

•

> Giving your sales force firepower – This
> chapter is about providing the sales force
> with sufficient help and authority for their
> claims. Relying on the salesman's quick wits,
> word of mouth, and technical knowledge to
> win sales is nowhere good enough

Q.1 *After a customer meeting you should:*

(a) Provide him and yourself with a copy of the meeting report.
(b) Send him a letter thanking him for his attention.
(c) Come back to him when you have something new to say.
(d) Send him some new literature.

Q.2 *What is the highest source of credibility for a salesman's claim?*

(a) A government statement to parliament.
(b) The salesman's personal word.
(c) Research from a university department.
(d) Confirmation from the salesman's competitors.

Q.3 *Clarity in writing. Which of the following factors are used by journalists writing for popular newspapers so their stories can be read easily and quickly by the great unwashed.*

(a) Short sentences.
(b) The use of words of few syllables.
(c) The use of personal pronouns, personal names.
(d) Repetition.

ANSWERS

Q.1 (a) 5 points — It may be tedious, but it takes only a few seconds to dictate in the car after the meeting. You should send the customer a copy of your meeting report. Remember, the secretary of the committee who takes the minutes, also controls the shape of the decisions.

(b) 2 points — A kindly thought. Heavily into meaningful social interaction, are you?

(c) 2 points — Can't argue with it. It is just not enough.

(d) 2 points — Boring. What can your literature do which you could not? Your literature can't listen to him or his problems, it cannot put him right where he goes wrong, it cannot construct a presentation around his needs.

Q.2 (a) −5 points — No comment. (Actually, to be taken seriously, it is a very good authority. Don't take any notice of my cynicism about governments. Still, give yourself minus five points.)

(b) 3 points — It needs more backing. By itself it is weak.

(c) 4 points — This one is really worth five but you must also think about the (d) option which is worth the maximum.

(d) 5 points — Some competitors actually do recommend their rivals and it is powerfully credible. Think of all those computer clones which claimed to be IBM-compatible. How about the standing that gave to IBM?

Q.3 Catch question. You can get full points for all the first three answers. Popular paper journalists do all these three things.

(a) 5 points — Right.

(b) 5 points — Right again.

(c) 5 points — Right again.

(d) 2 points — No, by and large they do not use this as a technique for clarity, only for emphasis.

● ● ●

This is a story for stout hearts and strong stomachs. It's not one to read tucked up with your Ovaltine at bedtime. It shows how I lost £100 000 of my own money in twenty seconds.

You see now why you need to have a stiff whisky beside you as you read. It is about a personal loss – not a loss of company money. Good heavens, if it was simply about some company decision that went wrong, then I wouldn't be too worried about it. In business 80/80 is what we aim for: we try to get 80 per cent of our decisions 80 per cent right. I reckon that if you aim to run a mistake-free business then you will not get any innovation. You can't learn without making mistakes.

But back to this one hundred grand of my own cash which went adrift. It all came about because I couldn't entirely understand what a salesman was telling me. If I had heard him emphasize the crucial bits I might be £100 000 better off now. I did not credit his word with having sufficient clout. This chap makes an appointment to come and see me about starting a pension fund in my company a few years back. He was a really nice chap. He was very knowledgeable and very helpful. At that time what I knew about pensions you could write on the edge of a buyer's official order form. He told me something about being taxed at my highest rate of marginal tax, and that I would get relief on this. Since I was not bursting with tension at the time, relief was not a big selling point.

In the sales presentation he mentioned that the money would be paid into a fund and that the fund would not be taxed either. Again, this did not leave me on the edge of my chair with excitement. I didn't even understand it – then. He explained that his company was one of the best in the business and showed me a complicated table of all the companies in the business with his own company stuck in the middle and said 'You see what a record we have'.

Well, to be honest, I was not really grabbing what he said. His company should have been at the top of the list and there it was in the middle. He took the table away with him and it was only four years later that I realized that the table must have shown the companies in alphabetical order. I gave the business to someone else I knew. He was a friend and I knew I could trust him and I did not entirely trust all these fancy projections of future benefits I was supposed to earn at retirement age. That decision, which was made in twenty seconds has cost £100 000.

Four years afterwards, when I had made a thorough and complete study of the pensions market, I knew I had let the salesman from the best company go away without the business. I brought him back in the end and we now place a high proportion of our pension money with him. We trust the salesman absolutely and he has never let us down. If

I had done it right at the start, then the final fund at retirement age would be likely to be £100 000 bigger.

EASY FOR YOU, COMPLEX FOR THEM

This is not a story about pensions. This is a story about selling. It is about the importance of clarity in the salesman's story. It's about authority. The vast majority of readers are in technical companies selling quite complex ideas. At least they're not complex to you and your salesmen. But they are complex to your customers. If one of your salesmen asks a customer, 'Do you understand what I am saying?' nine times out of ten the customer will nod his head in agreement, even though he has got perhaps 40 per cent of it wrong. If you don't believe me, then let them try out their sales pitch with a friend. Afterwards, ask the friend to repeat back in his own words what he understands by the product of service. Then they will have a measure of their clarity.

The single biggest problem is being unable to understand the customer's frame of reference, the customer's mental 'map' of the subject. The next biggest problem is the use of technical language and company jargon which is completely meaningless to the customer. This was the problem with the pensions salesman. But it was not his fault. It was the fault of his managers. His managers had not trained him properly, not rehearsed him, not tried him out on customers under proper supervision. The company believed in the dictum that if the product is good enough, then you don't need to train salesmen in selling skills, you just need to give them product knowledge. And that is bunkum, absolute bunkum. The company failed also to provide the salesman with proof evidence of his claims. No proper handouts. No proper charts. No references. The salesman just had to rely on the weakest authority he could muster for his claims, word of mouth.

MAKING YOUR CLAIMS BELIEVABLE

Here are five things to look for to provide your salesman with credible proof of the claims you make. You cannot provide them all, but you should be able to provide some.

1 *The salesman's word*: The weakest in authority is the word of the salesman himself, with no other backing. The claims go in one ear and out the other. If this is all your salesmen can use as clout for their arguments, then at least make sure they can communicate effectively. Don't put technical people on the road without training and no other back-up.

2   *Written confirmation*: Stronger in authority is a written document. Leaflets with technical data are quite good but don't become complacent if this is all you produce. Leaflets are too general in their application. A written letter to the prospect, confirming the claims made, is much better. Better still is a meeting report, being the minutes of the discussion circulated to the customer afterwards. Best of all in this written form is a survey report given to the customer about his problems. Now you are getting some credibility into your selling.

3   *Hard facts and data*: But there are better things yet. Why not give your salesmen memos from your technical department on specific applications to the customer? Give them evidence and data from your quality-control system. Give them charts showing the reliability of your deliveries and despatches. And make them give these to the customers.

4   *Third-party references*: Better still is the use of third-party case histories of successful applications, with or without customer names included. Let the salesmen give out this data to customer prospects and name referee customers whom your prospect can contact. Use press cuttings and articles as hand-outs.

5   *Independent tests*: And if you can get your technical claims checked and tested by an independent body of repute, an institute, a university or laboratory, then you are hammering home a story that no one will disbelieve. Why not set up a special study to test your product? It need not be expensive. And if the study shows that some other company's product is better, then you've made a very, very wise investment. And you'd better get your product better than their's as fast as you can.

It's management's job to give salesmen the backing. To give them the confidence to do the job properly. They are being bashed the whole time by buyers who are constantly telling them that someone else's product is cheaper, that someone else can deliver faster, that someone else offers special facilities. It's an artillery barrage which buyers fire upon your salesmen's confidence. For heaven's sake, give them something to fire back with.

ACTION POINT IDEAS

1   Can you strengthen up the whole of your proposition by putting in some kind of a written survey of the customer's needs – or an overview – or a statement of what the customer is trying to achieve

– or a summary of his position. It will strengthen the credibility of your case, because you will be seen to be responding to his problem properly

2 Get third-party testimonials. Ask past customers for their views of your product, your service. Get a product report back from new customers after they have used it. Get editorial mentions. Have experts in your field comment about your products. Pay specialist concerns to test them. And then use the results thoroughly in your advertising and selling. Give your sales force copies of these items to hand out to customers. Keep mailing them.

3 Work up your competitive edge against your major opposition in the market. Try to measure the difference if you can. Use every possible means of identifying this difference. Then hammer home this edge through an authoritative channel.

4 Use persistence. Don't believe that because you have told him once he has believed it and will remember it. Keep going at the same message all the time. For years if necessary. Sixteen mailshots a year to the same person carrying the same message applied in different ways is not too much if the person is in the target market. Remember, when you get fed up with your promotion and find it boring and old hat, then that's the moment the recipient is beginning to see it for the first time.

YOUR MIND MAP

YOUR ACTION PLAN

Think about your credibility. In what ways can it be reinforced?

TEST YOUR FIREPOWER AND CREDIBILITY WITH NEW CUSTOMERS

Take the last new customer you opened up. Consider the various stages he went through before he decided 'yes' in your favour. For each stage, try to calculate the impact that your various messages might have had upon him, at that time. Just rank them in order of importance at that time. How far did they push the customer along to the next stage of what is called the adoption process?

You may have to mangle this table, change it around in any way to suit your company. Change the headings if you like. Change the stages in the adoption process. The purpose is to separate out the various stages and for you to judge (guess if you like) which are the most important influences at that stage. Now you can think about what and where you can improve.

	Identification of his need	Searching for suppliers	Screening evaluating suppliers	Deciding
Your salesman	————	————	————	————
Your advertising	————	————	————	————
Your reputation with others (word or mouth)	————	————	————	————
Your company literature	————	————	————	————
Previous experience with your company	————	————	————	————

Rank from 1–5 in order of importance in each vertical column.

26

The sale is not made until their money is in your bank

●

> Getting paid for what you do – Customers
> must abide by the terms of business you have
> agreed. Make sure you agree some. This is
> about having trouble with overdue accounts.

Q.1 *Someone owes you money. Assuming you are brave
enough to do it, then your most effective way of getting
paid would be:*

(a) Take them to court for the debt.
(b) Cut off their supplies if they do not pay.
(c) Write to their company chairman at his home address.
(d) Go and stand in their reception until they pay you.

Q.2 *The reason why most companies have long outstanding
debtors who owe them money is because:*

(a) They deal with big companies and big companies
delay payment.
(b) They do not sell them properly in the first place.
(c) Their account collection procedures are routine.
(d) They want future business from their customers.

Q.3 *The best kind of credit risks are:*

(a) Big companies.
(b) Fast-growing companies.
(c) Profitable companies.
(d) Companies where you know the boss well.

ANSWERS

Q.1 (a) 1 point   You may not succeed, and you will probably have big costs to pay. It is a lottery.

    (b) 3 points   But you must have the stronger bargaining power. They must need you in the long run more than you need them.

    (c) 3 points   Why not? But be careful not to run foul of the laws against harassment.

    (d) 5 points   This is the most effective subject in the comment in (c) and subject to your having enough gall. You could get your salespeople to do it. They will not open so many poor credit risk accounts in future.

Q.2 (a) 3 points   Big companies often *do* delay payment, but others pay on time.

    (b) 5 points   This is true. See the text and action point ideas.

    (c) 4 points   This also is true.

    (d) 3 points   It may be true but it is not the main reason.

Q.3 (a) 4 points   But they may delay payment.

    (b) 1 point   No, they might not be profitable, and they will definitely be starved of cash.

    (c) 5 points   Definitely. Look at their profit and loss accounts.

    (d) 2 points   It might help if there is a dispute.

SCORES

12–15 points	Tough one you are. Street wise.
8–11 points	You know the better class streets.
Up to 7 points	What a very nice, trusting, ethical person you are.

●   ●   ●

Crooks, shysters and plain ordinary thieves – there's a few of them around in everyone's market. Some markets have a high incidence of wickedness, and perhaps 10 per cent or more customers will twist you a little if they can.

We bought a graphic design business some years back. Instantly the news was out, a rash of their smaller customers improvised 'complaints' about their work and used this as a reason to refuse payment. The previous owners went away and we were left without evidence – that's part of the price you pay for picking up a business on the cheap. The chap we put in to run the business was so angry with some of the previous customers that he went around and stood on their office doorsteps demanding his money. Most of them paid up without a quibble.

One of them stuck it out though. A local hotel made it clear that it had no intention of paying, even though it acknowledged the existence of the debt. So the design company manager took a party of friends to dinner there one evening, ran up a bill for about £200, paid the £10 balance owing on the account, and said that the bill would be contra'd against the debt. It's not a nice way of doing business. But you get cheats in every world and you have to be ready for them.

There's only one thing that will really help you to handle the cheats – it's called experience. The training course is very long, you suffer some very expensive lessons, but you learn in the end. Nobody setting out in business worries a great deal about constructing his terms of business on day one. Life is too exciting for that. Three big bad debts later – all of which could have been avoided if he had sewn up his contract terms properly – and the fledgling businessman is busy learning how to be the world's best contracts lawyer. As I say, it takes a long time to learn and the training course can be very expensive.

Here are my four basic rules for keeping out of trouble. The first rule is the most important. It is not about credit control, and it is not about the law.

- *Rule 1*: Don't do business with people who don't do nice business. It sounds a bit simple, but honestly, when I look back, I could have spotted two-thirds of the cheats coming, if only I had wanted to read the signs. No, no, here was a new piece of business which sounded exciting and that was all the convincing I needed.

    We owned a public relations company when I started. A new client came along with big launch plans. Paid us promptly the first month, he did. And the second. Then nothing happened. We went for five months building expenditure until the campaign peaked, then crunch, a complete refusal to pay anything at all. He came to our office. 'Look', he said, 'we are very experienced at this kind of thing. If you pursue us, we will counter-claim and proceed against you for our legal costs as well. It's just another case for our lawyers.' Well, I don't know what you would do, but I took the easy way out and wrote it off.

- *Rule 2*: Deal with people who have got money. Don't deal with people who have none. Most people who turn crooked don't do so because they want to. Many of them are forced to because their business is in trouble. If they are short of money, worrying about how to pay the salaries, staying awake at night, they are going to twist and turn out of every commitment they can to stay afloat.
- *Rule 3*: Ensure you do a good job, the customer is happy with it and you can prove it. The other reason that people get into trouble over bad debts is that they bring the trouble on themselves. The work might be sloppy, the service poor. The deal might have been over-sold. An angry customer is going to make life difficult over payments. So in one way, perhaps bad debts are telling us something about our business that we ought to listen to.
- *Rule 4*: Get the terms of business organized properly. Sometimes, just occasionally, you might need to remind an errant customer of the terms he has signed. So, make sure he signs them, or at least sees them.

TWEAKING IN OVERDUE ACCOUNTS

Now this is a different game. In their own way, the people who keep you waiting for your money are cheats, too. After all, you have struck a bargain with them. You have agreed to supply your service in exchange for payment on a date. You do your side of the deal, and then they do not do theirs. I call it cheating – particularly when they rely on the fact that, because you want further business from them, you might not chase it up too hard. I never mess about with that. If they owe money, no matter how big a customer or client it is, I get them chased hard and often.

GETTING BLOOD FROM AN OVERDUE STONE

Tip one

It is important not to let overdue accounts go too long. We give them ten days' grace, followed by another ten. Then the account comes up to senior management for special attention. We use a number of techniques, but the simplest one, which pulls in most, is this. Just write a personal, handwritten letter to the most senior contact in the customer's company. If it is the managing director, so much the better. But he has got to know you, and the letter must not be typed. Explain that you realize that he himself doesn't know of this slow payment problem, but ask him, as a personal favour, to sort it out. It rarely fails, if you know senior people.

Tip two

Sometimes the overdue account is a large organization and you get the run-around between departments. The buyer does not want to know, the accounts department fob you off on a junior. 'The cheque has been sent, haven't you got it yet?' 'We have not received your invoice, send us a copy.' (This after four months of chasing. Oh yeah?) There are many ingenious lies. We were once told that the bought ledger girl had gone on holiday and had taken the keys of the safe with her, so they could not get to the cheque book!

Try this with large companies. Send a fax to the financial director. Don't specify a threat explicitly. Tell them that you cannot stop your board from taking an irreversible decision after the meeting next Thursday unless settlement is cleared through your bank by 15.30 the previous day (or something like that). Notice that the threat is not specific. Note also that the matter goes out of your hands, and that the timetable is very specific. All of this sounds pretty official and serious.

But here is the trick. Do not specify the account, or the invoice number and certainly not the total amount due. When they get the fax they'll have to hunt through their accounts department, and possibly through different sections, to trace your account. That puts them to a lot of work. The boss of the financial section will almost certainly clear the account for payment to save trouble. With big companies it is a very good tactic. Yes, they might get a bit upset at you. But they are the ones at fault. And with luck, they'll put you on a shorter payments list next time, because you cause them too much bother. There are variations on the technique but it is important not to specify a threat, such as going to court.

Tip three

The most important thing of all is to sell them properly in the first place. If your sales force are worried about selling the products in against competition, then they will not want to add to their fear of failure by telling customers explicitly about their terms of business.

Don't mess with that. Once the buyer has bought then the salesman should ask for an introduction to the financial controller, or even an introduction to Nellie in charge of the bought ledger. The salesman should then go and see the finance people and explain the terms. The business will not go away. He will not lose the sale. But he will get his cheques on time if the finance people have agreed.

THE SECRET OF WINNING DISPUTES

If an argument is brewing, and you know there is going to be trouble between you and your customer, you must document your side of the case as soon as it happens. Get people to write down telephone conversations with the other party. Get them to record facts on memos. Get them to take notes of meetings. All of these should be signed, witnessed and dated, then locked away in the file.

When the dispute comes to court – if it gets that far – it will be in nine months' time. They will have forgotten the precise details of what happened. The dispute moves into other people's hands. Their solicitor will decide whether the other party has a good case or not. But you, lucky you, will have everything documented. Even if your people have left, there you are with your facts carefully dated and recorded, and this can be produced in court as evidence. So who will the court believe? You, the party who has got everything carefully documented in your favour? Or your opponent, whose memory is not quite good enough to recall precise dates and circumstances? You win.

ACTION POINT IDEAS

1   Ensure that part of the overall sales department responsibility is to collect overdue accounts. Accounts function should be related to providing the information and running the routine. Then it should come back to sales quickly.

2   Have a meeting with your sales force to explain how you want them to open new accounts. Explain that £1000 written off as a bad debt is probably worth a £10000 or £20000 order. (You write it off against your net profits, that's why.) Teach the salesmen how to call on financial controllers to explain (not to sell!) their terms of business.

3   Don't let computers run your overdue accounts. Give the account a grace period of ten days, then start your procedures. Do it again

in a further three weeks. After that call the customer on the telephone.

4 Don't go to court with bad debts. Go to a credit agency which knows how to put the squeeze on and is experienced at threatening to put in winding up procedures. That usually frightens the life out of overdue accounts.

5 Also use the solicitor which the credit agency uses. Never use a normal solicitor. Only ever use one which specializes in this work and very little else. These people are trained to win. For you.

6 When an important account is overdue then look for little ways to put on some personal pressure. You'll get them more easily by mild embarrassment than by any other way.

7 If you are dealing with a very large company then put them to a great deal of work, and frustration. Go very high up, the company secretary, or the chairman's secretary for example. Don't be worried about it. These blighters are sitting on your money. It is in their bank. Your object is to get it into your bank. For them it is a routine procedure; for you it is near survival. So interrupt their routine procedure. (But be careful about too much harassment. You cannot display a sandwich board outside their offices saying they owe you money. That is a criminal offence.)

8 Don't let the account go for long. Your chances of collecting it are then very remote. You'll settle for half, after a year.

9 Don't let the sales chief write off bad debts on his own accord. *This* should come back to general management or the financial director. In all of this, sales must not be allowed to have an easy way out of their primary responsibility which is to open good sound accounts. Any mug can open bad accounts.

10 Remember, too many bad debts and there is probably something wrong with your product or service. If not, then there is certainly something wrong with your sales.

YOUR MIND MAP

YOUR ACTION PLAN

What should you do to re-jig your procedures?

THIS TEST WILL MAKE YOU THINK ABOUT YOUR CREDIT COLLECTION PROCEDURES

If an account is long overdue then the salesman collects it personally	1 2 3 4 5	Account collection is always the responsibility of the accounts department
Each overdue account is considered for special procedure within a short time	1 2 3 4 5	You use a standard accounts collection procedure. Only at the end do people become involved
You have various means of putting pressure on long-overdue accounts	1 2 3 4 5	You just take them to court, or discuss with sales whether to write it off
When the account is opened, the salesman has to explain the terms of business verbally	1 2 3 4 5	The terms are included with the acceptance of order of in other documents
Your salesmen are involved with the account collection procedure at all stages	1 2 3 4 5	The salesmen are hardly ever involved
Your salesmen have to say whether a new account is creditworthy in their opinon	1 2 3 4 5	You take the standard credit clearance procedures

If the account is more than a certain size then you should move the scales towards the left-hand side. Have you thought about putting in special procedures to your overdue accounts? And the salesmen should have some personal responsibility for credit clearance. They are the only ones who can see and talk to the customer personally. They are in the best position to judge.

27

Close them sweet, close them easy

●

> Pre-selling – How to land business without trying hard – The message is very simple. If you want to double your sales, then double your prospects.

Q.1 *To get new customers coming to you, you need to emphasize the following:*

(a) Making many calls per day by the sales force.
(b) Teaching the sales force techniques of 'opening'.
(c) Timing to tie in with a customer's problem.
(d) Use frequent advertising.

Q.2 *The best support you can give your sales force for landing new accounts is:*

(a) Clipped coupons from advertising, with the prospects' address.
(b) Meetings which the telesales team have arranged for the salesman.
(c) Prospects who have telephoned in cold, to you.
(d) Prospects who have been qualified by the salesman on the telephone first

Q.3 *Your company has just bought out another. You are put in to run their sales operation. Where do you look first for the best new business prospects to get quick results?*

(a) The major accounts you deal with now.
(b) New business leads and recent sales enquiries.
(c) Accounts held by your competitors.
(d) Your backlist of existing customers.

ANSWERS

Q.1   (a)   2 points   Yes, you want them to be energetic and to open new accounts. It is not the critical factor however.

        (b)   1 point   Yes, training them to 'open' well is useful. It is not the most critical factor.

        (c)   5 points   Hit the prospect when he has a problem; that's the only time he is really going to listen.

        (d)   4 points   With advertising you can either use impact (make a big splash) or frequency (lots of little splashes). To get them coming to you, you need frequency, in order to get them when they have a problem.

Q.2   (a)   2 points   OK I know this is what you go for. But surprisingly this often results in some very weak leads, and your sales force will rush around like headless chickens if you are not careful.

        (b)   3 points   If the girls are given objectives to make meetings, that is what they will make. But often you still get weak leads to new business.

        (c)   5 points   If you analyse your results from people who *telephone* you, or who *write in* to you, you will find your highest proportion of sales success.

        (d)   4 points   If the salesman qualifies the lead himself on the telephone first, he'll avoid the headless chicken syndrome.

Q.3   (a)   3 points   Yes, but it takes time to build these up. And you don't want to jeopardize the future by rushing them. OK though, good answer.

        (b)   2 points   The company has been chasing these for years, so what's new? It's OK if the follow-up has been poor up to now.

        (c)   1 point   Definitely a longer-term attack.

        (d)   5 points   Fish in the pond where the fish have been known to bite before and where they like your particular hooks. The smaller prospects will often produce *faster* results, but not necessarily the biggest and best results, of course.

SCORES

13–15 points	Yes, you are a believer in the old adage that 'Sales are too important to be left to the salesman'. Give salespeople support, and pre-sell the customers hard.
10–12 points	This whole question varies enormously with the type of business. Perhaps I've scored your unfairly.
Up to 9 points	I think we've got a personality clash.

● ● ●

CLOSE THEM SWEET, CLOSE THEM EASY

There are two kinds of customer prospects in my life, I don't know about yours. There are prospects who are easy to close. And there are those who are hard to close. It just might pay us to take a look at the differences between them.

If I jump in the car tomorrow morning and pop up the road to the nearby trading estate, I could call on all the companies there asking if anyone wants to buy what my company supplies. I don't mind telling you that I would find them difficult to close. I can knock on a hundred doors to land one client.

On the other hand, an old client was on the telephone yesterday afternoon. 'John' he said, 'We've got a bit of a problem coming up in our sales team. We need something to be done with them as quickly as possible. What dates have you got free for a training seminar next month?' I don't mind telling you that this is the kind of sale that I find easy to close. I land eight out of ten of this kind, and even then I reckon that could be improved on with more application. If they phone me with their problem, I've as good as got the business.

So why should one type of prospect get me a 1 per cent conversion rate of order to call; while the other kind gets me 80 per cent. It's got very little to do with any technique I might use in personal selling. It's got to do with strategy; the way the whole thing is planned and operated. That's one big difference between sales success and sales failure.

So here are the three big rules for lazy closers. First, sell to the people who know you well – the people you have sold to before. Next, get them to come to your office if you can. Finally, get a large number of prospects running for you. Then you will not have many closing problems.

OLD CUSTOMERS ARE THE BEST

In any business which is a sound business and which supplies good-quality products and a reliable service, then your previous customers are going to be your best prospects. They'll be easier to convert than any others. This applies in every single business I know except undertakers, and even then, word of mouth recommendation from satisfied families is important for new business.

Look at your mailing list. You will be lucky to get 0.5 per cent response from a cold, bought-in mailing list. But get a list of past customers – well, that's a different matter. We sent out a simple letter to selected past customers the other month and 40 per cent of them, yes, 40 per cent of them bought one or other of the things we were suggesting. Now that's an exceptional rate of return by any standards but it just proves the moral once again. The old customers are the best customers. You want more business in a hurry? Then go into your customer book. Even old ex prospects; even old complaining customers; even those to whom you submitted proposals and tenders and did not land the business – they are still better than cold calling on new prospects. And they always will be.

If you can, form a 'club' of existing customers, make friends with them. Write to them call them on the telephone, go and see them and if you have something new to sell them they'll buy. So develop a few add-on products. Sell them a Mark II version when they've bought Mark I, keep them tucked into your organization with good service, send them a newsletter, invite them to a function. They'll like you. And if your products make sense for them, they'll buy from you.

SEE THEM FACE TO FACE

If I try and sell them by writing to them, then that's hard. It's not impossible to close them this way, but it's hard. I find it easier to close prospects when I see them face to face. So there is another rule for finding prospects who are easy to close. See them face to face. The problem is it's expensive to see them face to face but cheap to write to them. But when I see them face to face on their own premises I find it more difficult to close them than when they come to my office. I am not saying it is easy to get them to come to my office, because that demands the exercise of a certain amount of power. What I am saying is that if an important purpose of my strategy is to get them to see me in front of my desk, then that results in a higher proportion of sales. Territory is an important aspect of bargaining power. Use it when you can. It makes it easier to close deals. If you want to unnerve the average car salesman then all you have to do is to ask him to go and see his prospects at their homes. He'll run a mile from doing that. He is a lot more comfortable when he gets them across his showroom floor. They are easier to close, when they visit him.

GROW A BIG PROSPECTS TREE

I find it easier to close prospects when I don't need the business. Now that might sound silly, because everyone needs business. Yes, but you see in my scheme of things I like to get so many prospects coming flooding in that I can pick and choose between them. It's just a numbers game.

Let me give you an example. We need ten new clients every year, because luckily the old ones keep coming back. (See? The advantage of keeping the old customer club going.) So we built up a prospect list. If we have fifteen proposals outstanding then I know that we will land twelve of them.

To get fifteen proposals we need about twenty-four good client contacts – a contact is one where there has been some interest expressed in doing business. So how many old leads and contacts do we have on our list of people to mail, to call from time to time, to keep in touch with, to advertise to? We have about 2000. Yes, as many as 2000 old contacts are kept going in order to land merely ten new clients a year. So it is much easier for us to pick and choose, easier for us to close the ones we want.

So when we need a bit of new business, we dream up a simple letter, mailing shot, new leaflet, or new service and we push it out to 2000 people who know us. We call it shaking the tree. You don't have to shake a tree of 2000 very hard to land twenty-four new contacts which result in ten new clients. It's all pre-selling really. You make more sales, and close more prospects if you are not desperate for the business. Keep your business resources small, build a big prospect tree; concentrate on keeping your old customers topped up and you'll find them easy to close.

ACTION PLAN IDEAS

1   Identify the sources of your new business prospects. Look at your brand new first-time customers. (You may have to make a sample survey, if you have too many of them; say, pick one in every ten. But be careful to draw the sample properly at random. Don't pick clusters of new business in a given time period or a given area otherwise you will get a wrong reading.)
    From each source of new business; word of mouth; referrals from existing customers; people who have known of you before;

people in the trade; competitors; advertising leads; exhibitions; direct mail; salesman etc. identify four factors:

(a)   The conversion rate of orders to initial enquiry.
(b)   The rate of recall before order, i.e. how many calls does each source need before they buy
(c)   The length of time between initial enquiry and the order.
(d)   The volume gained.

Now you know what gets you the best and easiest new business. Plan to generate more leads from this.

2   Work out your advertising and sales cost for each type of customer lead source and express it at a cost percentage versus sales revenue earned.

3   Work out a plan to generate many many more leads of all kinds, but also plan to 'qualify' these leads i.e. sort out which are good prospects and which are weak prospects, so you can dump your no-hopers quickly.

4   Build up your own compiled list of customer prospects, using your existing customers, and your backlist of past or ex-customers. Telephone every one of them and ask the switchboard for the names and initials of the key people who make decisions about your kind of product and service. Put at least three names for each prospect on to your computer list. Code them all by type of business, geographical area etc. (If you sort them by geographical codes before mailing you can get rebates on your stamps from the postal services.) Now mail them frequently, very frequently. Sixteen, twenty or more times a year. Simple mailings will do but vary them; use a lot of personalized letters on a word processor. Put in a telephone team to follow-up the enquiries you generate.

5   Grade all your prospects A, B, and C. Don't do much of the C grades, just mailings, and let them come to you because these are the small prospects. Put your field force on to the B grade prospects. But work the A grade prospects very hard. Make up your mind you are going to land them in the end. Research them. Contact them at high level. Keep going at them until you discover they have a problem which you can solve. If you are top of their mind at this time they will call you first. You want that, because these are the biggest customer prospects on your book. Land these and you have big business.

6   Develop a customer club. Mail them newsletters. Send them offers. See if you can provide them with extra services, advice, technical support. Give them deals that they can get only if they are in your customer club. (Turn it into an institute and charge them a membership fee if you can.)

YOUR MIND MAP

YOUR ACTION PLAN

Which are your best lead sources to new business? How can you get more of them, many, many more? How can you dump your weak prospects quickly?

TEST YOURSELF ON PRE-SELLING

Buyer's decision-making stage	Opportunity for you to pre-sell	Rate yourself versus competition 1 = poor 5 = excellent
New ideas, generated within the company	Image advertising	1 2 3 4 5
Generated from outside the company	Product advertising	1 2 3 4 5
Identification of need or problem to be solved		
Decision to meet need or solve problem	Your company reputation is known to decision-makers and influencers	1 2 3 4 5
Search for suppliers. Screening of suppliers	Telephone reception, internal sales enquiry, literature	1 2 3 4 5
Selected shortlist of suppliers	Sales force, quotations, proposals, technical problem-solvers' skills	1 2 3 4 5
Negotiations of purchase. Selection of supplier	Sales force; skills in competitive edge and price negotiations	1 2 3 4 5

Q. What do you have to do to improve?

28

Losing the sale before you start selling

●

> Handling incoming calls from prospects –
> The initial reception of the prospect is
> critical. It can make the prospect view you as
> the best supplier, it can close off the
> competition before they ever get involved. Or
> it can lose you the business before you start.

Q.1 *If you set a standard for the telephone, how many times should it ring before being answered?*

   (a)   It depends upon the amount of telephone traffic.
   (b)   Twice.
   (c)   Should be answered immediately.
   (d)   Once.

Q.2 *What is the purpose of internal sales staff who deal with customers over the telephone?*

   (a)   To provide technical support.
   (b)   To give prices and terms.
   (c)   To answer customer complaints and queries.
   (d)   To identify customer needs.

Q.3 *A business plans to check upon its own service by making dummy telephone calls as if from customers and then reporting back to staff afterwards. Staff object. Who should win?*

   (a)   Staff say it's unfair for bosses to do this to them.
   (b)   Bosses say that setting standards and making sure they are met is part of the business.
   (c)   Staff should do their own performance monitoring.
   (d)   Bosses should ask customers to do the checking for them.

ANSWERS

Q.1	(a)	1 point	Although the standard may not be met all the time because of the telephone traffic, this is no reason for not having any standard at all. Without a standard, any performance will do.
	(b)	5 points	Or three times if you prefer.
	(c)	1 point	Too quick. Neither you nor the switchboard person have time to settle down and become adjusted to the conversation.
	(d)	1 point	Still too quick. If you don't believe me, then try out the test yourself. You'll find that two or three rings before answering is the most comfortable for the caller.
Q.2	(a)	2 points	Lovely idea, but you have to find out their needs first.
	(b)	1 point	This is what customers ask for all the time. But this is not in your interest to supply to them until you have found out their needs. Under this system, only the lowest price will win the business.
	(c)	2 points	It may be the objective, but you still have to find out needs first.
	(d)	5 points	All the time. That is what the game is about
Q.3	(a)	1 point	Whoever said this was a fair world? Lots of things are unfair. It is unfair for some people to have to go to work at all.
	(b)	5 points	Of course it is.
	(c)	1 point	The people who will be affected by the results of any measurement or control process must not be allowed to do the measuring themselves. They will bend the results so that they come out well. That is why quality control departments are usually run by someone other than the head of the production plant involved.
	(d)	2 points	Don't like it too much, but if you've got a couple of tame customers, then OK.

SCORES (These tests are easy)

15 points	You must score all three right to get a brilliant pass. It is not difficult.
12–14 points	OK so you made a small slip.
Up to 11 points	So perhaps you made quite a few slips.

● ● ●

In general, buyers start buying before sellers start selling. Just be a buyer for a moment. You want to purchase something you do not usually buy – office furniture for example. So what do you do?

You start looking up buyers guides, Yellow Pages, Kompass Register. You ask around the office for anyone who has bought furniture before. You call up the person who usually supplies your office sundries. You ask suppliers to send you leaflets and price lists. Already, even without seeing the price lists you are establishing a 'pecking order' for the deal. One company handles you well – another does not seem to know what you are talking about – another does not answer the phone for a long time. Another promises to send you material but you don't receive it. You started out with five suppliers as prospects and already they are whittled down to two. Three of them lose the business before they ever got going.

Most of the people who lose the deals for you are not salesmen. They are juniors – they are the office staff who handle the queries – they are the girls who answer the phone. Half the time, because they are not salesmen, they don't know the right things to say. The junior staff do not even know the product range properly. They are light years away from establishing customer's needs, identifying the appropriate benefits and handling objections. You can't blame them. No one ever trained them properly.

We bought office furniture recently. We telephoned three local suppliers, all dealers, and asked them to send us material. We went to see the range which we liked the look of. We asked about terms. Five per cent we got from one dealer, 10 per cent we got from another. The total deal was worth about £3000 so we thought we would try a bit harder. The salesman for our usual dealer came to see us. We said that he could order the equipment from his supplier, have it sent straight to us without stocking it, but he had to give us a substantial discount to get the business. He came back with $22^1/_2$ per cent. We asked him to go back to his boss and explain that we could pay cash with the order but that he could get two months credit from the supplier so that would have to be worth an extra discount wouldn't it? He gave us another $2^1/_2$ per cent. He could have closed the deal then if he liked – we were ready to buy. But he let us think about it for a day or so. That is why he lost it.

My colleague who was doing the buying thought he would make one more try at getting a better price. So he telephoned the supplier. He asked the switchboard girl for the name of the best girl they had in the sales department. The conversation with the salesgirl ran like this.

'Is that Jennie, Jennie Thompson? Jennie, I've been told that you are the one person who can help me with this problem.'
'What's the problem?' she said.
'You see, we want to buy some goods from you – by the way have you got these items in stock?' and we quoted the list numbers.
'Yes? Well, the difficulty is that your dealers can't meet our budget limits and it means that to stay within our budget we shall have to buy elsewhere even though we want to buy from you.'
'Jennie, if you were us, and wanted to get the best possible deal, how would you go about it?'
'It's a pity you are not a dealer,' she said, 'because then you could get $33^1/_3$ per cent if you bought direct from us.'
'Jennie, for money we can be anything, what do we have to do?'

She told us all we had to do was to write in with an official order and say this is part of our usual trade and no one would check up. So we did, and saved ourselves £1,000 off the list price. The point about the story is not that Jennie was wrong – she got the deal – though her dealers might be upset if they ever found out. No, the point is that any one of five local firms could have got the deal too and could have stopped us from pursuing it if only their office staff, the telephone people, had been trained properly.

Do you set a standard in your company for the telephone? Try this as a routine – it is very simple and even non-sales staff can do it. First, set a standard of three rings of the telephone before it is answered. Don't answer it immediately, give the caller and the respondent a little time to prepare. If it is an internal telephone, then the standard is two rings. The person answering must sound happy and cheerful. That is important and this includes internal staff as well. People should be told off for answering the phone with grunts – often this is the boss himself and it is a mistake, a bad mistake. The person answering should give their name, including their Christian name. This includes all secretaries. People must feel they are important, their name is important to them, and the name is important to the person making the call. It gives him someone to hold on to. Give them the information they want but always get their name and telephone number early in the call. 'Just in case we get cut off, so I can telephone you back.'

If they have to quote prices they should ask the caller how much does he know about the products and would he like to be told? This will tell them whether he is shopping around, or whether he is knowledgeable, and if they handle him nicely on the phone, it might be enough to stop him from going to other suppliers. Every company is different, of course, and you will have to make up a routine that suits your particular business. The important thing is to find out something about the caller and his needs. Before quoting the price.

Then, if they have to quote the price over the phone (better to make an appointment for the sales executive in some cases) they should always do so by quoting, first of all, a benefit they are offering, then the price, then add a further benefit such as 'We would give you 30 days credit with that, so you do not have to pay immediately.' (Or free delivery, or it includes packing and insurance cost, or it includes after-sales service or whatever suits you.) Sandwich the price between benefits. Most people answering the phone do not quote benefits. They just quote prices. And they will argue until the cows come home that this is all the customer is interested in and this is all he asks for. Just ask your staff if they can list the benefits, even if they were asked, and most of them will be unable to do so. The benefits are what will sell the deal – not the price. Your price will always be beaten by a competitor somewhere.

Finally, you must, must, must check up on your own performance. Get a few friends to telephone in to your offices after the training session as if they were customers. Tell your staff you are going to do this so they do not feel caught out. They'll improve, you watch. And so will your sales.

ACTION PLAN IDEAS

1   Examine every point at which your customers contact the company. Accounts, technical, sales, transport, management etc. First do a sample survey in each section of the material being passed through by correspondence or by telephone. Examine correspondence for:

(a)   Speed of response.
(b)   Accuracy of reply, appropriateness.
(c)   Quality of English, spelling, typing etc.

Examine the telephone routine by calling in yourself with dummy calls. Make a record of all conversations. Now you have your survey results, establish a set of standards for each section.

Now launch your quality improvement scheme. Show staff the results of the survey, without naming names or identifying individuals. Show them the standard you are setting, invite comments, make changes as necessary.

Run tests, and feedback the information to them all. Have it all open and above board, but do not blame individuals. Set competitions for improvements against standard. This is a brilliant way to improve people's performance.

2   Get a simple home video camera. Take one day to make up a studio set in an office. Have a series of simple scripts for the people who answer the telephone. Get your staff to role play different types of conversation. Do them the wrong way, then the right way. Use yourself on the film summarizing what the purpose is, what should be done and how to do it.

Let the film be made warts and all, wiggles with the camera are OK, bad cuts are OK, leave funny unexpected sequences in. Call it a Crummy Film. (It's an internal training film made on the cheap and everyone can see that.)

Now draw up a questionnaire of fifty questions, drawn from the material in the film. When your staff have watched the film, then give them half of the questions to answer. Tell them that they must score 80 per cent pass marks, otherwise they'll have to watch the film again and do the test again. Most will fail. So they'll have to see the film again. This time they will pay attention, make notes and will get 80 per cent of the other questions right. Now you have set standards, and trained them.

3   Get your service working brilliantly. Set your standards, get your people working to them. Then advertise them to your customers. Challenge your customers to break your standards of service. Some will, of course. But your reputation for quality will be superb. All your competitors will be frightened of it. And your staff will be proud to have been advertised in this way. They will do you proud. You see.

4   The ultimate technique is to publish a photograph of your company chairman. Put in his direct line number. Advertise that if anyone of your customers has any difficulty at all, then he has the right to contact your chairman directly on his personal line. That will do the trick. Do you dare?

5   Train everyone in product knowledge. Everyone. From transport to accounts, to technical, to production. Everyone should know about customers, about the market, about the competition, about the products. Make a simple video training film about these things. Show it to everyone, and give them tests on it. That way, your whole staff will feel confident of dealing with any customer at any time. And customers will be very impressed. You'll block off the competition before they ever get into the act.

YOUR MIND MAP

YOUR ACTION PLAN

What are you going to do to improve standards of customer service?

A SEARCHING TEST OF THE FACE OF YOUR COMPANY

Here are some real difficulties. Give your company an honest rating on each; then go out and test it for yourself. You can change the questions to make them more appropriate for your business.

But before you start, look at each question in turn and rank them in order of importance to your business performance, or in order of importance to your customer. (Don't bother with the questions which don't matter — just the ones which do matter.)

Rank these issues in order of importance From 1–9	Don't know	How do you rate? Average			Brilliant
Your switchboard can put people through accurately, swiftly, and to the right person even when the enquiry is vague.	1	2	3	4	5
Your switchboard people know what the company does and its products and departments.	1	2	3	4	5
Your sales admin/technical department can handle all the technical queries about your products *even in the lunch-hour break.*	1	2	3	4	5
You have someone to help callers after 5.30pm in the evening and before 8.30am.	1	2	3	4	5
You know your customers' correspondence is handled quickly, accurately, and you can measure the performance.	1	2	3	4	5
Your accounts department know the customers applications of the product.	1	2	3	4	5

Your transport people have product, customer, and competition knowledge.	1	2	3	4	5
When your managers, senior executives and directors answer the phone, they give their own name and answer with a smile. Always.	1	2	3	4	5
No customer is ever held waiting on the telephone without someone coming back to him every 20 seconds.	1	2	3	4	5

29

Terror: the salesman's fallback position

●

> The fear of rejection and how to deal with it.
> The salesman is away from home, the
> customer is powerful, new prospects are
> difficult. So salesmen are afraid of rejection
> particularly when they are exposed to cold
> canvassing. This chapter is about coping
> with it.

Q.1 *You are a famous sex therapist. This young man has been
sent to you by his GP. His problem is that he is afraid of girls.
How do you anticipate he will behave when talking about
the problem?*

(a) Eagerly.
(b) Awkward, shy, not easy to understand.
(c) Avoidance of eye contact.
(d) Not saying anything much at all.

Q.2 *His sister gets him to dance with her at a disco. Does she*

(a) Listen to him with great interest.
(b) Do most of the talking.
(c) Find him awkward.
(d) Enjoy the experience.

Q.3 *Instead of sexual rejection, imagine a salesman being
afraid of the buyer. Would he*

(a) Behave in a similar way to your answer to question 1.
(b) Tend to go for small, easy accounts.
(c) Try for meeting buyers he liked, old customers,
friendly people.

(d)   Go for a few deals, but big ones.
(e)   Cause his buyers to behave in a way similar to the girl in
       your answer to question 2.

ANSWERS

Q.1	(a)	1 point	
	(b)	5 points	Dead easy this question.
	(c)	5 points	And this.
	(d)	3 points	Maybe, maybe not.
Q.2	(a)	1 point	You must be joking. Long time bachelor are you?
	(b)	4 points	Can't give you 5 points. She might be afraid of men. Then they'll have a pretty silent dance together.
	(c)	5 points	
	(d)	1 point	Oh come on!
Q.3	(a)	4 points	Depends on your answer to question 1, but frankly you can hardly miss.
	(b)	4 points	Probably.
	(c)	5 points	He will go into the easiest bolt hole available.
	(d)	1 point	You must have misunderstood the question.
	(e)	5 points	But only if you answered (c) to question 1. Otherwise you get 4 points. You get nothing if you answered (a) or (d).

SCORES

13–15 points	Easy. This is a sensitizing process. The purpose is to indicate how damaging rejection can be, if it is not handled properly.
Up to 12 points	Keep on with the pills.

●   ●   ●

REJECTION – THE SALESMAN'S HIDDEN FEAR

They will never tell you of course, but the more gregarious and sociable they are, the more they fear being rejected. If you live in the world of ideas, rather than the world of people, the big R is not a problem. But it is for most salesmen.

Walk down a queue outside the Job Centre in Toxteth, Liverpool. It's a long walk, usually. Ask the people there if they would like to do a job that earns them between £10,000 and £15,000 a year. Tell them they'll get an expense account, they will be left free for most of the time to get results in their own way, they will even get a car. Not all the queue will rush for the job, but many of them will. And just as many will turn away, as soon as you tell them they will have to sell things. Most people fear rejection: and that is what the salesman lives with all his life.

So do we all. But as we grow up in management, we learn how to avoid being exposed to it too often. We develop very specific behaviour strategies to counter the problem. If the salesman cannot learn how to cope with rejection, then he or she leaves the job. The problem is as big as that.

UNHELPFUL ATTITUDES

Weaker salespeople mask their reactions to rejection. They say: 'You've got to take some knocks in this business', or 'You can't win them all'. Often they rationalize the knocks they take from others. They complain to their manager: 'Our price was too high, that's why we lost it', or 'The customer doesn't need my product'. These are just cop-outs – they are not very helpful in developing a sound sales technique for handling rejection.

HELPFUL TECHNIQUES

More helpful to the salesman is to develop some positive reactions. Can he do the same thing to the customer that the customer is doing to him? And can he do it professionally, even courteously, perhaps? Does he keep the customer waiting if he knows the customer is always going to keep him waiting? A sound technique for dealing with this is helpful. Can he cope with rudeness and insults with dignity, and even redirect the pressure on the customer? Has he got some bite of his own? Does he make the customer a little wary of him?

But the best techniques of all concern his selling strategy, the whole approach. When he is being kept waiting in reception for forty-five minutes, it's too late to recover. The trick is not to allow this to happen. Easier said than done, you might say. But let's have a look at some possibilities. Can he arrange a meeting away from the prospect's office, in his own office perhaps or at least on neutral ground? This weakens the prospect's ability to do him down.

He will get less rejection from selling to his own past customers – it's the new ones which are the problem. That is why it is so difficult to get salesmen to call on new prospects. Can he pre-sell the new prospects beforehand? Can he build up his own image with them before they ever meet him? Or can his company do this for him? Does the prospect get a letter in advance? Does he know something of the track record of the person coming to see him? What is the quality of advance publicity for the salesman himself, and for his product? It is a great help if the customer himself asks for the meeting.

Can the office help him to avoid rejection – by making appointments, by asking for the prospect's literature beforehand, by confirming the meeting in writing. And could the salesman himself use a two-step or three-step selling approach? The first meeting is to re-search the prospect thoroughly, to find out his problems and ask about his people. Then the approach to the right people can be made firmly, with confidence – and this will convey itself to the prospect. You do not want two-step meetings if you can land them in one, but if the prospect is big enough and important enough, it will be worth the effort to spend the time researching properly.

PLAYING THE POWER GAME

Having gone through all the problems in the early years, you yourself use a number of subtle techniques to ensure that you are not put down by prospects. Could your salesmen use any of these?

You insulate yourself from trivial tasks and do less for yourself. You are busy and active, and it may be quite difficult to get appointments with you. Why? Partly because you are a busy person, but partly it is a personal power game you play too. It does not do any harm to your prestige. You might even arrive a little late at some meetings. You like to be kept informed without involving yourself. You arrange meetings on your home ground, at times which suit you. You are quite difficult to please, and you are not afraid to state your view and argue it – even against the odds. You tend to draw meetings to a close.

In discussions you often sit still, with steady eyes, with quiet hands, and use a firm voice. Your answers tend to be short and direct. You make quite strong demands and concede little. You set limits on trouble-makers.

You feel quite confident, and within your own group you are fairly powerful. This is how you show it. I know this to be true because Dr Mark Silber, an industrial psychologist of international renown, has made a study of powerful people and these are his observations of their behaviour. I also know it to be true from personal experience, because I have watched you do it, and you are not rejected by others as a result. Quite the reverse. Your power acts like a magnet. I must learn to keep my hands still, talk less, and keep eye contact with other people. And I hope the receptionist brings me a cup of tea soon as I wait here outside your office.

ACTION PLAN IDEAS

1   Too much rejection is damaging to the selling effort. It can lead to a high personnel turnover, and poor results. So try to identify how much damage it is causing. Ask your salespeople to discuss buyers they do not like, customers they do not like. Ask for examples of rejection, ask for ideas on how they learn to cope with it. Everyone has personal methods which they will reveal. Tell them their ideas will help you with training newcomers to the sales force. They will tell you then.

2   Be very thorough with new people and also with those whose results are not good. Work with them closely. Don't put pressure on them for results. Give them plenty of training, and close supervision.

3   Give them existing accounts to deal with at the start, but with a few new prospects to cut their teeth on.

4   Give them specific advice and counselling on avoiding rejection, or coping with it. Show them how to use the technique of reflection (doing to the other person what he is doing to you) and give them the confidence to avoid being too submissive in the face of threatening situations. Praise them for getting a little tough themselves.

5   Let them have plenty of interaction with other salespeople: two-person sales presentations, meetings, and reinforce success. They are never going to turn into stars until they have the courage to get tough, and to take risks.

6   If there is a high level of rejection in your selling operation (Jehovah's Witnesses, double glazing, *Encyclopedia Britannica*, insurance) and an individual salesman has not learned effectively how to cope with it after six months, move him to a more productive job. He will not succeed in the firing line.

YOUR MIND MAP

YOUR ACTION PLAN

How can you train your sales force to be more powerful individuals, more confident, and not able to be put down easily?

YOU ARE NOT OK!

Terror sensitivity test.

Watch one person criticizing another. It may be in a meeting; it may be a buyer in a shop; it may involve a discussion with the boss; it may involve you yourself.

Look for the non-verbal signs which accompany the verbal arguments. These are the signs which victims read when they know they are being rejected.

SIGNS OF HOSTILITY	leading to	REACTIONS
Extra space between people, posture turned away, (particularly showing back)		Fighting back, counter criticisms, emotional response.
Folded arms, avoidance of eye contact, tapping fingers on desk.		Avoidance, withdrawal, no eye contact, shifting body movements.
Keeping the time short, keeping junior waiting, bringing the meeting to a close.		Increase of gestures, leaning forward.
Using fake arguments, using a facade (friendly or hostile), false smiles.		Hurried speech, speech pattern interruptions.

Watch for these signs in groups of people you cannot hear. (Trains, hotels, bars, department stores). Through watching groups of people talking together, you will gradually understand all the relationships between them.

People who are friends tend to behave similarly to one another, same gestures, postures etc. Their eye contact is high.

30

To reach the heights of mediocrity just do what everyone else does

●

> Making competitive presentations – If you sell against competition then you should aim to be different from them in the way you do it. Otherwise, if you do what everyone else does, you will just get average results.

Q.1 *Your product is bog-standard, the same as everyone else's product. So is your service. How should you win competitive bids for business?*

(a) By having the lowest price.
(b) By having good literature.
(c) The salesman should be smart and knowledgeable, and turn up on time.
(d) By making your sales presentation different from everyone else.

Q.2 *To make your presentation different from the others, you should*

(a) Introduce drama, the unexpected.
(b) Sell them something different.
(c) Use persistence.
(d) Concentrate upon the customer's position to find your difference.

Q.3 *When lady salesmen sell to men buyers they should*

(a) Behave like a man, with no difference between the sexes.

(b) Flirt and tease a little, if the man is willing.
(c) Know their products better than male salesmen.
(d) Deal with the buyer in the way they would with any other man.

ANSWERS

Q.1 (a) 5 points   This is *not* in conflict with other chapters about price. The fact is that if you and everyone else is selling absolutely the same thing with the same back up in a competitive market, then the best route is to have a slightly lower price than everyone else, *plus* all these other answers.

(b) 3 points   Yes, but it is a bit like being in favour of motherhood.

(c) 3 points   Love us, I must be getting too generous with these points in my old age.

(d) 4 points   Caught you. Look at the answer to (a) first. You thought you were on to an easy winner here, didn't you?

Q.2 (a) 2 points   Yes, do all of these three things, and (b) and (c). But they are not enough.

(b) 2 points   Yes. Not enough though.

(c) 2 points   Yes. Not enough though.

(d) 5 points   Absolutely.

Q.3 (a) 3 points   This is a bit rational. You would be throwing away a unique difference before you start if the buyer is used to dealing only with men.

(b) 1 point   And you knew it was the wrong answer.

(c) 5 points   Lady salesmen have an easier approach, but get tested harder by buyers on their product knowledge.

(d) 5 points   Stay in character. Absolutely.

SCORES

14–15 points	Easy to get nearly top marks here.
10–13 points	But one tiny little error takes you off the top.
Up to 9 points	All these tiny little errors, add down.

● ● ●

Her ankles were certainly an asset. They were part of the whole proposition Sandra was putting forward, but her ankles were not her unique selling proposition. First of all, compared to the other 20 shortlist candidates for the job, her ankles were among the best but were not outstanding. The same went for her smile and her manner. She was a pleasant, well-mannered, pretty girl applying for a job in the art department of an advertising agency. But her ankles were not unique.

This might seem all very sexist. But the fact is that this is the way the world is. And selling has to deal with the way the world is, not the way it should be. Girls' ankles are part of it. If you've got it, as the saying goes, flaunt it. Look at the odds against this girl getting the job. Sandra was twenty and fresh out of art college. She did not even complete the course because she found it too boring and remote from the real world of advertising.

Sandra had another problem. Her work was not particularly brilliant. You could say, with some understatement, that she was up against heavy odds. But she did get herself into advertising against huge competition which was much better qualified. She sold herself into the job by making the buyer want to buy.

ENGINEERING THE INTRO

Here's how. First she realized that most advertising agency jobs went out to friends of employees. The good jobs are not advertised. So together with a pal, she went up to London and to the reception desks of the top ten agencies. She found out first where the art boys went for a drink after work. She went to the pub with her pal and talked to them there about how to get a job in their agency. Soon enough she got an introduction to an agency art director about a job. She went along on the Monday for the interview. They chatted. He was bored – seen it all a thousand times before, pretty, lively, keen, eager, like hundreds of students he had interviewed in his career. He asked to see her work. She began to open her case and then shut it immediately.

'What's wrong?' he said.
'It's no good showing you this,' she replied. 'It's not relevant. I could

have taken months to produce these drawings and you've seen
hundreds like this before.'
'Well, how can I judge if you are any good?' said the art director. By
now he had a higher degree of attention than before.
'Tell you what,' she said. 'When are you going to make the
decision?'
'Friday.'
'OK. This is what I suggest. Give me a job to do now. Invent one,
any one. I'll take the brief, go away and do it and bring it back to you
late Thursday afternoon. Then you will see if I'm any good.'

By this time the art director was taking real notice. This applicant was
different. She was inventive. Her work might be ordinary but her
motivation was good. She was willing to be tested and would work all
week on the job. By the time Thursday came, she had got the job
almost before she showed him the result. She had stayed top of his
mind all week. The rest of the kids never had a prayer.

The point is that she had tracked in to what he wanted. He was
looking for motivation, willingness, something a bit different, a co-
operative personality. You would have taken her on too, wouldn't
you? Sandra will go on getting any job she wants for the rest of her
career. So how do some salesmen do it against the odds, time after
time? They do it by refusing to allow the big prospect to intimidate
them.

THINK BIG, THINK DIFFERENTLY

Don't let the big prospect roll over you – you will never win them by
creeping to them. But just do it differently from your competitors.
Track into the customer needs. Go see their lower-level staff first and
find out their problems. Before you make the sales call proper, do the
research. Then construct your proposition around them, and only
them. This gives you a huge advantage for a start because practically
all your competitors are trying to sell themselves.

One enormous contract for services has just been landed against all
the odds by a small company who competes with giants in the industry. The new company asked permission to pitch for the business.
They asked if they could meet with the marketing managers of the
customer beforehand. Quietly, they constructed a specialized presentation which was put on to a video film. They spent £1000 on the
presentation.

The customer's top management were all invited to their own
theatre to see the film. The film was all about them, the customers.

There were future market projections, future profit projections, future projections showing how much extra business would have to be done in different markets if profits were to be improved. All of the data had been worked from the client's own figures. The film then showed six imaginative, new ways in which revenue and profits could be increased with the use of the supplier's services. These innovations would give the customer a strong edge in his own market. The customers waxed enthusiastic over the presentation. They agreed to pursue the ideas. They threw out their existing service and put in the small supplier. They didn't care about their ankles, either.

ACTION PLAN IDEAS

1   Keep a file of all the good ideas you get from others. Write down notes of what other people do, the stories you hear of other companies, publicity ideas, magazine ads, good headlines, catch phrases. Use this file as a 'starter' to get you going with your big new presentation ideas.
2   Get the organization idea-conscious. Use brainstorming at meetings to get everyone thinking differently. Reward ideas with praise; don't knock them down with criticism.
3   Constantly change what you are doing now. Never allow anyone to think that a routine is in for ever. Everyone must know that things will be different in the future and they must contribute.
4   *Best idea of all:* use your crises and mishaps and emergencies to test out new ideas. Under pressure, facing defeat, then this will force out new schemes.
      The following schemes were all produced by companies who were facing defeat on a major account bid.

- A sandwich board man with a relevant message was hired for a day to patrol outside the offices of a customer who was refusing to see the supplier.
- A five minute video film was made cheaply showing the offices of the customer's competition and with a suitable short message from the sales director relevant to the prospect's committee which was making the decision.
- A special advertisement was drawn up naming the customer's board of directors, saying 'We are customers of yours, why are you not customers of ours?' This was printed as a dummy (it looked real) by the London *Evening Standard* and taken by special messenger to the offices of the customer. That gained attention.

- One company with a plastic product always tried to engineer an objection that the product looked fragile. The salesman would then stand up and throw it across the room or out of the window. That's drama!
- The menu in the restaurant was made up with dishes involving the customer's name. A small touch, but memorable.

YOUR MIND MAP

YOUR ACTION PLAN

How are you going to get ideas going in your company at all levels including top management and in sales? What about changing a few pitches to important prospects where you have little hope of winning, anyway.

HOW CREATIVE ARE YOU WITH YOUR BIG CUSTOMER PRESENTATIONS?

A searching 6-point test. There is no middle way. You have to come down on one side or the other.

Tick the nearest to your feeling on the subject.

1 Your sales people are encouraged by you to do things differently, and they have a budget they can use for this.	Over your dead body.	Yes, they have money to spend.
2 In your company, everyone at *every level* is encouraged to have ideas, and to suggest changes.	This presents difficulties.	Absolutely true.
3 Ideas fly round your organization thick and fast.	Can't truly say so.	All the time.
4 In your organization mistakes are tolerated, in the pursuit of results.	Our efficiency is critical to our success.	In the pursuit of fun and success we make the odd boob or two.
5 You love winning major deals against competition by doing it differently from them.	Would prefer to have it right, rather than to have it different.	Love being different.
6 People tell you, you are full of ideas.	No, they don't.	Yes, they do.

Now get three other people including sales staff to fill in the table. See if they share your views of your situation.

31

'You are going to buy this even if it kills you'

●

> Creating options — Boxing your customers
> into a corner so they must say 'yes' or 'no' to
> your particular deal is a certain way of losing
> a lot of sales. Think harder about the
> alternatives you can offer

Q.1 *You believe in letting customers make up their own minds. How do you offer them your propositions?*

- (a) A range of options from which they can select.
- (b) One single recommendation pointing out there are alternatives.
- (c) Dedicate to your one recommendation and just convince him.
- (d) A choice of two alternatives.

Q.2 *In what way should you offer your sales propositions to customers?*

- (a) Explain who you are, what your product is about, handle their objections and close the sale.
- (b) Explain who you are, listen to their problems, recommend your solutions.
- (c) Explain who you are, and generally see how it pans out from there with the customer making the running if he wants to.
- (d) Explain who you are, listen to their problems, explain that there are several means of solving the problem and giving one specific example of one customer's solution.

Q.3 *You know what they should buy. But they prefer some other solution which you can supply but you know it is not the best for them. What do you recommend?*

(a)   The solution which you know is right for them.
(b)   Let them buy the solution they prefer.
(c)   Tell them your preference, but also sell them the one they want.
(d)   Say as little as possible so you do not commit yourself.

ANSWERS

Q.1 (a) 1 point   Far too much confusion. This is called selling by a shopping list. Bad news.

(b) 5 points   Yes, find out his needs first. Then, if you are an expert and have credibility with him then you will produce the right choice for him and he should accept it. But indicating that there are other methods of solving his problem does not box you into a corner.

(c) 2 points   Boxes you into a corner. Difficult to switch when he says 'no'. But there are exceptions.

(d) 4 points   Don't like it overmuch – neither do advertising agents. It seems you cannot make up your mind. Advertising agents find that if they put up two schemes then clients will want them to produce more and more – it damages their credibility as experts. So the top agents actually go for one scheme and argue for it fiercely (option (c)). But theirs is a special case.

Q.2 (a) 1 point   You are too smart to be caught with this one.

(b) 4 points   Most people say 'yes' to this, but have a look at option (d).

(c) 3 points   It's not bad – in some fields you have to play it like this. But mostly it is better if you control the events by asking questions.

(d) 5 points   Sneaky answer. If you try a flyer by using a third-party reference, you can actually suggest several different means without being hooked up on one. If you make a recommendation, particularly too early, they will argue with you. They always do. But they can volunteer their preference on the basis of your other customers' solutions. *Then* you recommend.

Q.3   This is a classical dilemma in a Johari Window test, to see how manipulative you are or how concerned with your own wants. No one right answer – different people do different things.

(a) 4 points   This is you imposing your view – but you might lose the sale. With an established customer where there is mutual respect I do this. With a new customer with little rapport yet established, I box more cautiously than this.

(b) 4 points   This is the manipulative you. The salesman is paid to sell, he is not paid to be judge, jury or consultant. If they want to buy it – fine, sell it to them. (Unless it is totally unsuitable, of course.)

(c) 5 points   I'll go for this most of the time. They are the boss.

(d) 3 points   The manipulation here makes me feel uneasy. You, too?

SCORES

13–15 points   Yes, you'll have a nice touch and will not box yourself into a corner.

10–12 points   Keep it all a bit looser. You might be a bit hard-nosed.

Up to 9 points   The lowest scores here generally see themselves as serving the customer with what he wants. The posture is a bit too weak. Too much *caveat emptor*.

●   ●   ●

CREATING OPTIONS

There's a few, very few, photographers who have made a name for themselves around the world. And even fewer of them have made significant money – David Bailey would be an exception on both counts, but he's the only one I can think of.

If you took the average holiday snap photographer and put him into a little village in a remote part of the North Island of New Zealand, then he'd die for want of customers. Particularly in New Zealand which is hardly well known for hustling. New Zealand is a beautiful country with some marvellous people, but selling it does not. As far as marketing is concerned, fifteen million sheep can't be wrong.

So a customer walks in to Graeme Rodley's small instant developing print shop in Paihia, a little holiday village in the Bay of Islands, New Zealand. Graeme looks up and says 'Oh, I'm sorry, your photographs haven't come out, but don't worry, we'll give you someone else's. It's a lady who hasn't returned for hers and she took some very nice pictures, and I'm sure you'll be very pleased with them.' All done with a big smile. The customer is taken aback but then he realizes that Graeme is kidding and laughs.

'What do you want with your films, sir?' he asks. 'A 20 per cent discount, a free film, or a wash and a haircut?' To another customer, 'You can have large prints, or a budget price, or a kiss from one of the staff.' Another customer joins in the spirit of the thing and says 'Can I borrow your wife for a night?' 'No' replies Graeme, 'the minimum commitment there is a week.' The next customer is offered a warm handshake, or a cup of tea, or double prints with his film. If he prefers, the customer can have a free watch.

Now it sounds as if Graeme is larking about and that's the spirit of the thing. He keeps all the banter light and easy, he takes it easy with people who look very serious, but he keeps most of his customers happy and smiling. The point is that Graeme has built in a large number of options from which his customers can choose when they bring their prints into his shop. He really does offer them either super large prints, or double prints or a free film, or a free watch. Or else they can have a 20 per cent discount if they prefer. If they want a real budget price then they can have that too, but they have to leave their prints in over Tuesday, Wednesday and Thursday, when his demand is light and he likes to stack up some prints for handling in the shop.

Behind all the kidding there is deadly serious intent. Out of one little shop he makes himself enough money to go car racing every weekend and that's not a cheap pursuit. His shop in the town is full, and the other competitor's shop is empty. He mixes up his prices so that it's very difficult for customers to compare his prices with the competitor's prices. His pricing points are all different. His actual margins are very high because he keeps his prices high, he just discounts off the top, so he gives everyone the impression of getting very good value for money, and they enjoy the chat as well. If he has to quote a price then he'll quote his rock bottom budget price if someone is shopping around for the best deal.

In his sales patter he won't often mention the large prints offer because that's the most expensive option for him, but he does advertise that on the list. His site is a good one. He's got car parking outside and it's fifteen yards off the seafront road in the village centre. It took him seven different moves of premises before he got into the site he's in now.

He's built all the connections with the local fishing boats and fishing clubs to take their photographs of the tour trips which he fits in during the day. As the boats take off in the morning he stands on top of an island waving at them. When they wave back he takes their photographs and when they come back in the afternoon, he goes on board with their prints. He keeps a lot of customers very happy and he sells a lot of prints. He's made me £200,000 in my business because I can see that we can re-market a part of what we do to make it much more appealing and actually it will save us cost as well. It's just from the way that Graeme generates options. Graeme hassles and thinks, hassles and thinks the whole time. That's one good way of making money.

Here's another way. One of the local fishermen takes parties out to go sport fishing. He uses a twenty-five foot boat with a couple of powerful engines and charges customers the going rate of £30 per head per day which is competitive for the area. But when they turn up on board, he tells them that he hasn't got enough to make up a full boat load unless they pay him an extra £6 per head. Because they're committed, they always do. It's 7 o'clock in the morning, you've managed to get away from the family for a day to go fishing, what would you do? You'd pay, wouldn't you? The catch is two hundred kilos of fish which will net the boat owner £300 around the hotels and restaurants. It's a very hard life but it makes a lot of money. It's a pity it has to be associated with a con trick as well.

And here's the way not to do it. A small chap at the end of the long beach was offering small catamaran dinghies for hire by the hour. A rival set up along the beach two miles away and started to underprice the established firm by 50p an hour, so the established man counter attacked by pricing his dinghies 50p below his rival. His rival countered again until, in the end, they were both offering dinghies during the high season at a price of less than £1 an hour. They both went out of business at the end of the season. Their objectives were wrong. They thought that their aim in life was to beat their rival. Two other companies have now taken over the concessions on the beach and the prices are now quite well up into the £8 an hour, with both of them charging the same and making a reasonable living out of it.

So keep your options open, spread your passes wide, keep it loose, play an entertaining game and remember where the goal is. And if you can get the customers to enjoy playing with you, they will pay a bit more for the privilege. But don't con them. And don't give it away either.

ACTION POINT IDEAS

1 Take your principal product or service. Develop alternative packages which you could switch to, if the customer says 'no'. Then do this with each of your products/services.

2 How do you build in the 'extras' and 'add-ons'? Do you package them all together as one complete bundle? Try de-packaging all the extras which you know he is going to buy later when he has got your main package, but build in to a single package all the discretionary things which he might or might not buy. Construct several different packages out of the alternatives.

3 When you sell him on your main item; pre-sell him on the next thing you want him to have. There should always be something new to go back to him with the next time.

4 For continuous service calls where there is a constant round of looking after customers who have already bought from you, make sure that you ration out your alternatives. Don't give him all the range the first time. You'll get too many turn-downs. Sell him what you can at the first go, then always have something new to sell him on the service calls; add-ons, extras, services, or other products. That way he'll always want to see you.

5 Identify any part of your selling process that the customer might see as unethical (e.g. The fisherman who 'cons' the customers into paying more when he has got them on board.) If you have a continuous relationship to be built then take care of such 'cornering' devices which you or your sales people might apply – however unwittingly.

YOUR MIND MAP

YOUR ACTION PLAN

Just think about how you can mix up your packages so that you get what you want from the deal and he gets what he wants – most of the time. Where can you fatten up the sale?

THE ETHICAL TEST

Think of three different salesmen. One sells life assurance. One sells financial services. One sells life-support drugs. (Just consider your stereotypes of these three, not three actual people.) How far would you expect each of them to carry out the following actions:

He would only sell you the thing he knows is right for you, whatever you want.

	Never	Rarely	Sometimes	Often	Always
Insurance	_____	_____	_____	_____	_____
Financial Services	_____	_____	_____	_____	_____
Drugs	_____	_____	_____	_____	_____
+1	_____	_____	_____	_____	_____
+2	_____	_____	_____	_____	_____

He would sell you the thing you want to buy.

	Never	Rarely	Sometimes	Often	Always
Insurance	_____	_____	_____	_____	_____
Financial Services	_____	_____	_____	_____	_____
Drugs	_____	_____	_____	_____	_____
+1	_____	_____	_____	_____	_____
+2	_____	_____	_____	_____	_____

He would consult with you genuinely rather than push his products.

	Never	Rarely	Sometimes	Often	Always
Insurance	_____	_____	_____	_____	_____
Financial Services	_____	_____	_____	_____	_____
Drugs	_____	_____	_____	_____	_____
+1	_____	_____	_____	_____	_____
+2	_____	_____	_____	_____	_____

He would recommend a competitor's better product rather than his own.

	Never	Rarely	Sometimes	Often	Always
Insurance	_____	_____	_____	_____	_____
Financial Services	_____	_____	_____	_____	_____
Drugs	_____	_____	_____	_____	_____
+1	_____	_____	_____	_____	_____
+2	_____	_____	_____	_____	_____

If he thinks you are wrong he would tell you so – though nicely.

	Never	Rarely	Sometimes	Often	Always
Insurance	_____	_____	_____	_____	_____
Financial Services	_____	_____	_____	_____	_____
Drugs	_____	_____	_____	_____	_____
+1	_____	_____	_____	_____	_____
+2	_____	_____	_____	_____	_____

He would rather lose the sale than have you buy something which is not quite right for you.

	Never	Rarely	Sometimes	Often	Always
Insurance	_____	_____	_____	_____	_____
Financial Services	_____	_____	_____	_____	_____
Drugs	_____	_____	_____	_____	_____
+1	_____	_____	_____	_____	_____
+2	_____	_____	_____	_____	_____

Most people score the insurance salesman low on this rating; both the financial services and the drugs salesman being scored higher.

In practice, these stereotypes go too far. Insurance sales people are not as bad as people think they are, and finance salesmen folks can be a bit wicked at times.

+1   How do you think other people not familiar with your industry would score your industry's salespeople on this rating? Score again.

+2   How do you score yourself? (Don't tell fibs. Do it properly.)

Part Five

Seven Tactics in Sales Technique

32

The stuff that stars used to be made of

●

> How star salespeople differ from the rest –
> There have been countless studies trying to
> identify what star salespeople do differently
> to the rest. We are finally approaching an
> answer.

Q.1 *Have a guess. What do star salespeople do in their technique which is different from the rest? At least in complex major sales situations.*

(a) Ask more open questions.
(b) Close more effectively.
(c) Handle objections more thoroughly.
(d) Build up the problem in the buyer's mind.

Q.2 *According to classical sales theory, which of these still holds good today if you want to recruit people with star sales potential – you need to find:*

(a) People who can mop up pressure and stress.
(b) People with enquiring minds.
(c) People who are highly motivated towards success.
(d) People who get on well with others.

Q.3 *How should you win sales?*

(a) By winning arguments.
(b) By winning the close.
(c) By winning friends.
(d) By winning respect.

ANSWERS

Q.1 (a) 1 point   'Fraid not.
    (b) 1 point   'Fraid not.
    (c) 1 point   'Fraid not.
    (d) 5 points   'Fraid so.

Q.2 (a) 1 point   Salespeople often create their own stress.
    (b) 2 points   With technical selling it's more important.
    (c) 5 points   You knew all the time, didn't you.
    (d) 2 points   You can take this for granted really.

Q.3 (a) 5 points   Win arguments and you'll lose sales.
    (b) 3 points   Partly right.
    (c) 4 points   Nearly right.
    (d) 5 points   Got to be right.

SCORES

Tough marking but the questions are easy, apart from question 1.

13–15 points   Did you read the proofs before the book came out?

6–12 points   What can I say?

Up to 5 points   I'm not saying a thing.

●   ●   ●

People have been trying to analyse what makes for star sales performance ever since 1925. The early studies showed that salespeople needed to be self-starters. They needed to have empathy with their customers. And they needed to have a strong drive towards success.

So the advertisements for sales executives all used to emphasize these characteristics. 'Are you a go-getter? Can you work without supervision? Are you energetic and forceful? Do you want success badly?' This is what the sales ads were saying right up to the 1950s – you can still see some of them today. At that time the emphasis was on calls per day, to be followed later by an emphasis upon converting calls to orders. At this stage, the trainers concentrated upon methods of handling objections, and methods of closing sales successfully. If you look at some of the big training roadshows which go around the country today exhorting sales people to greater success, they are still concentrating on closing techniques. It's bunkum, but it does not stop people teaching it.

In the 1960s, a great deal of work was done by industrial and social psychologists on the subject of identifying personality traits in salespeople which led to success. They did not quarrel with the earlier evidence of the need for a strong drive, but they added something else. They added the need for understanding customers' needs properly and for establishing rapport. This led to a new trend in recruiting salespeople, and in some aspects of industrial selling it is very strong today. Many organizations try and recruit their sales staff out of personnel who have worked in the customer's industry. This gives them a great lift in terms of results, because their sales staff understand their customers' problems, they can identify with their difficulties and they know their way around customers' organizations. If you add product knowledge and selling skills training to the salespeople you employ from the customer's industry, then you should get successful results – they must still be ambitious, though.

But the need for making many calls per day drops away. And in consultative selling where the salesperson is a problem-solver, the need for converting calls to orders takes second place against developing profitable big business from existing accounts. As for heavy closing techniques, the only ones these folks need are the quick dash for the bar before 'last orders' are called.

Then in the mid 1970s came a man called Neil Rackham. A psychologist by training and specializing in selling by choice, he set up an organization which was devoted to studying the selling process in a scientific way, drawing lessons from the process, and developing new ideas to help organizations sell more. In the course of his work he had to persuade major corporations around the world to put up some big funds for his studies – but they did. So, for the first time, we have a significant advance in our knowledge of what makes sales stars. And I, for one, am absolutely convinced that Neil Rackham is right.

If you study the selling process in a scientific way, you have to sort out a few problems. No one sale is like another, customers are different, products and services vary enormously, and so do salespeople themselves. You even have to define accurately what you mean by 'success', if you are going to study it. What Rackham has done is to make a big distinction between ordinary, commonplace, everyday sales which he calls 'simple' sales. It is not so much that the products are simple or even cheap, it is more that the selling process itself is simple and fairly uncomplicated. These tend to be one-off sales of products which are understood quite well.

Most of you out there sell quite complicated ideas. Sometimes you have a lot of explaining to do; sometimes you have to solve customers' problems. Sometimes your customers change their decision-making procedure – perhaps one of your key problems might be to find out who is going to take the decision or influence it a lot in your target prospect's company. Others of you build steady long term relationships because your customers buy from you over and over again.

Try using a heavy or coercive closing technique to 'force' a regular buyer to buy from you. What is he going to do to you the next time you want to sell him something? That's right, he is going to get revenge. The Rackham research has found some very, very interesting results when they come to measure these 'major' or complex sales.

They have found that half the ideas of traditional sales trainers are up the chute for a start. For major sales, the heavy use of deliberate closing techniques is actually counter-productive. If you try, try, try again to close, the buyer is increasingly likely to back off the more you try. If you feel you have a closing problem, then what it means is that you have not convinced the buyer effectively and the fault lies in the early part of your technique. Actually, there is evidence from elsewhere that when selling to those buyers who have a personality profile involving a high degree of insecurity, then walking away from them, giving them room to think and make up their mind, is likely to be much, much more effective than pressurizing them.

The same is true of handling objections. Rackham explains that many sales trainers actually believe that if the buyer is giving plenty of objections then this is a good sign for the seller. That's bunkum, too. If a buyer is giving me objection after objection, then I know I've got trouble and he is probably going somewhere else. The customers I sell to give very little trouble. And that is true of all sales people. Ask yourself, do you 'win' sales by having lots of arguments with customers? Or do you win sales by understanding his problems, suggesting solutions that he likes – by collaboration, if you like.

ACTION POINT IDEAS

1   If yours is a simple selling process, then these ideas might help. The simple sales we are talking about, involve a process whereby the result of a sales visit is either a *sale* or a *no sale*. If there is any follow-up work, if the business is regularly obtained, if several meetings are involved, then this becomes a complex sale.

2   In most businesses there are elements of simple sales around. For these you have four routes to building an effective sales force; this is:
   - By recruiting the right person to start with.
   - By training them well.
   - By motivating them properly.
   - By managing and controlling them properly.

3   If it is drive and energy you need, then this can only be done by recruiting the right people to start with. The proper level of motivation will help, but recruitment is overwhelming.

4   If it is ability to empathize with the customer, this again involves recruitment to a great extent. You must have the right kind of personality and one which can understand the customer's business easily. But training them properly will help.

5   Ability to work without supervision. Here it can be found partly in recruitment (people with high drive want to be left alone to get results). But management and control is particularly important here, and training and motivation might also help.

6   To handle objections effectively. Basically you want to reconstruct the selling so that you get few objections. This is going to be down to training and supervision.

7   Ability to close. Your recruits with high drive for success will close sales. But training helps, of course, so does motivation, so does management and control. To land the business you need everything running for you.

YOUR MIND MAP

YOUR ACTION PLAN

How can you improve the simple sales part of your process?

CAN YOU BE AN OLD-TIME SALES STAR?

The old-fashioned test, for a simple sale.

Look at these five factors. Comparing yourself to other people whom you know in your business, give yourself a rating out of 10 on each factor. (10 = very good indeed. No one better)

	A Give yourself marks out of 10	B The importance of this	C Calculate result
Self-motivating, self-starting	_____	_____	_____
Ability to empathize with customer	_____	_____	_____
Ability to work without supervision	_____	_____	_____
Ability to handle objections	_____	_____	_____
Ability to close sales effectively	_____	_____	_____

Now, having scored yourself, give each factor a rating out of 10 for its importance in your own selling process. (10 = very important indeed, nothing more important.)

Subtract B from A. This shows you where you ought to improve your personal sales ability.

33

The stuff that stars are now made of

●

> For major and complex sales, the techniques
> are different – Using commonplace sales
> techniques, suitable for one shot deals, the
> salesman can find himself in trouble when he
> goes for major sales deals. He must re-learn
> his business.

Q.1 *Have a guess. What does the latest research tell us about star salespeople when they make major sales, with a continuing relationship with customers?*

(a) Sell the benefits well.
(b) Make effective sales presentations.
(c) Uncover customers' explicit needs.
(d) Build close relationships.

Q.2 *To handle objections thoroughly, you should:*

(a) Know your product and market well.
(b) Sell them so the objections do not arise.
(c) Have a battery of techniques available.
(d) Tell the customer the truth.

Q.3 *When selling benefits to customers, you should:*

(a) Put them in fairly early to arouse his interest.
(b) Explain them as being the use to which features can be put.
(c) Show them as cost savings.
(d) Get the customer to tell you what they are.

ANSWERS

Q.1 (a) 3 points Benefits are important all the way through, but they are not *the* important thing.

(b) 2 points How can it ever be effective when you do not know what their problems are?

(c) 5 points Yes, if you can take him from his difficulties and problems (implied needs) through to his expressed desire for something new or better or more fitted for his purpose (explicit needs) then you are 80 per cent of the way to getting the business.

(d) 3 points I'm not going to quarrel. But it is not the major thing.

Q.2 (a) 3 points Fine. Can't argue with this. Like trying to argue against the idea of motherhood.

(b) 5 points Absolutely. And it *can* be done.

(c) 3 points Another score for motherhood.

(d) Hello Mum.

Q.3 (a) 2 points There is some evidence from the research that this may be counter productive if it is done too early.

(b) 2 points A feature is an advantage, which may or may not be a benefit. It can only be a benefit if it ties in with what he needs.

(c) 3 points OK. Back to good old motherhood again.

(d) 5 points Mother knew the answer all the time.

SCORES

13–15 points Only one slip allowed for the top score this time. You star, you.

9–12 points You can have three slips from perfection for this score. No more.

Up to 8 points Have as many slips as you can get in.

● ● ●

How do gigantic consultancy firms sell themselves? Big or small, the successful ones all follow the same routine. Someone high up gets a meeting with a client prospect, preferably at chairman/chief executive level. The client's chairman admits he has a problem, which he would like some help with.

'We do not know if we actually can help with your problem, sir, but we would like the opportunity to study it first, without commitment on your part. If we cannot help you, we will tell you.' (The only client prospect who has ever been told by a consultant that the consultant cannot solve the problem is the client who has no money and who is probably going bust.)

So the consultant puts in a team of researchers. Their job is to talk with directors and executives at senior level, and some at a slightly more junior level. They always ask the same question. 'What do you think are the problems around here?'

They then turn the answers over to their specialist copywriter. His is a skilled job. He must rewrite the problems in a different way, putting the two or three different angles and writing the whole lot up in a report. This report will land the business.

In the first paragraph or two, they must praise the client company but not too much. If they are dealing with the original owner, then they point out references to his wisdom, foresight, creative flair and drive which has enabled the company to reach the powerful position it is in today. If they are dealing with new owners, they can afford to rubbish the previous executives. This gives the new owner confidence he can do better.

So the object is to get the chief executive to nod his way through the opening paragraphs. 'This will not be too unpleasant,' he thinks. Then they hit the problems. These are all defined from different angles so that they look different from the way the company sees them now. If they just repeat the company problems without a different angle then there is no need for a consultant.

The report consists of page after page of problems. The chairman nods his head, then more vigorously he begins to agree. He calls in a colleague, 'Have a look at this, George,' he says, 'These people seem to understand us. They were only here for a couple of days, but they seem to have got the hang of it.' The consultants know that if you can get the client to nod his way through the problems, he will nod his way through the proposals, and nod his way through the costs and terms of business. And then the consultants are in.

And if you think I am being overly cynical about the process, I am not. For this is what makes for star sales people. It is the build up and understanding of the problem which matters. Particularly for major sales. The Rackham research shows it very clearly indeed. The poor or average salesperson does two things he should not do. It is not so much that he asks the wrong questions – it's more that he does not ask the right ones. And, having identified a problem, he rushes in far too quickly with the solution.

The research covers literally thousands of selling interviews both here and in the USA. And the results show that building up the problem so that the client prospect sees it to be a much bigger problem than he thought it was, is the key to star sales ability. Rackham finds no correlation between sales success and asking open-ended or closed-ended questions. Stars ask both kinds, and so do failures.

The type of questions asked by salespeople need redefining to be of any use. First, Rackham defines what he calls 'situational questions'. They are of the fact-gathering kind. 'How many people do you employ; what are your annual sales; to whom do you sell; how many plants do you operate?' and so on. Rackham finds that stars ask some of these questions, but only those which actually help him or her to develop a major sale. The star does not ask irrelevant questions.

But the novice often does ask irrelevant questions. Such questions are easy to ask. The client prospect will answer them happily – at least the first few. They pose no threat of rejection for the salesperson asking them. So the failure babbles on, asking questions which become steadily more irrelevant because they are not leading anywhere towards the customer's needs. In the end the customer becomes irritated, the salesman loses confidence and then becomes a failure.

But even if the salesperson goes on to develop a problem, his troubles may not be over. Suppose he asks the prospect to name his principal problem. The prospect does so. Then the failure leaps in immediately with his own solutions to the problem. If he does this, he will immediately attract a mass of objections. First of all, the salesperson will not have completely understood all the ramifications of the problem. Secondly, the prospect himself will have only selected a small part of the overall problem and will not himself see how big the problem really is.

So, by training the sales force to handle objections, we have managed to avoid training them to sell properly. Because if they get a mass of objections, it is undoubtedly their own fault. They will not have understood the problems fully, and they may not have convinced the prospect of the size of the problem. So the Rackham studies do not say that asking fact-finding questions are wrong – all stars ask some situational questions. What the study shows is that failures often ask too many of these, and they are often irrelevant. But the biggest single error is to leap in at the first mention of a problem and to suggest solutions. This may be acceptable for simple sales but not for major sales.

It is not just an issue between open questions which lead the prospect to answer at length or closed questions which lead to specific answers. The ultimate purpose of the questions is to uncover needs. So they have got to track into difficulties he is experiencing now, irritations or dissatisfaction with what he is doing at present. If this can be seen to be a big problem, by careful probing of all the ramifications problem and its effect upon the organization, then we have a chance of selling to him. Why? Because the prospect starts to perceive that he has real and practical difficulties to resolve and he needs help.

If we do not rush in too quickly with our proposed solution, if we take him carefully by questions through possible alternative solutions then he stops making objections. Also benefits become clearer – it is noticeable in the Rackham research that the star salesmen actually get the customer to nominate the principal benefits himself.

There is no need for closing techniques either. Actually, if a salesman uses any kind of force to secure an order, any kind of pressure, then the customer in a complex sale is likely to be turned off. The customer is actually making a commitment towards a long-term relationship. If you pressurize him, he thinks twice about working with you. In other words, what does a star salesman do, which normal mortals don't do? The star *gets the customer to sell himself.* He does not push. He gets the customer to pull. And he does it through developing more questions about the problem. It really could not be easier. And that's what you stars out there have been doing for years, isn't it?

ACTION POINT IDEAS

1   Get hold of the Rackham book, *Making Major Sales*, study it in detail, relate it to your own situation. Train yourself and the sales force on it.
2   Don't ask successful salesmen how they do it, because they don't know. You will have to observe them yourself. Compare what they do in practice over a dozen sales calls with what the new theory says. You'll see it working.
3   In your preparation, before the call, identify three problems which the customer might possibly have. Develop some key questions to uncover such problems. Train yourself to stop selling him immediately he has named one. Build up the problem first.
4   On each call, have in mind a specific objective which will advance the customer's business to the next stage. It must involve the customer in making some commitment, however wild, to take an action (setting up the next meeting is fine, if it progresses the sale.)

5   For complex sales forget any forcing techniques. If the business
    is there to be done then fine, take it, don't leave it. But don't
    threaten the future by using some trick closing device. He will
    spot you coming a mile off. Even if he buys then and there, he
    will be wary in the future. (There is specific evidence on this
    from the research.) On the other hand, don't be naive and fail
    to take an order if he is willing for the commitment.

YOUR MIND MAP

YOUR ACTION PLAN

How are you going to turn yourself and others into even greater stars, than you are now?

CAN YOU BE A MODERN DAY SALES STAR?

Today's search for the super star.

A Look at the factors. Comparing yourself to other people whom you know in your business, give yourself a rating out of 10 on each factor. (10 = very good indeed.)

B Now, having scored yourself, give each factor a rating out of 10 for its importance for your own selling process. (10 = very important indeed.)

C Subtract B from A. This shows you where you ought to improve your personal sales ability.

	A Give yourself marks out of 10	B The importance of this	C Calculate the result
1 Do you always get the customer to explain his problem	___	___	___
2 Do you probe his problem until he sees it as a big one?	___	___	___
3 Do you always get him to explain and to tell you of his explicit needs?	___	___	___
4 Does he end up by selling himself?	___	___	___
5 Do you get very few objections?	___	___	___
6 Does *he* tell *you* what the benefits are?	___	___	___
7 Does closing the deal always seem quite natural and unforced, somehow you both know it is right?	___	___	___
8 Is selling to people very very easy for you?	___	___	___
9 Do your customers come back to you again and again?	___	___	___
10 Do your customers come to depend upon you?	___	___	___

34

Are your salespeople saints or sinners? Prepare yourself

●

> Preparation, research and planning are the
> groundwork upon which success is built –
> Salespeople need to be shown, trained,
> motivated and controlled for their
> preparation and planning.

Q.1 *You want your salespeople to think about what they do, who they call on. You want them to be professional. Which of the following personality characteristics are likely to reveal the best 'planner'?*

 (a) A quiet, reserved type who was good at maths in school.
 (b) A warm friendly type who was great at art in school.
 (c) A lively assertive type who was captain of the school.
 (d) A married woman, with children.

Q.2 *How should the industrial salesman prepare for his calls?*

 (a) With appointments first.
 (b) With no appointment.
 (c) Concentrating upon big prospects.
 (d) With a mixture of appointments, telephone fill-ins and calling casually.

Q.3 *Opening new accounts. For an industrial or commercial salesman should these be done by:*

 (a) Cold calling.
 (b) Telephone selling by an office specialist to make appointments.
 (c) From enquiries generated by direct mail coupons.
 (d) From the salesman himself, through referrals.

ANSWERS

Q.1 (a) 5 points   This type does not necessarily make a good salesman but he will make a good planner probably.

   (b) 2 points   Often a 'salesman' type, but usually poor at planning.

   (c) 3 points   These assertive types can be good at planning when it suits them, otherwise they cut corners.

   (d) 4 points   Life has trained her. Ever balanced a budget, purchased supplies, controlled three kids, been a lover and run a Mash clinic at the same time?

Q.2 (a) 3 points   Bit cumbersome, will get you a low call rate per day.

   (b) 2 points   Creaming the surface stuff. Lot of calls per day but very few big orders.

   (c) 4 points   But there are others, too.

   (d) 5 points   It's obvious when you think about it.

Q.3 (a) 2 points   Very wasteful, but OK for fill-in calls in between your appointments.

   (b) 4 points   But if the salesman does not qualify the leads he will waste time on many poor prospects, with no hope.

   (c) 3 points   OK but again there will be many weak prospects amongst this lot.

   (d) 4 points   Quite good, this one. Could spend a lot of time chasing no hopers, though.

The right answer was not listed. It should be a mixture of all of these ways. You cannot lay down firm rules. If you didn't answer the question then go straight to the top of the class and give yourself 10.

SCORES

12–20 points   (Yes it is possible. Work it out. I didn't say it was likely, though, did I?)

8–11 points   Stupid questions, weren't they? They always are when you miss out on the top marks.

Up to 7 points   Stupid author.

●   ●   ●

MANAGERS, SORT OUT YOUR SHEEP FROM YOUR GOATS!

St Peter stands at the Pearly Gates. 'Did you close?' he says. 'No, I didn't', says the salesman. Doom.

'Did you find out who was making the decision?'
'No', says the salesman.
Doom.

'Did you plan the call thoroughly?'
'No, I waited to see what would happen.'
'What happens, my son, is Doom.'

Recognize the types? Have you got these types in your sales force? If so, they are headed for a hot hereafter.

Here's a good wheeze for getting a grip on your salesmen's technique. We are going to give you three sections based on the 'saints or sinners' theme. This one is about preparation and planning; the second will be about behaviour; and the third about sales technique.

In each we'll provide a small table each with six common salesmen's problems listed. Get each of your salesmen in turn to fill in the table with what they believe to be their own scores. You fill it in too. Then have a discussion about it to see where they can improve. It's not nasty; it's not critical. And, if you avoid turning it into a punch-up session, your salesmen will see where their next area of improvement lies.

PLANNING AND PREPARATION: SAINT OR SINNER?

	Very good	Average	Poor	
1 Good call preparation	5 4	3	2 1	Takes a chance on the call
2 Pre-sells the prospect	5 4	3	2 1	Tries to hit it in one
3 Researches the prospect	5 4	3	2 1	No customer knowledge
4 Finds the decision-makers	5 4	3	2 1	Relies on the 'buyer'
5 Good territory planning	5 4	3	2 1	Poor self-management
6 Good pioneering	5 4	3	2 1	Dodges new prospects

Total score must be 18.

What you do is this. Ask each salesman what he is best at on the list and what he is worst at. We can't all be perfect at everything so force out some differences. On his 'best' things give him a score of four or five. A score of one or two is for his worst things. But here's the rub: his total score for the whole test must be 18. It means that if you score a 4 for something then you must get a 2 somewhere else. (Score a five, then you must get a one or two twos.)

See how it works? It is not a competition between different members of your sales force. It provides a profile of one salesman's skills and aptitudes, a profile he can agree with you, and then work on his weaker areas. Because you are not comparing him with anyone else, he will not feel criticized. After all, even the weakest salesman will get a four or a five for something because the scores are only relative to his own performance, not anyone else's.

WHY SALES MANAGERS LOSE THEIR HAIR

Let's now look at each of these six items in turn.

1 *Call preparation:* If I could collect all the handfuls of hair torn out by managers who despair at getting their salesmen to plan better, I could carpet Britain. Planning means taking those precious few moments to work out what it is you want to achieve from the call; what information you need from the prospect. It means sorting out a priority list of what you plan to sell them. And it means a system for finding out the volume potential in their business and then calculating your goals around that. If you don't aim properly, then you can shoot yourself in the foot as easily as anywhere else.

2 *Pre-selling:* How many salesmen try to hit the sale in one? They are so busy chasing around, going from call to call, that they don't have time to sit back a bit and think. Get them to sort out their priority calls where there is serious volume available, then carefully to nurse that piece of business. They must cultivate the necessary relationships with the people who matter and dig that spade in deep.

Most customers need pre-selling. They work up to a decision. They get used to your ideas and finally take them on. The salesman who tries to hit it in one is doomed — most of the time.

3 *Research:* The man who knows his customers well will always beat the man who does not try to find out about them. So often a deal is cracked because someone does his homework better.

The man must know about the company, what they do, how they do it, how they use his product, who the bosses are, and all about the person he is to see. Some companies go further; some who sell high-value goods get the prospect's balance sheets and profit and loss accounts before the salesmen go in. But that's exceptional.

Make out a list of all the basics which ought to be known about the prospect and which you would expect your salesmen to know. Work out a system whereby they can get this information in advance, preferably from someone other than the buyer. And make them write it on a record card. That gives them good customer knowledge.

WHERE 60 PER CENT OF REPS GO WRONG

4   *Finding decision-makers:* Do you realize that 60 per cent of industrial salesmen are tripping around the country in their fancy Sierras calling on the wrong people? So many salesmen believe that it is buyers who buy. You and I know different. Only in a very few cases does the buyer not have to refer to someone else. Normal, pedestrian, mundane things – routine purchases which no one cares about – that's what a buyer buys on his own. But most purchases involve him in discussions with other people. Technicians exert a powerful influence; so do production directors and other managers behind the scenes. Sometimes the finance people will be involved, sometimes members of the board.

The buyer is only one of a group of people making the decision – and he is not usually regarded as being very senior in management terms. He can be a shy retiring violet with his colleagues although with your salesman he turns into Godzilla. So get your salesmen to look beyond the buyers. Get them to seek out the people who know what is going on and who influence or make the decision.

Often this means establishing contact high up in the organization, but sometimes people lower down the line will be just as useful. They know what is happening, the chiefs often don't. So talk with your salesmen about whether they are losing some deals because people behind the scenes who they do not know are pushing contracts to competitors.

5   *Territory planning:* If sales managers have any hair left, then they pick it out strand by strand whenever they see the way their salesmen plan their routes and journeys. St Peter love us, but this stuff goes back to 1935 and it is still just as valid today. The saints will get their first call in at 9 o'clock – the time the sinners are starting in the office. The saints prepare a plan around sensible routings leaving some flexibility for urgent calls. They make appointments in advance. They fill in with telephone calls to other prospects in the territory. The sinners go where they are sent and come straight back.

The saints grade their calls into A, B and C grade calls, paying more frequent attention to the A grades. The sinners think to themselves, 'That's a good idea' and then forget about it. The saints organize a four-day or five-day clover-leaf pattern to minimize their journeys.

Question: Using sound territory planning methods, how many more effective calls could your salesmen make? I bet it's another 15 per cent. Well then, that's 15 per cent of your money being wasted through not thinking at the simplest level.

SELLERS OR ORDER-TAKERS?

6   *Pioneering:* Lots of salesmen are afraid of difficult calls. What's a difficult call? A call on someone you haven't met before. The problem is that the salesman begins to rely on his old contacts. He sees himself in the role of providing customer service. And that's bunkum, because he should be selling. However well we service old accounts, some will die away and need replacing. In the long run, all will die off, so all need replacing. Also the company ought to want to grow. It makes life so much easier if we have floods of work pouring in. That's what effective selling can get for us. All salesmen should have their due quota of pioneering calls to make. They should all be capable of bringing in new business.

You may be saying at this point, 'But that's what all my people do anyway'. That's fine – but other people actually do have a problem with their sales forces in this way. And even if you are happy about the new business your people are bringing in, is there any more they can do? Are some people producing more than others? Should you not dig into it? It's your job to ensure your salesmen get to Heaven.

ACTION POINT IDEAS

1   Most sales managers control sales after the event. They compare results with targets. Few of them do what ought to be done, which is to get involved *before* the sale is made. Discuss the major accounts which are coming up in the next selling cycle. Agree how the sale is to be prepared. What is the objective to be? How is the deal going to go? What is the salesman going to try for? This will be enormously helpful to the salesman.

2   Put in sales coordinators to your team. Their job should be to follow up well qualified leads to new business and to make appointments for sales people to visit. This ensures your sales people make cold calls on new prospects.

3   If you have a series of difficult accounts in a territory, then consider backing your sales executive with another sort of personality, one who is good at planning, good at the detail. You can only afford this on the biggest business – on the other hand you cannot afford not to have a sound team managing the biggest business.

4   Get them to mix up their calls. Some timed appointments, surrounded with some recalls, and filled in with a few research calls for new business. Pass them over to your sales co-ordinator, to make appointments.

5   Sort out your biggest prospects and make out good detailed record cards for them, identifying the key decision makers and influencers. For each call, have an objective in mind which will move that call on to the next stage. Do not make service calls – always have something to move them towards.

6   Sort out their time management for them and their priorities. Determine how much time they should spend driving, how much in face-to-face selling, how much in paperwork, how much in the office. For their face-to-face time, how much is needed on new prospects, how much on present prospects and leads, how much on service calls to old prospects. Make them keep time sheets, so you can compare actuals to targets. Just keep this going for a while until they have got grooved in to new habits.

7   Keep a territory or two for experimentation. Always keep your sales team unsettled with new ideas, new schemes. But you need somewhere to test out your ideas, theories. You can spread such tests around your individual sales people. Take *their* results and use these to monitor and control the whole team after the test has been proven.

8   Ensure that into your biggest customer prospects your sales team researches low into the organization at junior levels in order to find out information, survey the prospect properly, establish the facts and problems and then construct propositions to suit the company from this data. Go low for information. Go high for decisions.

YOUR MIND MAP

YOUR ACTION PLAN

How are you going to get your team to plan, research and prepare better?

35

Are your salespeople saints or sinners? Behave yourself

●

> The wrong kind of behaviour in front of the
> customer can ruin the sale – Salespeople can
> be too strong. They can be too weak. They
> need to give the customer confidence.

Q.1 *You want your salespeople to get on well with others, but
not to be an easy pushover for a tough buyer. Which of the
following personality characteristics would you hire, if
building customer rapport was an important part of your
selling operation?*

    (a) A quiet, reserved type, very sound on product
knowledge.

    (b) A warm, outgoing personality, an easy mixer.

    (c) A restless individual, highly motivated towards
results.

    (d) A married woman, with children.

Q.2 *All the following behaviours are needed in selling. Which
would you pick as the most important for results in a service
industry?*

    (a) Gentle persistence.

    (b) Closing ability.

    (c) Self assured, unafraid of rejection.

    (d) Putting customers at their ease.

Q.3 *What actions are most likely to create confidence in the
customer's mind?*

    (a) Making an effective sales presentation.

    (b) Handling objections well.

    (c) Sound product knowledge.

    (d) Exploring the customer's problem.

ANSWERS

Q.1 (a) 3 points   You have to hire the right kind of personality for the job. If the customer is technical himself, then this kind will do well probably.

(b) 4 points   OK for most people, but they can irritate a tough buyer.

(c) 2 points   For the answer to the question on rapport this would score low. On the other hand this one is a winner. It depends how important rapport is to you.

(d) 5 points   If we go on like this we will be hiring our sales forces only consisting of women with children. But this is not guaranteed for success, either. She is going to be hard pressed on her technical knowledge, authority and competence by a tough buyer. But if she wins through this, then the respect she earns will last.

Q.2 (a) 5 points   No doubt at all.

(b) 3 points

(c) 4 points

(d) 4 points   Remember it is a service industry where people skills are going to count.

Q.3 (a) 3 points   It's impressive but better to talk about *their* needs.

(b) 2 points   If you sell well you rarely get objections.

(c) 4 points   Yes. No doubt about creating confidence.

(d) 5 points   This is best of all.

SCORES

14–15 points   No room for errors in this result.

10–13 points   Sorry. Top scores are very tight today.

Up to 9 points   (Have you ever thought about reading the answers, first, than doing the question? You would improve your scores.)

●   ●   ●

There's one single thing in sales management which beats all others. It beats motivation programmes, it beats commission, it beats management style, it beats target setting, it beats supervision and it beats training. All those things are important, sure, but this one thing is even more important.

It is recruiting the right sales executive initially. You can't make stars out of nothing. They have got to have the potential to start with. When was the last time you bought from someone who upset you? When did you last buy from someone who was boring? Or from someone aggressive? And have you not had hundreds of sales pitches from people who only have their own self-interest in mind, not yours as the buyer?

Question: Do any of your salespeople bore you? If so, then he or she bores the customers too. Is one of them aggressive? Then he or she will make your customers sales-resistant. Is one of your sales staff dedicated to his or her own self-interest? Then that's how he or she will be coming across to your customers. They will sell your product here and there. After all, if they call on enough live prospects or past customers, then a few will be bound to buy. Not because of your salesperson's skill, but because the prospect wants your product. You have bought from a boring salesperson in the past, haven't you, when you wanted the product badly enough?

FERRET OUT THEIR STRENGTHS AND WEAKNESSES

Use the same scoring system as in the previous chapter to measure each of your sales executives' behaviour in each of six categories over the page. Give them each a score out of 5. A score of 1 is very weak, 5 is very good, 3 is average. But the total score must add up to 18 for the six items taken together shown on the next page.

In other words, this is not competitive scoring between different people in the team. This gives you an idea of their individual 'behaviour profile'. It makes you work out their strengths and their weaknesses – for each member of the team. So, which of these things is he or she strongest at, and which weakest? Score them appropriately.

1 Creating confidence: It is very important to be able to put the other party, the customer, at their ease. To know one's product, to know the market and to have a confident manner. If the sales executive has little presence, or has a boring personality, this will make it difficult for customers to have confidence in them. They will not be able to create that all-important 'bond', particularly at the start of the interview.

2 Empathizing with the customer: People who are dedicated to their own self-interest do not make star salesmen – because it shows. You

can tell in the way they talk about themselves and their products –
rather than asking questions about the customer and his needs. People
often imagine that it is good selling to talk about themselves all the
time.

But the star salesman is a very fine listener. He listens with his eyes as
well as his ears. He can tell exactly how his prospect is feeling at any
one time. He does so from the gestures, the posture, the movement.
And he knows exactly when to shut up and listen, and when to
propose. He is, above all, sensitive to his customer's situation.

Question: Which of your salesmen are what you would call sensitive to your situation, your problem as the boss? Score those that are
good on this count high – and score the self-centred ones low.

SALES BEHAVIOUR: SAINT OR SINNER?

	Very good	Average	Poor	
1 Creates confidence and immediately puts customer at ease	5 4 3	2	1	Poor at creating initial empathy: makes prospect feel uneasy
2 Thinks mainly about the customer's need to buy	5 4 3	2	1	Thinks mainly about his own need to sell
3 Accepts rejection philosophically as part of the job	5 4 3	2	1	Uses avoidance tactics ducking the difficult situations
4 Seeks to be respected by prospects	5 4 3	2	1	Seeks to be liked by prospects, courts popularity
5 Patient and persistent	5 4 3	2	1	Aggressive, pushes too hard
6 Respectfully sceptical	5 4 3	2	1	Takes everything the buyer says at face value

Total score must be 18

3 Unafraid of rejection: Are any of your sales executives afraid of
difficult situations? Any of them nervous of tough buyers? Do any of
them avoid calling up the line to senior people in your customers'

organizations, such as technical directors, managing directors? Or do they settle instead for the safety of dealing with junior management in your customers' organizations? This is a great problem – the fear of rejection.

The signs to look for are a willingness to go after new business, to open up new accounts. A willingness to try for high-level interviews. Are your salesmen relaxed with their prospects or do they look and sound tentative and restrained – or even nervous?

If they are weak on this issue then nurse them along carefully with the motivation of success. Don't force them into too many failure-potential, high-threat situations. Set them lowish targets but keep pushing them along. Not too much at any one moment – but bit by bit, you'll improve their confidence. If you think they are all a bit tentative about difficult situations, then I should have a look at your product training and product knowledge. If salespeople are nervous of being asked a question they cannot answer, then they will be afraid of the prospect.

4 Earning respect: All your sales executives would like to be liked by their customers. Who does not want to be popular? But it can go too far. Some sales executives take the customer's side on nearly everything – indeed, they can start working against their own company. Particularly is this true if they are a long way away from their manager, or away from head office, or have very little supervision. Their only friends in business are the customers they cultivate. So take care with your sales executives if you do not see them often. Are they working more for the customer than they are for you?

PUSHINESS IS FATAL

5 Persistence, not aggression: Some salespeople have little patience. They try and do all their deals at one go. They grab the business and run. They push too hard, all the time. There are times for pushing, of course, but most of the time you need persistence rather than aggression, and sometimes having patience is the most important of all.

Yes, of course they must try and close the business when they can – but it is fatal to misjudge it, rush it too hard, get the timing wrong and blow it altogether. Only use very assertive salespeople for simple one-shot sales.

6 Respectfully sceptical: Buyers are tricky. They are sometimes greedy – 'I've got a cheaper quote, can you do something about the price?' They are fibbers when they try to get out of awkward situations. 'Sorry, I have not got the money left in the budget.' This is the hoary old put-off for the buyer who cannot think of a decent excuse for not buying. 'You'll have to do better than that', says the buyer who wants to squeeze in extras to the specification. Some buyers just leave other suppliers' quotes around where the salesmen can see them.

These moves are sometimes genuine and sometimes not. It takes a skilled judge to pick out the times when he is being conned by a buyer and to take his words with a pinch of salt. But the good sales executive will do just that. The weak one takes what the buyer says at face value.

Take each of your sales executives in turn. Go through each of these questions with them if you like. Discuss the issues. Ask them to score themselves on what they think they are best at and what they are worst at. Get them to give themselves marks. It is not a painful exercise. We are all better at some things than at others. Looking at themselves objectively is part of a salesman's job – athletes have to do it, so why not sales executives?

ACTION POINT IDEAS

1   Put the right kind of salesman into the job. Identify the behaviour you want in selling, and then recruit people just for that.
2   Work them at their product knowledge. Test them on it. Keep them talking about it. Run meetings on it. Test their applications knowledge. If they do not know what their products are, they cannot possibly create confidence.
3   Look to your customer's industry to recruit your salesmen. Bring a buyer of your products into your company as a salesman to sell to the kind of company he previously worked for. He will be very confident about the industry, be completely at home.
4   If your salesmen can be pushed over by you, if they won't say boo to your goose, then they'll be pushed over by the customers, too. You need a bit of fight, a bit of spirit in your team.
5   Look at your sales people. Are they street-wise? Do they know what tricks the customers can get up to? Or do they think they are in the customer service business?
6   Watch out for the 'Thank you for giving me the opportunity to come here and present our ...' brigade. It's submissive rubbish. It is OK so long as they don't mean it. But if they think that selling is all about creeping to customers for business, then you have got a team that is boring the pants off the market.
7   Do you find any of your salespeople boring? So do your customers. Even boring customers will find them boring.

YOUR MIND MAP

YOUR ACTION PLAN

Have your sales team got the right attitude, the right behaviour? What should you do to improve things?

36

Are your salespeople saints or sinners? The six deadly sins

●

> Here are the six main errors made by
> salespeople – Whether through nerves, poor
> training, bad experiences or never having
> been shown the right way, many experienced
> salesmen can commit these errors without
> realizing it.

Q.1 *The most common error made by salesmen out of this list is:*

(a) Selling features of the product, not the benefits.
(b) Failing to close properly.
(c) Not knowing the profitability of the sale.
(d) Not showing proofs of claims.

Q.2 *Which is an even bigger error made by salesmen, even beyond the above list?*

(a) Not making enough calls.
(b) Failing to see decision-makers.
(c) Failing to meet sales targets.
(d) Failing to uncover real needs.

Q.3 *If Purgatory exists in the after life for salesmen, what is the punishment likely to consist of?*

(a) Buyers who say, 'Leave it with me, I'll think it over?'
(b) Buyers who say, 'Your price is too high, my son.'

(c) Buyers who say, 'I'm very happy with my existing service.'

(d) Sales managers who say, 'I'll reduce your target next time, my son, so you'll have an easier time in meeting it.'

ANSWERS

Q.1	(a)	5 points	Out of the list, believe it or not this is the most common problem. It is widespread – probably 70 per cent of salespeople make this mistake. Just listen to them.
	(b)	3 points	If the job has been done well, you should not need closing techniques. But some salesmen are afraid to go for it at all. That's a different matter.
	(c)	3 points	It *is* true that this is widespread, but not many companies require their salespeople to know profitability. I do not recommend it. I *do* recommend, however, that salespeople should know that A is more profitable than B, and B is more profitable than C.
	(d)	3 points	This is also widespread. But management must supply the data to salespeople.
Q.2	(a)	2 points	Mundane.
	(b)	4 points	Yes, very serious problem.
	(c)	2 points	Depends upon how tough the sales targets are.
	(d)	5 points	This is *it*: the number one *deadly sin*.
Q.3	(a)	3 points	Nasty problem, but many complex sales are like this, and you *cannot* close them there and then. It is normal everyday punishment for sales folks.
	(b)	2 points	So they play games in Purgatory? Sounds like a lot of fun, to me.
	(c)	5 points	'Oh no. Not again, St Peter. Give me the flagellation, any day.'
	(d)	1 point	You've made a mistake here. This is *Heaven*. They sent you to the wrong place.

SCORES

12–15 points	Some of these are a bit tricky. So I'll be flexible on the top scores.
8–11 points	I know your business is different to the one I'm thinking about, and in *your* business your answers are all right. Tough. You still don't get into top marks.
Up to 7 points.	Look, I don't care how different your business is, your answers are still wrong.

● ● ●

SIX PEARLS OF SELLING WISDOM FROM ST PETER

'So you think you deserve to get past the Pearly Gates, my son', says St Peter.
'Oh yes', says the salesman. 'I used to be a technical man before going on to selling, so I know all about the products.'
'And did you tell the customers?' asks the saintly boss man.
'Oh yes', says the salesman.
'All of it?' muses the Saint, sliding his halo back.
'Every single bit.'
'Sorry, son', says St Peter. 'You'll have to do better than that.'

Here's a table with six common technical faults made by sales representatives. It's part of the analysis of salespeople's strengths and weaknesses – under the 'saints and sinners' theme. Get your salespeople to fill in their own scores – what they are good at, and what they are bad at. You fill in your view of their ability as well, then use it to have a serious discussion about their sales technique.

Have each of your sales executives say which of these items he thinks he is best at, and which he thinks he is worst at. Let him score himself four or five for the good things, but these must be balanced by ones and twos somewhere else. After all, we all have weaknesses somewhere. The total score for all six items must add up to 18.

SALES SKILLS: SAINT OR SINNER?

		Very good Average Poor	
1	Sells benefits to the customer	5 4 3 2 1	Sells technical features
2	Has something new to say on each call	5 4 3 2 1	Uses same approach and story all the time
3	Shows firm proofs of benefits claimed	5 4 3 2 1	Relies upon customers believing him
4	Goes for a commitment or closes well	5 4 3 2 1	Lacks the killer touch.
5	Sells quality against competitor's prices	5 4 3 2 1	Tries to match price or gives in on discounts
6	Knows his product priorities, sells profitably	5 4 3 2 1	Sells only what customers demand

Total score must be 18

1 *Benefits or features*: It's amazing how many people come into our office and think that, so long as they tell us all about how their product is made and its price, then we will buy. This is a particular fault with people employed first in a technical capacity and who are then 'sent out to sell'. Just a moment's thought will show that what the buyer is interested in is himself. How does this technical gobbledygook fit in with his needs? That's what he wants to know. What are the benefits?

And if you don't believe me, you have not tried buying a microcomputer for the office. I watched a small builder talk to a computer salesgirl the other day. 'Will it do a project costing for me?' he asked.

'Oh yes', she said. 'You can put all your accounts on it, too. It's got enough memory to do all your management figures and graphics as well. If you want more storage or faster loading, then we recommend you use a hard disk.'

'Yes, but can it do a costing for me?'

'Well, if you have a spreadsheet program, then you can use it for forecasting, budgeting and for cash flow as well', she said. 'Your accountant can help you set it up.'

He walked out. Very slowly. Shaking his head.

Nasty question for you. Have you got anyone who sells like this? They are headed underground after they meet St Peter.

LEAVE SOMETHING OUT

2 *Saying something new*: If your sales executives make regular calls on buyers it's very easy for them to slip into the 'Have you anything for me today?' syndrome. Even when following up quotes, it is important for the sales executive to have something new to say – every time. If you ask St Peter how much you should tell the customer, he'll say 'Just enough to land the business, my son.'

The saintly old male chauvinist goes on: 'Leave something out of your story – an additional benefit, a different application, a new angle, so you can use it on the re-call.' Every time the buyer sees or hears him, your salesman should have something different to say.

3 *Proving it*: Word of mouth is the weakest authority of all. The claims go in the buyer's one ear and out the other. Confirmed afterwards in writing, they are more credible, but only just. Using a third-party reference – a testimonial, a referee – is better. Better still is using hard factual data – particularly if it has been produced by an independent testing authority. Showing the customer your technical press cuttings makes your claims much, more more believable.

Don't let your salespeople just make claims. Give them the evidence – so they can prove their story.

4 *The killer touch*: Sometimes sales executives just walk away from deals. They leave the buyer to think about it, when he is perfectly prepared to place the business. If he thinks about it, he might just try for one more quote, see one more sales executive, and then your rep has lost the business. He'll never know why he lost it, either. If they are nervous or afraid, then they simply will not close.

5 *Price – the big bogey*: For some sales executives, price is the big bogey. They lie in wait for it, dreading the moment the buyer whistles through his teeth and says, 'That's too much'.

Someone sold my wife and I a carpet the other day. Out of every range he showed us he assumed we wanted the cheapest. He took a lot of convincing that we actually wanted the top of his range. We bought it – once we'd squeezed him on the price, of course. After all, he seemed to expect price pressure and we didn't want to disappoint him. He'd got it sold anyway whether he gave us a discount or not. You know the story – you do the same when you buy. Don't you?

6 *Product priorities*: Now it's all very well selling what the customer wants – but we should know our own priorities too. What is most profitable for us to sell, what is least unprofitable. We should know something about the cost of the things we include in free service.

N.B. I don't recommend the sales executives should know the full story on profitability – that's generally bad news if they are facing greedy and rapacious buyers (i.e., most big buyers and quite a few little ones!). But we should know what it suits the company to sell. Have targets on it, too. So that where we get the chance to influence the buying decision, we can improve our company profitability. So, add up all your scores. Have you got more saints or a majority of sinners? St Peter would like to know 'cos he's preparing his forecasts.

ACTION POINT IDEAS

1 *Benefits and features*: This can be very, very confusing. If I say we offer faster delivery, is that a feature or a benefit? Most people say it is a benefit (because it seems obvious). But actually it is a feature until I go on to point out that the customer can then keep his stocks lower, or replace his stocks quicker, or order later, or use us for emergencies. These are all benefits.

   Make a list of all the features (which answer the questions, 'How does it do that?' or 'What does it do?') Extend each one into extending the statement for the customer 'And this means that you can…' Then train your salespeople over and over again with the differences. It *is* tricky, sometimes.

2 *Leave something out*: In their sales plans, always build in some advantage or some additional factor which they can use the second time around. When you supervise their calls just ensure that they tell the customer enough to land the business or to get it to the next stage. They must leave themselves with a way back in, later.

3 *Proving your claims*: Develop case histories of successful customer cases. Give them some customer names and telephone numbers so prospects can call. Give them evidence from your own laboratory tests. Give them press cuttings. Give them results of independent tests. Give them every piece of documentary evidence you can think of which they can use to back their claims.

4 *Closing*. They must not think they are simply advisers or consultants or counsellors or whatever. They must land business. They must see the object and be confident enough to go for it. If you have a salesman who is not closing properly, then either he is too soft and lacks the drive for success; or else you have not trained him properly and his confidence is low.

5 *Price*: Give them training in price negotiation techniques. Use the other chapters in this book on the subject to form the basis of your training programme adapted for your own business.

6 *Product priorities*: Don't tell them all about the costs. Just tell them what you want them to sell more of and how it benefits the company. Build the product priorities into their sales plan.

YOUR MIND MAP

YOUR ACTION PLAN

How are you going to zap up your sales techniques and avoid these errors?

37

Kamikaze selling

●

> Some sales forces commit suicide – While
> there are no guaranteed ways to gain success
> in selling, there are a number of ways to send
> the salesman to his doom.

Q.1 *The customer is thinking of buying a cheap product, which
you know to be inferior to yours. Do you,*

(a) Tell him this directly.
(b) Let him find out for himself.
(c) Compare specifications, like with like.
(d) Tell him of some general problems which customers
sometimes experience and which your product
avoids.

Q.2 *You know the customer is going to agree. You are very
pleased. He offers to buy lunch for you. Do you,*

(a) Apologize saying you have another appointment but
perhaps next time.
(b) Accept, offer to pay, in order to tell him more about
your product and company background.
(c) Use the opportunity to explore for future business.
(d) Make sure that he has really understood everything
you have said while you have lunch.

Q.3 *You are facing a group of people who are likely to give you a
hard time. They are likely to be resistant to your proposal.
How do you play it?*

(a) Make a sales presentation then ask for questions.
(b) Turning the meeting over to them, and just answering
their questions as they think of them.

(c) Concentrate mostly upon the boss, getting the decision-maker involved in your sales pitch.

(d) Ask them to think up the most difficult questions which should be asked of companies such as yours.

ANSWERS

Q.1 (a) 1 point   Knocking. You have to take care. Read the chapter.

(b) 1 point   Some adviser you'd make if you leave him to fend for himself.

(c) 5 points   Great. But make sure you know the competitor's product specification inside out, and make sure that you take the customer through the specifications line by line while both bits of paper are there.

(d) 4 points   This is recommended in the chapter rather than (c) because you can seldom get the two product specifications out side by side.

Q.2 (a) 5 points   Yes. Cut and run. Nicely, though.

(b) 2 points   You've got the deal. How can you improve on that? But you still have time to lose it though.

(c) 3 points   Bit crummy this. He is paying for lunch. He is going to buy from you. And he is going to get more pounding for future business. How high up are you on the sensitivity scale?

(d) 1 point   If you want to be sure, do it now. Do it later, you will raise doubts when you are relaxed and start rambling on about your poor results this month, and how you work for Mr Ghengis, and isn't this a lovely brandy.

Q.3 (a) 3 points   Just because this is what most people do, does not mean you have to follow the herd, does it?

(b)   2 points   Try getting into control after this.
                     Everything you say will sound like an
                     excuse.

(c)   1 point   The boss can say yes, but all the others
                     can say no. And there is more of them
                     than there is of the boss. And they *will*
                     say no, mark my words.

(d)   5 points   Great. *You've* asked for the difficult
                     questions and you'll get them. But you
                     know which ones they'll be, don't you?
                     What a confident start. You suss out the
                     audience, find out who is pro you and
                     who is con, draw their fire, then you go
                     into your presentation nicely moulded
                     around their points. You have total
                     control. Actually, it's worth 6 points.
                     Give yourself a bonus.

SCORES

13–15 points   I'm getting tough in my old age. Possible to
                    bomb out here and get low scores. You were
                    getting too confident anyway.

9–12 points   Not getting over-confident are we?

Up to 8 points   Lots of people score here on this test. So
                    don't feel too bad about it. You need a bit of
                    a confidence booster.

● ● ●

HOW TO AVOID BEING A KAMIKAZE SALESMAN

Being a crazy salesman is one thing. That's when you break the rules in order to win. But being a kamikaze salesman is bad, really bad. Have you got any salesmen who dive towards their own doom?

There is a standard exercise we use in training seminars. We get the participants to make a number of telephone calls to their own sales offices as if they were prospective customers. They have to score their own salespeople on the telephone out of five. For example, how many rings are there before the phone is answered? Does the person get their name and telephone number for calling back? Is the person interested in them? Do they have product knowledge?

Don't name your competitors

Here comes the tricky one. They ask about the price. When they are given a price, they then ask, without any pressure at all, if the salesperson knows where they can buy it cheaper. I tell you, in absolute truth, that 5 per cent of the salespeople who are asked this question will proceed to do a marvellous selling job for their competitors! It is as if they were on their competitors' payroll. Some kamikaze salespeople actually recommend other people's products in preference to their own, when their own fits the bill perfectly well. If that isn't kamikaze selling, I don't know what is.

There is quite a good rule on this business of competitors. Don't name any competitors yourself or even assume the job is competitive unless you have been given the signal by the buyer. But if he mentions a competitor, you must find out who you are up against, what his specification is and what his price is. If the buyer tells you it's competitive, then the gloves are off.

Don't knock the competition

I asked my secretary a few years ago, to sort out which word processor we should buy for our personal office. I asked her to examine any ones she liked, go to exhibitions, but she must have a look at the market leader and the number two. After all, there must be a reason why one supplier is market leader, and the number two is probably pretty good, too. This is normal buyer strategy.

It was taking a long time. I asked her if she was close to a decision. She was grumpy with me. 'It's a terrible job, this,' she said. 'All the computer salesmen come in and all they do is to criticize the competition. They all say where their machine is better, faster, bigger or whatever, and they point out the other machines as being faulty. I honestly don't know where I am.'

'Well, you've got to decide on one of them,' said I.

'I'm going to look at the Apple machine and then decide,' she said.

I asked her why knowing that Apple was not on our original list of machines because it uses a different operating system. (Early days of personal computers, this was.) She said to me, 'Yes, I know that. But all the salesmen seem to compare themselves against Apple. They all say how much better they are than Apple. So I had better have a look at Apple.'

You see what had happened. By knocking and naming the competition, they had put the buyer right off. She thought they were all a bunch of crooks. But she ended up looking at the one they mentioned most. The selling job for Apple had been done by their competitors knocking it.

We waited a while, and bought IBM instead. The machine was much more expensive than we needed to have paid. It was slower and had less capacity than other cheaper versions on the market. But at least with IBM you know they are still going to be on the market in ten years time. Against all the odds they became brand leader within the year of launch.

But on the other hand

If you want to knock the competition, here is the way to do it. If you want to plant a worry in the customer's mind, then simply say, 'Well, I don't know about the company or product you have just named, but I do know that some other machines have a problem with their doofer plungers, which hang too low ... and this causes ...' You have not knocked the competitor specifically, but you will make the customer chase up on their doofer plunger hanging specifications.

Sometimes, I might ask a prospect to think of the six hardest questions he can put to a company like mine. The six questions should have me squirming. I will give him a suggestion of four of them for starters. They will be four on which we are clean but which are true competitive advantages of ours. And at the end, I'll ask him in fairness to ask the competitors the same questions. This works well, particularly if you are selling to a group of people and you challenge them to fire difficult questions at you.

Don't indicate you are willing to trade

The number one rule in bargaining is, 'Don't bargain if you don't have to bargain.' If you can get all you want without dealing, then get it. But a lot of salesmen, when facing a buyer who is walking away from them, will try and land them on price. 'Oh, and I can get you a discount', they jabber. Now this teaches the buyer that all he has to do to force the salesman to reduce the price is to walk away. This is hopeless. In fact, it's worse than hopeless. It's kamikaze selling.

If he doesn't want to buy, then no amount of price reduction is going to make him. You've got to get him on his needs, and on your benefit story. And if he is going to buy from you, but is playing games, you are merely teaching him to make life difficult for you. So name your price when you know he is going to buy. There is, of course, a whole game to be played on price negotiations, but the guaranteed way to lose is to give an indication early in the conversation that price reductions are possible.

Don't give them a shopping list

'Would you like some of these, then?' asks the salesman. The buyer shakes his head. 'Well, we have a very nice line in these others, and they come in several colours.' Slowly, item by item, the salesman goes through his shopping list of products. The buyer just sits there shaking his head and is bored out of his tiny mind. How many times do buyers get salesmen coming to them with this kind of approach? Far, far too many.

You've got to get the prospect involved. You've got to get him talking. Talking about his problems, talking about his needs. Then, when you have his requirements lined up, you can select the thing that suits him. But have an alternative up your sleeve.

Ask buyers what kind of salesmen they dislike most, and they'll tell you it's the shopping-list merchant. They find him totally insensitive. This kind of selling is very wasteful, and this kind of salesman is no better than a leaflet about the product range. You can print 1000 leaflets for £60; 1000 shopping-list calls from personal salespeople will cost you £20 000. So don't hire walking shopping lists.

Talking your way out of the deal

A salesman was talking to my wife about a carpet the other day. Selling her with explanations about a particular grade. She chose the colour and chose the grade, having been assured that it was the right quality. The chap could have taken the order there and then, but instead he went on chatting, like a chump.

He told her that there were other grades available in that colour. Now this confused her. 'What are the other grades?' she asked him. 'Well, one is higher quality and one is lower', he replied vaguely. 'What's the difference, compared to the one we've got?' she asked, becoming more agitated. He examined the carpet we had and said it was difficult to tell. I chipped in then from around the corner and asked what was the difference in price of these other grades. He told us. My wife said we would discuss it and come back to him.

When he had left, without the order, she was really concerned. 'Do you think we are doing the right thing?' she asked me. 'He didn't seem to know which one to recommend.' I was furious as well. This chump had got the order and we were quite happy, but he had gone on talking about it afterwards and had now managed to talk us out of it. When you've got the business, if you go on talking, you can only lose it.

ACTION POINT IDEAS

1   Ask your sales people individually to fill in this questionnaire. Compare their answers with yours. Discuss with them.

2   Identify from this list about six major faults. Ask the sales team as a group to mark themselves out of ten on each of these faults. A high mark is for a good performance, a low mark is for bad. Call this A list. Now ask them to take your six faults and to mark them out of ten for importance in the selling process. Call this B list. Subtract A from B. The highest scores are now where the salesman should concentrate upon what he is doing wrong.

3   Ask your sales force to write down four major difficulties they face when selling. Buyers' objections, etc. Taking examples from each person, list them on a board. Now get the team as a whole to vote on these, give them three votes each, for the three most difficult problems. Get them to score themselves on how they think they perform on these problems. Have them discuss this in pairs. Each pair should then say what solutions should be found for these problems.

4   Have them sorted into groups with $1\frac{1}{2}$–2 hours to spare. Make a tape recording with the buyer raising these problems, and the seller has to handle the difficulties. The aim is to produce a perfect tape. The tape should last for a maximum of eight minutes. Have the whole team listen to each tape, making notes about what they think is bad, what is good, and where any opportunities existed which were not exploited. Let the group which made each tape have a right of reply at the end.

5   Work the poorest salesmen hard with more joint visits, tighter target limits (not harder, just tighter, i.e. limited price discretion). Don't be negative with them, help them. But in the end they must either leave or improve.

7   Get them to phone you with their plans for each major call just as they are going in to it. With car telephones these days, this is easy.

YOUR MIND MAP

YOUR ACTION PLAN

Identify their weaknesses. How are you going to improve them?

EIGHTEEN SUICIDE STEPS IN SELLING

How frequently do your salespeople shoot themselves in the mouth with these bullets?

	Never	Rarely	Some-times	Often	Very often
Assuming the customer knows all about the product and your company	___	___	___	___	___
Matching competitors' price instead of the quality	___	___	___	___	___
Failing to get all of the possible business	___	___	___	___	___
Selling technology instead of benefits	___	___	___	___	___
Not using presentation aids, not producing evidence, not supplying proofs of your claims	___	___	___	___	___
Being liked and popular rather than being respected and tough when necessary	___	___	___	___	___
Running away from complaints and trouble	___	___	___	___	___
Giving in to a no too easily	___	___	___	___	___
Being too self-centred	___	___	___	___	___
Not asking the boss for help when needed	___	___	___	___	___
Selling only the products they are familiar with	___	___	___	___	___
Lacking customer knowledge	___	___	___	___	___
Being afraid to sell to the top person	___	___	___	___	___
Not using their sales training	___	___	___	___	___
Rushing the big deal	___	___	___	___	___
Breaking the company rules	___	___	___	___	___
Not calculating facts, figures, profits, beforehand	___	___	___	___	___
or the big one:	___	___	___	___	___
NOT PREPARING THOROUGHLY ENOUGH	___	___	___	___	___

38

Crazy selling

●

> Sometimes you have to break the rules in
> order to win business – When to use
> specialized tactics in order to overcome
> obstacles. When to go into reverse on your
> sales training.

Q.1 *Your long-standing customer has been cheating a bit. You
have made good your promises, but he has not been com-
pleting his side of the bargain. And he has not been paying
your bills on time. How are you going to handle it?*

(a) Showdown time. You tell him fairly straight what is
wrong, up front, but remain polite.
(b) Let the problem drift until you have got the next order
then raise it.
(c) Try not to raise the problem at all. See if you can get
someone else to handle it instead of you.
(d) Threaten him with a lawsuit, and put him on the stop
list until he behaves.

Q.2 *You have four competitors all putting in quotations. When
do you want to see the customer?*

(a) Early on, to give him prices.
(b) Right at the end, after the others.
(c) Doesn't matter, so long as your prices are right.
(d) See him first, *and* last if you can manage it.

Q.3 *The buyer is threatening you. He says he is going to get rid
of you as a supplier unless you do something he wants.
What do you do? He is ridiculing your company unfairly. His
demands are heavy.*

(a) Go quiet until he has finished, and then resume selling.

(b)   Prepare to leave, politely saying you never negotiate under threat.

(c)   Point out the deficiencies in his personality and intellect and demand to see his superior.

(d)   Pick holes in his organization, too. Show him you can hand it out as well as him.

ANSWERS

Q.1   (a)   5 points   It's right. Remain cool, calm and collected, but your demands on him must go up front before you do more selling. Otherwise you will never get the relationship right. You can do it. Have courage. (And have a boss who agrees to your strategy first.)

(b)   3 points   This is what most people do. And buyers continue to get away with murder.

(c)   3 points   This is where both the buyer *and* you get away with murder. Who is this chump who is going to do the nasty work for you. Oh, it's your boss, is it? Well, that's all right then. If you want the boss to take over all your difficult accounts, that's fine.

(d)   1 point   If it has gone as far as that then the relationship is at an end. But for this to work, you must have extraordinary bargaining power. Question: if things have gone this far, has he got the ability to do what you want? Has he got any money, for example. This could be a stone which contains no blood.

Q.2   (a)   2 points   Yes, see him early. But not to give him firm prices. Every competitor with an ounce of nous will come after you, rubbish your proposition nicely, find out your prices and undercut you.

(b)   4 points   But his mind might be mostly made up by then. But close to his deadline is a good strategic position for you.

	(c)	3 points	It does matter. And prices are not everything – it is your quality related to his needs which matters.
	(d)	5 points	What a wonderful strategist you are. You really think about things.
Q.3	(a)	3 points	Aren't you the laidback one?
	(b)	5 points	Yes, providing it is polite.
	(c)	1 point	Makes you feel great uh? So does losing the customer.
	(d)	3 points	I am not totally against this provided it is done with great control, extreme politeness, even a little charm. You could, just could, get away with it. But for the rest of us earthly mortals it is a loser.

SCORES

11–15 points	Not too easy this lot. Makes you think a bit.
8–10 points	Take comfort. They are not easy issues.
Up to 7 points	Don't take any comfort.

● ● ●

LEARNING THE ART OF CRAZY SELLING

The techniques examined here can only be handled by real experts. This is not the stuff of which sales training courses are made. But these are the kind of ideas which can win business, big business, in the hands of people who have been through the basic training mill and who have great confidence and experience.

Sales training in most organizations is too simplistic. It is based on getting newcomers to selling grooved into a number of standard patterns of thought and behaviour which will help them. No one can quarrel with ideas like selling benefits and not features. No one can quarrel with the idea of finding out customers' needs and developing propositions around them. Actually, most salesmen would be far more effective if they followed these rules. And they are such basic rules that none of the experts ignore them.

Selling technique is a mass of customs, so-called rules and preju-dices. For instance, the salesman should be a self-starter. He should identify needs. He should counter objections. He should present ben-efits. He should close. He should secure 'yes' responses. He should ask open-ended questions. Of course he should – most of the time. But there are times when he should break the rules. He has got a mind of his own – he must respond to circumstances. If you want him to sell with robotic-like precision, then you have not got a salesman, you've got a mobile mailshot.

Here are the times to break the rules in order to come out winning. And if you don't break the rules at these times, then you stand a big chance of losing.

When you should not close

'Always be closing' said the old rule – they used to call it the ABC of selling. If you spot a chance then take it. And if it does not work first time, try again later. But I put a big question mark over this repetition of closing attempts. No one could ever sell to my wife Gillian like that – the more the salesman pushes, the more she walks away. She is the type of customer who should be handled with care. She has a very high steadiness factor in her personality. It makes her wary. The more eager someone is for her to do something, the more wary she is. She is like many buyers. They need a lot of space for their decision. If you identify this high steadiness type, back off and don't push too hard for the deal. Don't worry, they'll come after you. It's fine to close other types of personality, but take it easy with this group.

When you should avoid quoting prices

The order in which your quotation and those of your rivals go into the customer is very important. The customer tends to remember the first salesman who comes in. But the problem is that everyone coming in afterwards can investigate what the buyer has in mind and find out what competitors' quotes are – or at least get an idea. Then they are in a position to cover them. They can kill their rivals' benefits stories, sell against their weaknesses, and undercut them on price. So it might seem that a good place to be in the queue for quotes is last. But the problem is that by then the buyer is bored with the whole affair and has probably already made up his mind. Wresting the business away from the favoured supplier at that point is a tough job.

So where should you be in the list of those quoting? Simple. You should be first and last. You should set them up with the excitement of your proposition and its benefits early in the process, by being the first or one of the first to present. But then you should aim for a re-bid. Give them only a 'quote for budgeting purposes'. Give them a ballpark figure because you have not managed to work out the final figures yet.

Ask them when their decision is to be made and make an appointment for that time. Excite them by telling them that when you come back you will have a marvellous deal for them. And give them this marvellous deal after all the others have bid. You will stand a good chance of landing it through being first and last. So don't put your real quote in too early.

When you should not sell

When there is very high sales resistance, stop selling. Go into anti-sell. Tell them you are not there to sell them anything, you are just asking them for information. Ask them for their counsel. But above all stop selling. Win their confidence first, give them reassurance, and come back and sell to them later.

Try pressure selling *Encyclopedia Britannica* and see how far it gets you. One top sales executive I know stops her presentation, shuts up the book and says, 'No, I can't do it.' 'Do what?', says the prospect. 'Sell you this encyclopedia', she says. 'Why not?', says the prospect. 'Because you have got better things to spend your money on, and you should not afford this', she says. That was her closing technique: the anti-sell. She was one of their star sales executives.

When you should walk away

When an important buyer is pressurizing you with demands or threats, just say your company never negotiates under threat. Close up your papers and prepare to walk away. If you are facing extreme demands then you must prepare to go into reverse. He may let you go. You may live to fight another day. But one thing is certain, if you stay and negotiate in the face of heavy demands, you will lose. Just call his bluff. Nine times out of ten, that's what it is. And if, when you walk away, you can leave yourself with a way back later, that's ideal. It will be a different game next time. You'll be dealing as equals.

When you should admit your deficiencies

In every presentation it is a good thing to admit your deficiencies, but you must get the timing right. Where you want to build trust, you can do so by opening up a bit, but don't be naive. I watched an American in a chemicals company in Ohio training his salesmen to open up with a new buyer by saying that if the buyer wanted to buy certain kinds of products, then although the company supplied them, there were much better specialist suppliers in the market. On the other hand, if the buyer wanted another product, his company might or might not be best – it depended on the specific application. *But* if the buyer wanted to buy this product, or this, or this, or this one, he should not look anywhere else, because his company was the best specialist supplier of these products in the world.

It all sounds pretty crummy when written down like this. But you should hear the sales pitch in practice. It was tremendous. Why? Because everything the salesman said was true. He knew it, and the customer knew it too. Being truthful is important, but watch your timing. If you have to get across some awkward things about your product or service, the time to do it is just after the buyer has agreed to buy. And you should do it by summarizing all the good points in your favour, adding the bad points so that he cannot afterwards say that you misled him, and finally adding another couple of good points. Then you will tie up your deals nicely.

When you want the buyer to say 'no'

Some top salesmen actually try to get the buyer saying 'no'. Now that sounds crazy, but this is what they do. They go through their sales pitch and have a relaxed two-way conversation until the buyer says 'What do you recommend for us?' or something similar. Then they use the alternative close. This is familiar to all you experienced folks out there – it simply means that you offer him either this proposal or an alternative proposal and ask which one he prefers. In this way the prospect finds it hard not to buy.

What the star does is to recommend that the prospect selects one particular proposal. And he promotes the one which he thinks the prospect will turn down. He sells him this one, and gets his 'no'. Then he brings out the one which he thinks the prospect will buy and suggests that as a compromise. The prospect is far more likely to take this one, having had a chance to argue and refute what the salesman has been suggesting. So the star puts up the unacceptable proposal, gets his 'no' and then sells him on the proper one. Buyers like saying 'no'. It puts them in charge. So give them this satisfaction.

When you should stop selling

Some salesmen find it pays to stop being persuasive at certain times. Most of the time, the seller finds himself in a position of mild inferiority to the buyer. Not all the time, and not with all buyers, of course. But there comes a time when being nice, being pleasant, proposing solutions to buyers' problems just doesn't work. These are the times when the buyer is not doing his side of the deal.

Often you will find that you, as the seller, make good your side of the bargain, but the other side cheats a bit. They don't do what they agreed to do. They mess you about with special demands. They do not pay their account on time. When you are in dispute, or when you have to bring the buyer to heel over something, it pays to stop being persuasive.

You become the buyer instead. Do it early in the meeting, but tell him straight what is wrong. Don't leave it until later. Make sure you can prove your case. Supply the evidence and press the buyer hard to make good the deficiencies. Stop selling. When the buyer has agreed to make good whatever is wrong, then you can go back to your old pleasant ways again.

There is no one more persuasive or nicer than a finance man when he wants to lend you money for something, such as a new car, particularly if he is in competition for your business. But if you fall behind with your payments, see how he changes when he comes to repossess the vehicle or to get the payments. Salesman? More like Attila the Hun.

When to turn up late

Some star salesmen find it useful to turn up late at some meetings. Have you ever been kept waiting by a buyer? It's demeaning, is it not? It puts you off guard and it unsettles you. Well, some top salespeople use the same technique on a buyer who keeps them waiting.

If the meeting is for 10 am, they wait in reception until 10.15 and then walk out to their car after reminding the buyer's secretary that they are there. At 10.30 am they come back in again. If the buyer apologizes, they apologize and explain that they were just catching up on some work in the car. If the buyer does not apologize, neither do they. The technique is called 'reflection' by psychologists – doing back to them what they do to you. And it is a useful device.

When to go silent

Some salesmen break the rules by sometimes not saying anything at all. This sounds odd, but there are two occasions when silence is very, very useful.

The first is when the buyer says virtually nothing himself. This situation is unnerving for most salesmen. They feel they have to fill the gap with words, so they rabbit away without getting the buyer to participate.

So the really skilled seller, faced with a silent buyer, will turn again to reflection. He will simply go quiet too. He will make the minimum of conversation, ask a question and then go quiet. Two silent people facing each other can make for one hell of a lot of boredom. It can also take a long time. But it is important to bring the other person equally into the conversation. If you feel awkward with silence, then remember that he will feel awkward too after a time. So he will talk.

The other time to use the technique is shortly after you see a little blue light flashing in your rear-view mirror. You draw up to one side of the road and a man in a white hat gets out, examines your car and tells you that 'anything you say will be taken down and may be used in evidence against you.' At this time, star salesmen keep very quiet indeed.

ACTION POINT IDEAS

1   At your next sales meeting ask people for examples of times when they successfully did things the wrong way. Ask them for examples of when breaking the rules is necessary.
2   Ask your salespeople how and when they put across any deficiencies or disadvantages in your case.
3   Brief your salespeople as to the action you want them to take when they are threatened by a customer.
4   Work out tactics which you would support if the buyer puts them down heavily by criticizing the company, or by keeping them waiting for a long time. What do you do, yourself, about this? Can your sales people have the right to do the same thing?
5   How do you want them to handle the situation when the customer is cheating you? Brief them in advance as to how you want them to play it.
6   Work out whether you have the right person in the job to do the heavy work. When someone has to put in the boot, as it were, have you got the mugger there to do the job effectively?

YOUR MIND MAP

YOUR ACTION PLAN

How do you want your people to handle the difficult situation? How do you want to handle it yourself in the future? What tactics should they try out?

HOW DO YOU HANDLE THE REALLY TOUGH ONES?

Give yourself marks out of 10 across all three points on each question. These marks will show how frequently you like to relate to difficult customers in each of the three ways. Always use 10 points total. You can score 0 in a column if you want:

e.g. 7	0	3	10
<u>Col A</u>	<u>Col B</u>	<u>Col C</u>	

1 In getting along with difficult people I usually:

go along with their wishes for the moment	recognize this as a challenge to be overcome	respect their opinions as long as they respect mine	
_____	_____	_____	10

2 When the customer openly criticizes me, I:

want to cool down their anger and frustration	challenge their right to criticize me, particularly if it is unfair	pick out each criticism in detail to analyse their case carefully	
_____	_____	_____	10

3 If the customer is not doing what I want him to do, then I:

trust that things will work out if I keep persisting long enough	push harder, become more forceful	find another customer	
_____	_____	_____	10

4 If the customer strongly disagrees with my recommendation, then I:

give in, and do it his way	argue my case much more firmly	make sure of my position and stay detached	
_____	_____	_____	10

5 If someone has cheated me or my company, I feel that:

they are really the loser in the long run	I should even the score and seek revenge	work out how to avoid similar problems in the future	
_____	_____	_____	10

Total for each column			
Col A	Col B	Col C	50
_____	_____	_____	

ANALYSIS

0–15	16–25	26–35	36–50
Very mild	Quite mild	Quite strong	Very strong

Column A The higher the score the more you are a warm and friendly person, helpful to others, care for the feelings of others, but you would like to be more assertive and less fearful of pushing for your rights. You are a good person to calm and pacify others, but fighting your corner is not for you. Avoid the knock-down drag out battles, with tough opponents. You feel most discomfort with people who are hostile to you, or become angry with you, or who do not recognize your attempts to do well by them.

Column B The higher the score the more you are an assertive, strong, ambitious leader, who takes charge particularly in difficult situations. You understand the use of power in yourself and when others use it. You are responsive to others when they help you to achieve your aims. You would like to be more considerate of others' feelings, and you would sometimes like to think things through a bit more before acting. You feel most discomfort in people who do not fight back and friends who betray you or withdraw their loyalty from you.

Column C The higher the score the more you are a clear, logical, analytical sort of person who is self-reliant and a person of principle. You respect the integrity of others. You would like to trust people more, and to be less reserved about asserting your rights.
  You feel great discomfort if someone were to accuse you of being unprincipled or opportunistic. You do not like people who insist on helping you when you do not want it.

We are a mixture, of course, of all three types, but one type is usually predominant. If your scores are all roughly about the same, then you have a great deal of flexibility, you are a good all-rounder, and a good team player. You do not want to be subservient, nor do you wish to dominate others. You feel the greatest discomfort with others who let you down, or let themselves down, or let the whole team down. You can do without such people.

Index

●

PROFILE RESEARCH INTERNATIONAL
6 St Georges Place, Brighton, Sussex BN1 4GA
Tel: (0273) 570137   Fax: (0273) 570133

1. Profile is a simple but highly effective system designed to indicate your own perception of your characteristic style of behaviour at work.

   When you fill in this form think of yourself at WORK not at home or at leisure.

   You will, we are sure, find the results of Profile beneficial to you, but only if you complete the form honestly and correctly.

2. You will see to the left 16 groups of 5 words. Please rate the words in the following way. In the first group choose the word which you feel is 'most' like you, rate it as 'A'. Next choose the word which is least like you and grade that one as 'E'.

   From the remaining three words select the word that describes you best and rate it as 'B'. Take the least descriptive word and rate it as 'D'. This leaves one word that must be 'C'.

   In this example the most descriptive word is 'accurate' and the least descriptive word is 'inventive'.

3. Please complete each of the 16 groups in the same way. Try and complete the questionnaire fairly quickly, do not dwell too long over your choice. It is your immediate reaction we need. There are no right or wrong answers, and there are no trick questions.

EXAMPLE

	C	A	D	B	E
Composed	)				
Accurate		)			
Make things happen				)	
Mix with people			)		
Inventive					)

RATING

	S	C	D	E	T
Composed	)				
Accurate			)		
Make things happen					)
Mix with people				)	
Inventive					
Determined	)	)	)		
Conscientious					
Warm					
Credible	)				)
Imaginative					
Ingenious	)				
Rational			)		
Factual				)	
Lively					
Assertive			)	)	
Socially skilled					)
Full of ideas					
Balanced	)				
Ambitious			)		
Precise		)		)	
Careful	)				
Will to win			)		
Generous					

WINKLER MARKETING, 1990